2014

W9-AMO-400

And Morning Came

And Morning Came

Scriptures of the Resurrection

Megan McKenna

SHEED & WARD
Lanham, Chicago, New York, Toronto, and Oxford

Published by Sheed & Ward
An imprint of Rowman & Littlefield Publishers, Inc.
A wholly owned subsidary of the Rowman & Littlefield Publishing Group, Inc.
4501 Forbes Boulevard, Suite 200
Lanham, Maryland 20706

PO Box 317
Oxford
OX2 9RU, UK

Distributed by the National Book Network

Copyright © 2003 by Megan McKenna

All rights reserved. No part of this publication may be reproduced,
stored in a retrieval system, or transmitted in any form or by any
means, electronic, mechanical, photocopying, recording, or otherwise,
without the prior permission of the publisher, except by a reviewer
who may quote passages in a review.

Excerpt from "Burnt Norton" in *Four Quartets* by T. S. Eliot, copyright © 1963 by
Harcourt, Inc. and renewed 1964 by T. S. Eliot, reprinted by permission of the publisher.

Excerpt from "Poem #34" reprinted by permission of the publisher from *Antonio
Machado: Selected Poems*, translated by Alan S. Trueblood, p. 143, Cambridge, Mass.:
Harvard University Press, copyright © 1982 by the President of the Fellows of Harvard
College.

The scripture quotations contained herein are from the New Revised Standard Version
Bible, copyright © 1989, by the Division of the Christian Education of the National
Council of Churches of Christ in the U.S.A. Used by permission. All rights reserved.

Library of Congress Cataloging-in-Publication Data

McKenna, Megan
    And morning came : scriptures of the Resurrection / Megan
McKenna.
        p. cm.
    "A Sheed & Ward book."
    Includes bibliographical reference and index.
    ISBN 1-58051-141-4 (alk. paper)
    1. Jesus Christ—Resurrection. 2 Jesus Christ—Resurrection—Biblical teaching. I.
Title.
BT482 .M35 2003
232.9'7—dc21   2003011275

Printed in the United States of America

♾^TM The paper used in this publication meets the minimum requirements of
American National Standard for Information Sciences—Permanence of
Paper for Printed Library Materials, ANSI/NISO Z39.48-1992.

For Timothy A. Butler
With a grateful heart for our friendship and
abiding love in the Lord's presence

Contents

Introduction

The soul should always stand ajar, ready to welcome the ecstatic experience.

—Emily Dickinson

This is a book on the Scriptures of the Resurrection, concentrating on the accounts of the four Gospels, in the order they were written in the history of the church—Mark, Matthew, Luke, and John—and then how the understanding of this mystery developed in the practice of the community, in the rites of baptism, and in the experience of witnessing to belief under the guidance of the Spirit, as well as the persecution by those who did not believe. It presumes from the beginning that you already believe in the mystery of the Resurrection and are seeking to stake your very life on it, until the day you die. But it is mystery, in fact, the defining mystery of our religion, and as such is an endless source of awe, power, wisdom, and strength. It is believed in, first, by living it out, in singular commitment and baptismal vows, and communally as public witness as part of the living, suffering, and rising Body of Christ today in the world. All other statements of belief, spirituality and devotion, creed, and ritual revolve around the glory of resurrection: the reality that words seek to reveal and, because they are human and cultural, so often slur and stumble as they try to express the inexpressible. So, this is a book of theology, and yet it is also a series of stabs in the darkness, hoping that some pinpoint of light is opened to reveal a glint, a sparkle, a momentary bit of insight that results in an "ah!" that can then be translated into living, a way of being in the world based on that glimmer of faith seen and grasped and held dear.

Lawrence Kushner, a rabbi whose thinking about religion is defined by the Jewish tradition, speaks to all religions. He is concerned about what religion actually is and what it does for the one who seeks to practice it with others. He writes:

> Religion is a more or less organized way of remembering that every mystery points to a higher reality. A reality overarching and infusing this world with splendor. One pulsing through its veins. Unnoticed and unnamed. Of the Nameless One. A holiness so holy that it fills even our everyday illusions with spiritual meaning. (Quoted in the *Jewish Review of Books*)

The word *religion* means "to tie" or "to bind together," but not loosely as we might think. Religion is more like tendons, cords of muscles tying together bones, veins, and tissue. It is internal, providing a structure that enables movement and is primarily revealed in motion, and it is at its fundamental level a communal structure shared by many others moving and acting in the same way. Our religion as Christians, as followers of the Way (as we were first named), as Catholics is sourced in the Resurrection, the result of God becoming human, becoming flesh in the person of his beloved child, Jesus. In this mystery of the Incarnation our God was born, lived, breathed, ate, and walked the earth with us and then was betrayed, tortured, handed over to death, and murdered legally by crucifixion, a death so heinous and inhuman that it defies description. But God the Father, the God of Life, raised Jesus from the dead in the power of the Spirit, and now our God dwells with us in the presence of the Risen Lord, still one with us, praying with us in his Spirit to the Father until the fulfillment of time and the coming of God's kingdom of peace, born of justice for all. This is the first level of the mystery: God's raising of Jesus from the dead.

The second level of mystery is that God has shared this life of grace and power with us and, in Jesus, has promised that all of us will be raised from the dead, one day sharing in the fullness of life in God. And there is still more awesome depth to this mystery. Our resurrections begin now, here in our baptisms. We are buried with Christ in God and live now in the breath of the Spirit, living beyond the grasp of sin, evil, injustice, and death. This is our underlying, penetrating truth. We live resurrection life now, as a way, as a practice that continually converts us, transforms and transfigures us into the Body of Christ risen among us, in community, in the church, and in the Kingdom of God. And this mystery seeps into every moment of history, every person's body and life, into every aspect of creation and every experience in the world. It is the catalyst for continued regeneration, redemption, and freedom in the Spirit of God. This power is meant to issue into glory, the glory of God that can be seen and known by all on earth, and in our baptisms we pledge ourselves as witnesses to this Light, this Truth, this Life among us, as first gift of the Spirit to those who believe. Now we stand for God, stand with God, stand behind the revelation of God in Jesus, and stand together—our communion in the Body of Christ testimony to the presence of God with us on earth, for others to see, take comfort and heart in, and be drawn into this mystery themselves, until all are one in God, fulfilling Jesus's last prayer among his friends the night before he was crucified.

The Resurrection is not a single event, but a loosening of God's power and light into the earth and history that continues to alter all things, infusing them with the grace and power of God's own holiness. It is as though a door was opened, and what poured out will never be stopped, and the door cannot be closed. Jesus Christ, "the first born from the dead," goes before us, and we follow after him, and in our baptisms we are continuing, exchanging, and transforming our life at birth into the life of being born in the waters of the tomb and the breath of the Spirit of God. This life frees us from fear, from insecurity, from meaninglessness and from the powers of sin, evil, injustice, and death itself. What holds onto us now, what saves us, what seeps through our bodies and souls is the grace and power of God, and our lives are no longer our own, but we are God's, as Jesus is God's beloved child. We are now the beloved children of God, calling God Our Father with Jesus, praying and living on that same Spirit that came upon Jesus in fullness and shared now with us, as his body in the world. This mystery, the reality of what we seek to express, renders all existence altered, underlined now with hope, distilling love that is stronger than any other force on earth or in the heart. Death is shattered. Evil is empty. Injustice is null and void. Sin is shunted aside. Fear is useless. Insecurity is meaningless. Hate is pathetic. Suffering is turned inside out. Nothing is as it was, or will be ever again. There is a new order to creation; a new end to history; a new hope for the fullness of life for all; a new depth and even meaning to all that resists death and sin. All that is inhuman is undone. And when we have said all that, we have said little or nothing. The mystery is known in submission, in obedience, in shared struggle and enduring faithfulness that is first practiced with others on behalf of others or in the closing words of the Eucharistic Prayer: in him, and with him and through him—Jesus, in the Spirit to the glory of God the Father, until forever. Amen.

The title of this book is *And Morning Came*. I am indebted to Daniel Berrigan who used the cover of this book, painted by Sister Marie Celeste McFadden of the Carmel of the Mountains, in Reno, Nevada as the prayer card with these words for the funeral of his mother. The picture is Jesus, risen from the dead on that morning that did come after death, on the third day, looking out over the sea of Galilee, his disciples out on the lake, unaware as yet, that he is waiting for them, with breakfast and a new life, on the beach. It is a moment when Jesus is still alone, still with his Father and the Spirit in the stillness of morning, of silent glory, of life after death. His face is serene, yet incredibly sad. He has known life and death and another life altogether. He is peace incarnate and yet there is an awful rawness and vulnerability to him, human and divine in his body now. It is the unknown Jesus as human and God, the mysterious crucified and risen one hidden among us. It is Resurrection with the shadow of the cross and of death now in his eyes and face along with Easter's morning glory. It is Jesus inbetween what the disciples and the world knew and what they will slowly, until forever be invited in to know now. It is the Risen One.

It is the moments before knowing, before seeing, before the glory is tangible, able to be touched, before he eats with them and walks with Peter and before their lives are altered forever by his life, his Resurrection. It is from the ancient translation and refrain both proclaimed and sung on Easter at dawn and throughout the seven weeks of the season . . . and morning came, the third day. It is a phrase that seeks to be a bridge between all that has gone before in history and all that will be after this momenteous event of the life, death–crucifixion and resurrection of Jesus. We called all that has gone before the "old" or now the Earlier Testament and all that comes after the New Testament. Testament as in last will and testament, how all that God has given us in Jesus is handed on, treasured and cherished and put into practice by us now, in his place and with his own Spirit to encourage us and empower us to continue that work of redeeming and repairing the world. And in testimony as given by witnesses to what is and what they will swear to, stake their lives on and if need be, lay down their lives as protestation of truth and what they believe in and stand for in spite of suffering, sin, evil or injustice. We, as those baptized into the death and resurrection of Jesus are now the new testament, living truth, sworn witnesses, vowed to continue the words and the way of Jesus in the world today, here on the earth in the decades of the years 2000 and beyond.

God's presence in the Incarnation, the Resurrection, the Body of Christ, as both Eucharist and Church, in the Word of Scripture, in the community and in the poor and crucified of the earth, and the Trinity are mysteries of and in themselves but now by the will and plan of God, mysterious as it is, those mysteries are first known and experience in human beings, in the Church and the kingdom of God that encompasses all of creation. This is what we are baptized into and we live being unfolded, opened as a letter and read, being stretched in heart and mind and stretching and reaching out to others, in gratitude for our God opening the heart of Jesus, stretching his arms out on the cross and in opening the tomb so that the life of God could enter and recreate all things. Now it is death, sin, injustice, and evil and all that is aligned with them that are sealed in the tomb, their power conquered. Now as the beloved children of God, living in freedom and resisting all that is death and evil; we live only

under the sign of God's power: the sign of the cross, the sign of community—
our God, the Trinity, the Father, the Child and the Spirit wrapping their arms
around us as the shrouds of death are unwrapped from us.

And Morning came, the third day ... morning, dawn, the approach of the
light pushing back the night, illuminating, revealing, beginning, genesis, again.
It comes as it does every day, obeying the command of its Maker at the beginning of time. It comes as our God comes into the world as one of us, born
of a woman, a child who will grow to be a man, a believer, a Jew who knows
God as his Father and all human beings as his blood kin, blood of the cross and
blood let in truth telling. Now the family of God is birthed in the waters of
baptisms and our brothers and sisters are those who share belief, share bread
and wine, the body and blood of Jesus, who share suffering and persecution,
who share all things in common, who share the poverty and need of the least
among us, for in doing so we share the intimacy of the presence of God who
has, in his incarnation, chosen to share his closeness to us in remaining among
the poor, exhorting us to do for the poor what we would want to do for God.

It comes, this morning as freshness, as life without end, yet life that is continually transforming and bathing the world in splendor, reconstituting all of
life and not only calling it back to the original commands of the garden, but
to a command beyond imagining: Love one another as I have loved you and if
you do so, then I will call you friends. This morning after death, we are called
a new thing: the friends of God, the beloved children of God, God's peacemakers, God's reconciling presence in the world, God's ambassadors, God's justice and compassion to be given for the life of the world. God the Father now
loves to see and love in us what he saw and loved in his first-born child and
we follow in Jesus' footsteps along his way, all the way to the cross, and onto
the glory of that morning: the morning of Resurrection. And morning came,
and as the women left the tomb they saw him coming towards them. And
when we rise from the waters of the tomb of baptism, when we leave the
tombs of death and our old ways of life, riddled with sin and fear, injustice and
evil behind us, we see him coming towards us with the same words: Peace be
with you! This is our birthright blessing, our way of life:forgving, reconciling
and making peace, and our command to obey as well as our invitation to come
and dwell where God lives, in Jesus by the power of the Spirit, in the Trinity,
in the Word and Bread left among us as presences, in the community and
among the poor and the least, those who look like the crucified and risen one
still among us.

And morning came ... it still comes. Our God is here, Emmanual, among
us, always coming towards us, always standing behind us, always standing up for
us, always standing with us in solidarity and communion asking us to come
with him now, as disciple, as follower, as believer, as friend, as intimate beloved

child of God, now and forever. And now it is our privilege and responsibility to stand behind Jesus' words and life, to stand up for what we believe, to stand behind those who suffer, who speak the truth, who are caught in the web of injustice and death,and to stand with those that God has given us in faith, in need and in love, even those the world labels enemy but we know as those who are coming towards as in need of a friend who will come with them to God. This is our new life, this is the practice of Resurrection, the life we vow to live, until the coming of the end of our lives in death and our resurrection into the presence of the glory of God.

This is the life of God, resurrection life that is given to us in baptism and it is to mark us indelibly forever, to seep deep within our psyches, minds and souls, and our bodies so that we come into the world witnessing the glory, the light and freedom that we have been given to others. We are marked with this resurrection life as surely as we are smeared with oil and signed with the cross and Trinity, and plunged into the waters of the font, the tomb of Jesus. And we come forth from the waters, as Jesus came forth from the tomb, impossibly, un-believeably, joyously, gloriously marked as those who death has no hold over any longer. The palentologist Loren Eiseley was long an atheist but the detailed wonder of the natural world and the universe drew him into the mystery of the one who made all things. Philip Yancey writes of an experience Eiseley had in his book *Soul Survivor.*

> The naturalist Loren Eiseley tells of an event he calls the most significant learning experience of his long life. Caught on a beach in a sudden rain-storm, he sought shelter under a huge piece of driftwood where he found a tiny fox cub, maybe ten weeks old, which as yet had no fear of humans. Within a few minutes it had engaged Eiseley ina playful game of tug-of-war, with Eiseley holding one end of a chicken bone in his mouth and the baby fox pulling on the other end. The lesson he learned, said Eiseley, is that at the core of the universe, the face of God wears a smile. (from Daily Dig., Plough Publishing)

That is what Eiseley learned from the natural world about the face of God. What we learn from the Resurrection is far more astounding and pow-erful: the face of God is turned always towards us, the face of God is life-giving, life-enhancing, life-renewing; the face of God is freedom; the face of God is love unto death and beyond death iself. Resurrection says that no mat-ter what is happening in the world, no matter what we have done or anyone has done; the love of God is stronger and it is always coming towards us, in the person of Jesus but in all and everything redeemed by the love of God for us in Jesus extending out through all time through the Spirit lovingly given to us. Baptism is our initiation into that love. And you can see it loose in the world.

What does it look like? John XXIII prayed in his Christmas message of 1961 for what it looked like to be expressed ever more strongly and clearly: "Renew, O Lord, your wonders in our time, as though for a new Pentecost . . . increase the reign of the Divine Savior, the reign of truth and justice, the reign of love and peace." This is our birthright, our gift, our vocation, our glory and work, and we have the power of the Spirit of God to help us finish what Jesus has begun in his life, death and resurrection. We actually live that life now! This is the gift we have to share and give away to others and to live so that God keeps coming into the world, in every place, in every situation and time, in every person's life and heart. As God depended on Jesus to do his will, his work and to walk his way in the world, God now depends on us to do his will, his work and to walk his way in the world.

We are birthed into a life that is based on hope in the impossible! Everlasting life that begins now, seeded in us on earth, in our baptisms and growing ever-stronger daily, until we die, and flower into more life with God. Death is a reality, as it was for Jesus and we seek to explain it, live in terror of it, avoid it and yet it is there. But Karl Rahner wrote an essay called "On Christian Dying" something that consoles us, encourages us and gives us a glimpse of the power of Jesus' death in our own deaths.

> If we have been given the vocation and grace to die with Christ . . . then the everyday and banal occurrence which we call human death . . . has been elevated to a place among God's mysteries. In order to understand these mysteries and ot be able to put them into practice in the liturgy of our life we need only to look to the death of the crucified Lord, and hear the words that he spoke . . . words which we too can hear and repeat in life and death: 'My God, my God, why have you forsaken me? Into your hands I commend my spirit.' For if we understand death as supremely the state of abandonment by God in which we fall into the hands of the eternal God, then we have already understood and endured death itself. (*Theological Investigations*, Vol. 7, trans. D. Bourke, New York: Herder & herder, 1971, p. 293)

We die. We die as human beings but we die in Christ, with Christ and through Christ's death and resurrection. We die out of this life and more deeply into the life of God that was begun in us at baptism. Because of baptism, there is this side of life and death and there is the other side of life and death and we straddle the two. We live this side of death in the life of Christ and we have died to all else and we live on the other side of death in the life of Christ that we have been plunged into at baptism. We live in both, loving life here and loving the life of Christ's death and resurrection in us here and drawing us limitlessly and inexhaustibly into more deeply that can only be fulfilled after death. We, as Christians, are to die the way we live, in God, with God and for God, as Jesus did. We live in that radiance even now, though it is often shadowed and sometimes eclipsed by death, actual death, sin, evil and injustice all around us, and sometimes in us. Our lives by baptism is a plunging into and endless ocean of life stronger than death and we live absorbing that holiness God has shared with us in Jesus, resistance to all death that is not-life-giving, until our holy departures. We will in dying, be born into the presence of God we have always been able to see in everything God created, especially those given to us in need, in life and love and in those who opposed us and persecuted us, but we will see 'face-to-face' the glory shining on the face of God and know boundless life and love that defies any description. Bernard of Clairvaux speaks in one of his sermons on what it is like to seek God all our lives, and to seek him especially as the Word made flesh that dwells among us, introducing us to the endless journey, the endless treasure hunt, the pilgrimage that is our life and death until we die and, perhaps even after death.

> I have ascended to the highest in me,
> And look, the Word is towering about that.
>
> I have descended to explore my lowest depths,
> And I found Him deeper still.
>
> If I looked outside myself,
> I saw him stretching beyond the furthest I could see.
>
> And if I looked within,
> He was still further within.
> (Sermon 74 on the Song of Songs)

This is a book about living, about dying, about rising, about beginnings and endings and how to live resurrection now, practicing all the way home. This story says what is our calling, our vocation and our glory. It actually happened around 1997–98 in New York City. The virtuoso violinist Itzhak Perlman rarely appears in concert now, because of age but many see him as the greatest violinist of this century. He is admired as much for his triumph over terrible physical disability caused by childhood polio which left his legs underdevloped and paralyzed as he is for his incomparable skill and music. When he comes on stages, the audience is already seated, the orchestra is in place, even the conductor stands ready and then Itzhak Perlman makes his way across the stage, painstakingly dragging his legs in metal braces, leaning on metal crutches. Then he sits on his chair in front of the orchestra and lays his crutches down and unlocks his metal braces putting them on the floor. Then when settled he is handed his violin.

In one performance, when the music was chosen to showcase his range and ability to play there was a long piece that was the ending of the concert. He was playing a fiendishly difficult and passionate piece and suddenly, to everyone's horror, one of the four strings on his violin snapped, with a loud twang echoing in the air. The audience gasped aloud. The orchestra stopped playing. The conductor dropped his baton and whirled around in shock. But Perlman motioned to him to continue the piece. The orchestra began again, after a few bars and the piece continued. Perlman never missed a beat, or lost a note. To everyone's absolute amazement he finished the entire piece, more than six minutes. He used only three strings, instanteously transposing the music from the missing string onto the three strings he had left.

When the performace and the piece was over. The audience was stunned into silence. No one moved, or barely breathed. They just sat there awed by what had happened, unbelieveable and yet they had seen it and heard it. The sweat had poured from him and Perlman was dripping wet, sitting in his chair, violin and bow in one hand, dazed. After minutes the audience exploded. They leapt to their feet in ecstatic appreciation. The musicians banged on their music stands and stomped their feet. It went on it seemed forever. Itzhak bowed from his chair, his eyes somewhat glassy and shining. Then he gestured for a microphone. The crowd was immediately quiet. He addressed the audience saying: "This has been my vocation, my lifelong mission—to make music out of what remains." And he repeated his words: "This, this has been my vocation to make music out what remains." There was a moment of total silence and then once again the audience erupted into rapturous applause and there were tears in many eyes, and tears on Itzhak Perlman's face.

This is our vocation: to make music out of what remains. To dance, to burst into new life. From the moment of our baptism we are summoned to make music out of what remains: what remains of our lives, our loves and dreams, our hopes and fears, our sufferings and deaths, our struggles and our faithfulness, our communities and relationships. This music began with the Resurrection of Jesus and will continue now until the end of time. While we live it is played in us and we always are played with others for the benefit and appreciation of those who hear, who need to hear the music of the good news to the poor, the good news of life, of Resurrection life given to us in Jesus by the Father in the Spirit.

A poet once said "In our beginning is our end" and in our baptisms is our dying and rising begun, completed and begun again and again. This is our life and this is what we are summoned to as Jesus calls out to us: "If you wish to be my disciple, then begin by denying your very self, pick up your cross and come after me." (Mk 8) Come after me, all the way to the cross and on into the tomb, and come with me into the morning's glory. And morning came, the third day. This is where we live, where we dwell, where we stand . . . right here where morning comes, the third day. Christ is risen from the dead! He is alive! And they recounted how they had seen him on the road and come to know him in the breaking of the bread. And even as they spoke, he appeared in their midst saying: Peace be with you.

And we cry out: "He is alive! And we tell the stories once again how we meet him on the roads and come to recognize him in the breaking of the bread; and even as we tell the story, he appears among us saying: "Peace be with you!" Get ahold of yourself. It is I! And they rejoiced and he opened their minds to the Scriptures. And we open the scriptures, standing together, with Jesus standing in our midst, the tomb open and empty behind us, facing into the world opening before us, God coming towards us. And with each opening of the Word of God we plunge more deeply into this mystery of the Resurrection and our baptisms and we stand and profess: God the Father raised Jesus from the dead in the power of the Spirit and God will raise us from the dead in that same Spirit. And we believe that already we live hidden with Christ in God, living not for ourselves alone, but for your glory to be revealed in the world. This is our vocation, our lifelong mission, to make resurrection music out of what remains for us and for the world. Let us begin once again.

1

Resurrection

Not knowing when the dawn will come, I open every door.

—Emily Dickinson

*R*esurrection! How do we begin to speak of this core mystery of our faith, our liturgy, and the practice of our lives as believers in Jesus Christ, the Cruci-fied One, risen from the dead? And it is that word "mystery" that we must be-gin with, remember, and return to over and over again as we read the texts of Scripture, study past exegesis and midrash, and seek to reflect upon their mean-ing for us today. The word itself is from the Greek word *mysterion,* which ba-sically means the same as its Latin equivalent *sacramentum,* namely sacrament. But what is a mystery? Something unbelievable? Impossible? Extraordinary? Something that defies the laws of nature? Not rational? Something that cannot be explained? That is beyond our understanding? That must be believed in or-der to be understood? Ridiculous? Preposterous? All these statements or ques-tions have a glimmer of truth and yet do not begin to speak of what mystery might be.

There are mysteries of the universe, so vast and, for the most part, still in-comprehensible. Scientists themselves proclaim in awe the depth and expanse of our small galaxy and the innumerable other galaxies beyond us. Their task is enormous, perhaps impossible to fathom, and yet they seek answers, build on what has come before, make mistakes, and stumble into knowledge that forces them to change the way they define reality, as well as the way they ask ques-tions. Galileo lived with his head in the night skies, watching, and, with the aid of a telescope, discovered what people resisted knowing: that we are not the center of the universe and the world does not revolve around us! Since then, myriad discoveries in astronomy have revealed to us that we are actually a bit of dust in the universe, star dust, dust that is conscious and intelligent, but dust

1

nonetheless. Our true relation to the rest of creation reminds us of humility and cautions us against arrogance.

Today with the advent of huge telescopes that orbit the Earth, knowledge spirals out of the range even of scientists as they seek to describe the universe we inhabit. Listen to this short piece on dark matter:

> Dark Matter
> The universe really is invisible; We learn from the galaxies and from their motions in space that the universe is by its very nature largely unseen. More than 90 percent of it is composed of Dark Matter, stuff that has mass but is undetectable by anything it emits, reflects or absorbs. The more we look for meaning in the space between the stars, the more forcefully we reach the surprising conclusion that most of what is there we cannot see.
> The most beautiful thing we can experience is the mysterious. It is the source of all true art and science. He to whom this emotion is a stranger, who can no longer wonder and stand rapt in awe, is as good as dead; his eyes are closed. . . . This knowledge, this feeling, is at the center of true religiousness. In this sense, and in this sense only, I belong to the ranks of devoutly religious men. (Albert Einstein, "What I Believe," quoted in Malin, p. 14)

Still what is mystery? Perhaps it is a concept that enables us to search our languages, cultures, and experiences for what is true. This word teaches us that the more we know about something, the less we can explain it, and that any experience of mystery puts us in awe of what is and tells us bluntly that we know nothing at all, regardless of our study, our erudition, and our information. Mystery is something to fall into, to stumble upon, to be caught up in, to be carried by, and to submit to singularly and with the rest of humanity. Mystery is the envelope we dwell in and are always opening to find out what is still unknown, uncovered, and unrevealed to us. Life itself is a mystery. Being born and dying are mysteries, and all that happens in between is mysterious, dangerous, exhilarating, freeing, and devastating. Mystery is encounter with the unknown, or more precisely put, The Unknown.

Religion is by definition in the ancient languages that which ties and binds us together. What holds us as human beings, persons together within ourselves, with one another, with the earth and all that is created, and with the Maker and Keeper of all things: God. We belong to a mystery. We practice a religion of mystery. There are four tremendous overarching mysteries of our religion as Judeo-Christians: incarnation; resurrection; the Body of Christ, which is the life, crucifixion, death, and rising of Jesus in the Eucharist and the church; and the Trinity. We have a tendency to capitalize all of these mysteries because they are not just descriptions, but proclamations, like the Good News of God, the Scriptures, and they embrace us and hold us in being. We live in, move in and through, and are saturated with these mysteries. And we believe them, stake our lives on them, seek to practice them, and fervently hope that they will one day come to fruition in us.

Perhaps the crucial verb in that last sentence is "practice." We practice the mystery of the Incarnation, of being the Body of Christ, of dwelling in the Trinity, and we practice resurrection. This book will assume belief in these four defining mysteries, but concentrate, contemplate, and seek to be immersed in the mystery of the Resurrection and how we, as believers today, practice resurrection.

Most of us in our contemporary society are not adept in this practice. We are more pragmatic, demonstrative, rational, sensate, and involved in the daily tasks, humdrum and delightful, of just living, or for most of the world, just surviving day to day. And yet this practice, this discipline, this tao, this way of living is essential to religion, to the art of being and living consciously and vibrantly, whether we are alone or with others. And to practice resurrection! Now that is something else altogether! And so this book will be first of all practice in wonder, in questioning, in stretching our minds, in straining after words and stories, in delving into and sharing experiences and reaching past limitations and boundaries into the margins of life, growing a bit more at ease with the unknown, with mystery. Before we look at even the word "resurrection" and what it might mean in dictionaries and languages, we need to fall into a story that will begin the process of stretching our minds and hearts to hear and speak words differently and to dig into meaning and see with a third eye what might be right under our noses, yet of which we live unaware. The story aptly enough I call "Improbable, Impossible, Unbelievable!"

But first a few questions: Improbable? What, given our lives, our ages, our experience and knowledge, and just the state of the world, is highly improbable? What most probably won't happen to us? What will we most probably not do or know? Any answer to these questions is usually preceded by laughs, chuckles that are both rueful and reveal a bit of knowledge and past experience. Then, the quick responses, I'll win the lottery. I'll quit my job and live in luxury. I'll find a cure for cancer. I'll get married, or I'll get married again. I'll take a cruise around the world. And yet, improbable is not impossible. It is usually out of the realm of the usual, but whatever we answer often reveals our lack of imagination, our inability to reach beyond where we are and what we do and what is expected of us. It often says more of our limits, many self-imposed or culturally manifested, than it does of what could actually happen to us or what we could do. True, with the lottery in particular, the odds are stacked against us, but if you buy a ticket or two, who knows? And getting married or remarried? I had one woman adamantly tell me it was definitely in the impossible category, not an option. She was very clear about it. It was decided. And six months later, I got the funniest invitation to a wedding I'd received ever: what had been improbable, impossible, was suddenly happening.

Next question: given that the improbable is not impossible, that you just have to take a risk or stretch into the next level of living, or hoping and acting, then what is impossible? What is impossible for you, for us, for the United States, for the world? Since people now are thinking and straining against ordinary limits and concepts, the answers do not come as quickly, but then, the next thought and hope level kicks in and the responses are blurted out. Women will get ordained. A layperson will be the next pope. I'll get pregnant again. We'll cut the military budget in half. No one in the world will go to bed hungry tonight. Oddly enough, these answers often make people angry or sad, even a bit depressed. Perhaps because once again the answers reveal what has been concealed: the impossibility of changing existing reality significantly, or the places in our personal lives and society where we have come up against walls of indifference, of evil, and of acceptable behaviors and structures.

Impossible reveals to us where we stop. The points where we stop being converted, changing, hoping, working to shift perspectives, where we tolerate injustice, where we give in and give up on what is going on in the world. And that is always a dangerous place, a point it is crucial to recognize and come to a decision about, and so push the boundaries of living and of what is possible. Perhaps now is the time to listen to the story, and then we will pick up on impossible and unbelievable after it is told.

Once upon a time, in northern India, long ago, the Mongol tribes, described by their conquered peoples and slaves as brutal barbarians, invaded and destroyed the land, farms, families, cultures, religion. There was chaos, and many fled for their lives, leaving everything of value behind him. Many hurriedly buried their possessions, their money, and what they treasured, under their houses, in rice fields, some haphazardly, others making maps and hoping that one day this would all be over and they could return to their homelands and what remained of their lives, recover what was lost and begin again. But time passed and there was no retrieval and there were no better times. Most never returned, and their secrets and their treasures were buried with them in prisons and on foreign soil.

And so it happened that a very poor husband and wife, very young—no more than eighteen or nineteen—were weeding the rice in their small plot, while their young son, who was about two years old, was playing nearby. To their utter amazement, they came upon a stone, large and heavy, different from other rocks in the paddies. When it was cleaned, it sparkled in the sun, glinting with inner fire. The couple looked at each other wide eyed. What had they found? The husband whispered that he thought it was a ruby. Perhaps, she whispered back, it was one of those long-lost treasures that the old ones told stories about at night. They quickly tried to hide it, but their young inquisitive son wanted to know everything about the shiny stone. Now the trick was how to keep their talkative two-year-old quiet about their find, because once it was discovered that they had found it, the man and woman in charge of their village would take it for themselves and claim it as belonging to the leaders, not to them. If they could keep their find a secret, they would have to wait months before they could take it to another village when they went for market days and bring it to her brother who worked with jewels in the city and see if it was a ruby and what it was worth.

How could they keep him quiet about the stone? He had already picked up on their excitement and elation, and he would tell his friends, everybody in fact, as soon as he got to his morning work and play group, and then the head woman who was always listening and snooping around would find out too.

Usually, at this point I stop the story and ask the group what would they do? How do you ponder and reflect on what appears to be an impossible situation? Remember that you must both conceal the real and yet not harm your child. What follows in the discussion is often telling in itself, because it is so hard to come up with something quickly, almost intuitively, and not get bogged down in psychological responses to the situation. And what happens in the story itself takes everyone by surprise. The folk wisdom strikes us as humorous, but it also teaches much about God's ways among us and the depth of what lies hidden just underneath all our lives.

That night the child was kept indoors and kept busy until he was exhausted and put to bed. Then the woman moved quickly and told her husband to go to a villager's house and borrow an oven. She had been saving honey and cinnamon to make special cakes that her child delighted in and that she'd be making as many of them as she could all night. The two of them stretched the ingredients and made many thin, almost paper thin cinnamon and honey rice cakes.

Just before dawn she went outside and scattered the cakes all around, on the roof, on the ground, on the edges of the rice field, in the chicken coop, along the steps and porch, even in the bushes, the garden and garbage pit. Then she ran inside and woke her child. "Look!" she cried, "I think it rained cinnamon and honey cakes last night! Just the kind you like! Come quickly and help me gather them before the birds discover them!" Outside in the morning light, the two of them collected the cakes in bags, running around to collect as many as they could, while the birds feasted on them. They showed them to the father, ate some for breakfast, and then sent the boy out to his class and friends with enough for all of them in a small bag.

They waited and hoped their plan would work. And of course, the first thing the young boy did was talk! He had so much to talk about. Why, yesterday they had found a huge shiny rock in the rice fields, red and very heavy. Immediately, he was overheard by the head woman of the village. She interrupted the boy and began questioning him about the stone: Where exactly did they find it? What did it look like? How big? Where was it now? But he was anxious to get on with the rest of his story. "And that's not the best part!" he said, beaming. "It rained cinnamon and honey rice cakes at our house last night! We collected them this morning while the birds were fighting over them too and ate some for breakfast. And see, I have some for everybody here too!" He was delighted with himself.

And the head woman laughed. It was just a story. Children were always making up stories, and she went back to what she was doing and forgot all about the stone. The cakes were impossible; everyone knew that it hadn't rained anything the night before—not even rain! And as for that other story, it was merely a game the boy's parents played with him to keep him entertained, another story. What was rare or unexpected (the discovery of the stone) was now associated with the impossible (the rain of rice cakes), and both were relegated to the unbelievable; no one was the wiser on any score. But with time, the parents went to the city and found out how thoroughly the impossible could become reality. They had a ruby, a huge one. It was broken into pieces and shared among their family, their in-laws, distant cousins, neighbors, everyone in the villages for miles around, and the family's situation slowly improved. With time, there was better seed rice, more food, a chicken, a pair of sandals, a book, a piece of cloth, medicine, and all began to prosper and to live with hope. What was thought to be impossible was, of course, reality and very true. And what was never even thought about: the possibility of freedom—unbelievably—became a reality, not just a dream kept silent in their hearts, but spoken of and worked for together.

Reactions to the story begin with laughter, always indicative of truth that is suddenly seen, insight that reveals itself like a jack-in-the-box that magically springs out when the music comes to the right spot. What do we dream? What do we base our decisions, our lives, and our long-term plans on? What do we accept as the way things are? What do we chafe against and refuse to accept or tolerate? This is where we begin to look at belief, at what we stake our lives on and commit ourselves to publicly.

Impossible! There are two occasions in Luke's Gospel where the words "nothing is impossible with God" are uttered. It is good to start there, because if that statement is true, it lays the foundation for our religion based upon "the unbelievable." They are first spoken by the Angel Gabriel to Mary at the Annunciation or, more precisely, at the moment of the Incarnation after Mary has

submitted to the Word of the Lord and found her‍
tery of God becoming flesh among us. They are sp‍
beth, Mary's aged cousin, who is pregnant by the g‍
1:37). It is, we know, an intimation of more wond‍

And these same words are found later in Jesu‍
ciples, after the rich landowner turned away fron‍
luctance and sadness, but he also refused Jesus's ‍
and eternal life because of his great wealth and position and ᴜᴜ ᴜ‍
tachment to it. He could not part with it, or even share it with those in desperate need—the poor—and thereby lay up treasures in heaven.

Jesus too is sad and says to his followers, "How hard it is for those who
have wealth to enter the kingdom of God! Indeed, it is easier for a camel to go
through the eye of a needle than for someone who is rich to enter the kingdom of God." And the others respond, "Then who then can be saved?" Jesus
states, "What is impossible for mortals is possible for God" (Luke 18:24–26).
Or in older translations, the passage reads, "Nothing is impossible for God."
The disciples are distressed by Jesus's words about wealth and begin to panic
over whether or not they themselves stand a chance at entrance and long-term
residence in the kingdom. Yet, Jesus's words are a simple declarative sentence:
"Nothing is impossible with God."

What appears impossible—a camel passing through a needle's eye—is easier than some people heavily burdened with wealth entering the kingdom of
justice shared and mercy given. I have been told that the eye of the needle is a
gate in Jerusalem for travelers on foot leaving the city. It is narrow and low. A
camel can get through it, but only if it is unloaded of its cargo, hasn't drunk
water for its journey, and is pushed from behind! The image is lasting and the
reality improbable, but possible. What about the more impossible?

We have to linger with the impossible a bit before we move on to the unbelievable, the Resurrection, so that we can begin to get used to the stretching
and straining that we need to do to look at this mystery and begin to practice
it consciously and passionately as core to our lives. It seems the first insight of
Jesus's kingdom and power is that of conversion: the conversion of all, but the
conversion of those of us who are most secure, lax, self-righteous, waffling in
our commitments, and living with divided hearts, at ease in this world, and
maybe with a foot that dances in the Kingdom of God. And this insight is tied
to a second realization: heaven and earth are intimately bound together. What
we do for the poor here and now in our age lays up treasure in heaven. These
worlds overlap, and, as the Irish say, the dwelling place of the poor is one of
those places "where the veil of the world is very thin." It is semipermeable, a
threshold where the sacred can be touched and the holy seeps through, often
unnoticed.

version to sharing, to letting go of excess, and making friends with who lack what we have is not impossible with God, not impossible for he who is a disciple of Jesus. In fact, in Jesus's community, after his death d resurrection, it will be the usual practice of the church, and his disciples will be described, a bit amazingly, as loving others so carefully that "there are no poor among them"! Impossible? Improbable? Perhaps Incarnation proclaims that the merely improbable is easy, and what was thought to be impossible just takes time and conversion, a bit of practice, like some of us laying up treasure in heaven among the poor here and returning to the invitation of Jesus: now you can come and follow me. We have to start on the impossible together so that we can look at what is truly unbelievable, but nonetheless true.

What is unbelievable? Most of the basic truths that we accept in our baptisms into the Body of Christ, his church, are unbelievable—just not possible except by grace, by God's justice and mercy and design. Incarnation is the beginning: God becomes flesh and dwells among us. The Word of God is uttered, and the skin and bones and heart and mind of our God become visible among us. The invisible God is now seen, touched, known, misunderstood, used, taken for granted, loved, rejected, crucified and murdered, caught in history, politics, economics, conflicts, and hate. This Body of Christ is taken, blessed, broken, and shared around among his friends as food, as word and story, as presence and peace for all the world. This God made visible in Jesus the Beloved Child reveals his equally Beloved Father to his friends and clothes them with power from on high, wrapping them in the same Beloved Spirit that came upon him in fullness at his baptism, and we are introduced to the Trinity, our God that is Oneness in the Three, and Threeness in the One. But all these unbelievable, true mysteries are intertwined and rooted in the mystery of the Resurrection. This is the hinge, the lodestone, the pole star, the benchmark that all the other mysteries are steeped in and intimately bound up with, making it all one piece that is the mystery of God with us, for us, and in us, now and forever. This is the mystery, Paul says, "If Christ has not been raised, then our proclamation has been in vain and your faith has been in vain" (1 Cor. 15:14). Or, as it is phrased in more blunt renditions: "If Christ has not been raised from the dead, then we, of all people, are to be most pitied." We are either blessed beyond belief, or we are the most unfortunate and deluded of people. Not much leeway there on what is and is not reality.

What is resurrection? This entire book will speak of resurrection, of Jesus's resurrection, of our own resurrections, and of resurrection as a practice of our faith and a way of life. We begin with the most basic statement. We believe that God the Father in the power of the Spirit raised Jesus from the dead and that Jesus now lives in the power of God, dwelling among us. And we believe that what God the Father did for Jesus in the power of the Spirit, God will do for us. We will be raised from the dead, and our bodies will be given life everlasting with God. But there is more, much more, that is, in a sense, crucial to believing and to living in light of that belief now, until we know that fullness of resurrection in our own bodies. We believe that Jesus, the Crucified One, is alive now. And we believe that our resurrections begin in our baptisms. Our lives as believers in Jesus, the Word of God made flesh, in the Father, and in the Spirit, are meant to bear public witness to the presence of God among us, and so we spend our lives practicing resurrection life for all to see, take heart from, come to believe in, and accept or reject as truth, unbelievable as it may seem.

Belief in the Resurrection of the body is hard to find in the ancient world. This piece from Plato is as illusive as it is poetic, a romantic idea, but utterly lacking in any life after death.

> And after having thus framed the universe, he allotted to it souls equal in number to the stars, inserting each in each. . . . And he declared also, that after living well for the time appointed to him, each one should once more return to the habitation of his associate star, and spend a blessed and suitable existence. (Plato, *Timaeus,* quoted in Malin, p. 108)

Belief in bodily resurrection from the dead is part of the tradition of Judaism, but it is a later development of belief. There are rare point-blank statements in the older testament writings. The most blatant is found in the Book of Daniel the Prophet.

> At that time Michael, the great prince, the protector of your people, shall arise. There shall be a time of anguish, such as has never occurred since nations first came into existence. But at that time your people shall be delivered, everyone who is found written in the book. Many of those who sleep in the dust of the earth shall awake, some to everlasting life, and some to shame and everlasting contempt. Those who are wise shall shine like the brightness of the sky, and those who lead many to righteousness, like the stars for ever and ever. (Dan. 12:1–3)

The Book of Daniel is the last book of the older testament, chronologically. One of the other few references to an afterlife, or resurrection, is found in the Book of Maccabees (also a very late addition), when one of those who is being tortured to death for his faith cries out with incredible courage in the face of his torturer: "I got these from Heaven, and because of his laws I disdain them, and from him I hope to get them back again" (2 Mac. 7:11).

The Sadducees deny resurrection and mock Jesus in their absurd questions about who will be married to whom in the afterlife. And Jesus answers by telling them they have no understanding of their own belief. He replies:

> You are wrong, because you know neither the scriptures nor the power of God. For in the resurrection they neither marry nor are given in marriage, but are like angels in heaven. And as for the resurrection of the dead, have you not read what was said to you by God, "I am the God of Abraham, the God of Isaac, and the God of Jacob"? He is God not of the dead, but of the living. (Matt. 22:29–32)

This belief in resurrection, or hope in life after death as we think of it and believe in it, is rooted in Judaism's history, but N. T. Wright calls it, as a doctrine, "quite imprecise and unfocused." He writes:

> Josephus describes it, confusingly, in various incompatible ways. The rabbis discuss what, precisely, it will mean and how God will do it. Furthermore, the idea could be used metaphorically, particularly for the restoration of Israel after the Exile, as in Ezekiel 37, where the revived dry bones represent the House of Israel.
>
> The early Christian hope for bodily resurrection is clearly Jewish in origin, there being no possible pagan antecedent. Here, however, there is no spectrum of opinion: Earliest Christianity simply believed in resurrection, that is, the overcoming of death by the justice-bringing power of the creator God.
>
> For early Christians, resurrection was seen to consist of passing *through* death and out the other side into a new sort of bodily life. As Romans 8 shows, Paul clearly believed that God would give new life to the mortal bodies of Christians and indeed to the entire created world: "If the Spirit of God who raised Jesus from the dead dwells in you, he who raised the Messiah Jesus from the dead will give life to your mortal bodies also through his Spirit who lives in you." (Rom. 8:11) This is a radical mutation from within Jewish belief.
>
> Resurrection hope (as one would expect from its Jewish roots) turned those who believed it into a counter-empire, an alternative society that knew the worst that tyrants could do and knew that the true God had the answer. ["The Resurrection of Resurrection." *Bible Review* (August 2000): 10, 63]

This is the background for the theologically postulated belief in resurrection: Jesus's being raised from the dead by God the Father in the Spirit and Christians' belief that they will share in that resurrection through baptism and life in Christ.

Let us look now at the word "resurrection" and its meanings for insight into how to practice resurrection and live it now in our daily lives as witness and testimony, without words, declaring the power of life over death as fundamental to our very existence as human beings. Basically, at its roots and simply put, the word "resurrection" means "raised up," specifically from death, or the "sleep of death," as it is often called in the Judeo-Christian and other religious traditions. We are most familiar with it in relation to Jesus in the Paschal mystery of Jesus being rejected, crucified, and murdered, executed publicly, and of the empty tomb and the experienced presence of Jesus still with his disciples and friends. And we cling to the hope that death is not the end for any of us and that God in his merciful love truly is a God of life who will raise up our mortal bodies from the grave so that we will know eternal life in Christ. These are creedal statements, belief statements, dogma and doctrinal principles, and they speak reams, but they come forth from the Scriptures, the narratives of the Resurrection and the experience of those who know the Risen Lord, those who have gone before us in faith and those among us who live their lives predicated on that truth here and now.

We will attempt to look at resurrection in the words of Scripture, in the accounts of the four Gospels first, then in what I call intimations and hindsight, stories of the Gospels that speak of resurrection from the dead, those Jesus raised up and prophecies and statements that speak of Jesus's coming sufferings, death, and rising on the third day. Then we will look at the Acts, most often in sermons and statements of belief shared in public preaching and how the Resurrection was practiced by the first Christians. We will look at hymns and psalms, paeans of praise in the letters and epistles that reveal the worship of the Risen Lord and the Trinity. And lastly, we will delve into the mysteries of resurrection today, in the church and world of the twenty-first century.

Resurrection. The word means "to raise from the dead." But in many languages and ways of speaking it is more colloquial, more expressive. It seems to have three basic meanings, all derived from rising or standing up. The first is literally to stand up for—as though you were a character witness in a court trial, giving meaning and credibility to another's words or person. This is God the Father standing up for Jesus, witnessing and testifying to his words, stories, preaching, works, and very person. The Resurrection of Jesus is God validating and confirming the person of Jesus as the Beloved Son in whom he is well pleased, as all that he claims to be before God. In John's Gospel, when Jesus is preaching about witness and testimony, he declares, "the Father who sent me bears witness to me" (John 8:18b). The Resurrection is this ultimate unequivocal witness.

The second meaning is "to stand behind." Think of a wall, a power and presence that supports, protects, backs up, and gives strength. The Resurrection is God the Father in the power of the Spirit standing behind Jesus. There are devotional texts in the eastern church and by the early fathers that speak of

God standing behind Jesus as he died in agony on the cross; that say Jesus cried out and handed over his Spirit into the hands of his Father, and he fell into the waiting arms of God, who caught him up and held him in death. And that the Father, loving Jesus, his very own life, threw him back into life never to die again! Again we hear in John's Gospel, "The one who sent me is with me; has not left me alone; because I always do what is pleasing to him" (John 8:29). The Father's presence abides with Jesus throughout his life and, in and through his death, into another, truer life.

The third meaning is "to stand with," as though in solidarity or communion with another or others. The Resurrection proclaims for all time and all places that the Father stood in solidarity with, was in communion with Jesus on earth, was one with him always, standing with whom he stood in solidarity with and holding them, loved and known and forgiven, accepted as they experienced Jesus. This meaning of the word is used often in prayers and psalms. The psalmist prays, "O Lord, you have brought up my soul from Sheol, restored me to life that I should not go down to the pit" (Ps. 30:4). Often in the Psalms, the Holy One is described as "lifting up or raising up those who are oppressed, poor and barren." This is the sense of the phrase "to raise up or to stand with." Mary, the Mother of Jesus, uses it in her song of delight in what God will do for his people in her child when she prays steadfastly and confidently: "He has raised up all who are bowed down" (Luke 1:52b). All these define ways of looking at resurrection and what it could mean for us who believe and seek to put into practice that belief as a proclamation of the power of life over death.

This means that what God did for Jesus in standing up for him, standing behind him in life and in death, and standing in communion and solidarity with him, the Father also does for us, here and now, in our lives. Our Father, with Jesus in the Spirit, stands up for us, stands behind us in life and death, and stands in communion and solidarity with us who believe and are baptized into Christ's Body, the church, who are to stand in communion with the poor and those of the earth in need of justice and the judgment of God, declared by our presence with them. Just these ideas will take chapters to examine and integrate into our words and practice.

It was the practice of the early church liturgically to celebrate and proclaim the Resurrection very publicly during the Easter season. *The Didache*, a first-century document that describes much of the liturgy and daily practice of prayer and the sacraments within the community, proclaimed that no believer should kneel to pray from the beginning of the Paschal vigil (Holy Saturday) until after the feast of the Pentecost. That for those fifty days the church was to stand in the presence of God and stand for what they believed God had done for his people in Jesus by raising Jesus from the dead. Further, it went on to say that the priest, like a shepherd with the sheep, should gather the flock around the altar to celebrate the Eucharist and to sing the Eucharistic prayer, and to dance it "as he was able." Even today, in one of the Eucharistic prayers we say, "We give you thanks, O God, for the privilege and honor of standing in your presence and serving you." More often than not, these words are spoken, and the congregation is firmly kneeling, not standing at all. The Easter season seems especially potent for demonstrating that we believe, and we stand up for that belief, firmly proclaiming that our Father, God, stands behind us, Jesus stands with us, and the Spirit stands in communion with us and all those who are one in the faith that we are baptized into, live into, and die into the fullness of resurrection with.

There is a basilica in Istanbul that I have never seen, but of which many send me postcards; it depicts a lesser-known and -celebrated mystery, named by the early church as the harrowing of hell. It portrays the Risen Jesus as Lord standing astride the tombs of Adam and Eve, breaking open the gates of hell and bringing forth all the souls since Adam and Eve into life. The patriarchs and matriarchs, prophets, kings, and people are gathered to enter heaven. Maria Boulding, in her book *Marked for Life: Prayer in the Easter Christ,* describes it thus:

> In Istanbul in the little church of Kariye Camii there is an early fourteenth-century painting of the Resurrection. According to Byzantine custom this is presented as a descent of Christ into the underworld. One of the most striking features of this beautiful work is the sense of rhythm and movement it conveys: Christ appears strong and active; with his right hand he grasps Adam's wrist and with his left Eve's, pulling them out of their graves. There is a vivid impression of dancing, as though he were drawing them into his dance of life. (p. 23)

Even in the small postcards, it appears as though he is dancing with them—the dance of resurrection life that breaks the hold of death forever. This is the harrowing of hell!

We will look at many images of resurrection from the history of the church and spirituality and the Scriptures. We will just glance at one now (but in more detail in the chapter on "Intimations: Stories That Prepare for Resurrection"), that of Lazarus, the one whom Jesus loved and raised from the dead, as told in John's Gospel (John 11). Lazarus dies, and Jesus is away. He waits two days, and by the time he returns, Lazarus has been dead and buried for four days. His sisters, Martha and Mary, mourn him, along with countless others in Bethany and Jerusalem, and this is one of the rare occasions when, we are told, Jesus weeps for his beloved Lazarus. He stands before the stone that encloses him in the tomb and tells those around him to roll away the stone. Even

Lazarus's sister balks at the suggestion, telling Jesus rather bluntly that he's been in the tomb so long that there will be a terrible stench. But Jesus firmly repeats the order and rebukes her for her lack of belief in his words and life, which she had so recently and perhaps glibly professed. The tomb is opened and Lazarus, who was most probably standing in his grave, wrapped in his burial sheet, is visible to all. Tombs generally were the size of a man, long and narrow so that as one body decayed the bones could be pushed to the rear of the tomb and the next put inside.

And then the Word of God made flesh cries out, "Lazarus! Come forth!" and to everyone's astonishment and fear, he does! He was wrapped and bound hand and foot, like a mummy, a cloth over his face. How did he come forth? I often picture him rather comically wobbling on feet bound together. But he most probably fell out on his face before the crowd of witnesses. And Jesus commands them, "Unbind him and set him free!" Who moved? Culturally and religiously, the Jewish community cringed from touching a dead body because they themselves would become unclean. Who moved? Since it doesn't mention the apostles, they probably did not obey Jesus's words. Surely it was the women, his sisters, Martha and Mary, and their friends, who had originally prepared the body for burial. They had nothing to lose; they were already unclean, and they had everything to hope for from their obedience. They would have rushed forward to the form on the ground and painstakingly unwrapped what they had carefully bound in grief, unwinding, around and around, until his limbs were loosed, and lifted the covering from his head. They would have stood him up, wonderingly, and turned him to face Jesus. He was raised up, standing on his feet. And fear and trembling and awe, disbelief, horror, cynicism, any number of reactions would have been expressed by the crowd. But Lazarus is alive!

The word or name "Lazarus" means "one who has been raised from the dead." Obviously, it is not his given name! Lazarus symbolizes everyone who has ever been baptized and raised from the dead by the sound of the Word of God laying claim to us. "I claim you for God, in Christ" are the words of the one who welcomes the catechumen before the waters of the fount of baptism. Every fifth Sunday of Lent, we hear this gospel proclaimed, for what happened to Lazarus will happen to those preparing for baptism. They will go down into the tomb, the waters of the fount, and be raised up to life in the words "I baptize you in the name of the Father, the Son, and the Holy Spirit. And they too will die and will be raised up, alive in Christ Jesus the Lord."

This is baptism, which we have all shared in and the power of which we have known in our lives. Lazarus was dead, but is now alive. He lives, but he will die again. We have died to our old ways of life, to the ways of evil and sin, and have been raised to the life of the Spirit of God, and are being raised as the children of God, knowing the same relationship to God the Father as his beloved child, Jesus, knew. Death has no more power over us and cannot hold us. But we, like Lazarus, will die again. When we die, we will die in Christ, as we have lived in Christ. But from the moment of our baptisms, we live until we die as Lazarus lived from the moment he was called forth from the grave by the sound of the Word of God made flesh, until he too died again and was laid to rest with his ancestors. What we do between our baptisms and our deaths is practice resurrection!

What is the opposite of death? Often the immediate response to this straightforward question is life! And that is the wrong answer. Oh, it is the answer much of our culture and society would have us thoughtlessly buy into, but it is not the truth. The opposite of death is birth, and what happens in between is life. There is life in the womb, before we are brought forth, but that life is categorically different from the life we experience and grow in consciously all through our years. And there is life in and after death, as well. Especially for those who believe, we stake our lives on a life that is truer, dearer, and more complete and whole than this one we know now. This life is set in motion in our bodies and our souls—this life in God begins at our baptisms and matures, grows, develops, and is formed in us until our last breath into the waiting arms of our God of Life, as he once caught his other beloved child, his first born, Jesus, the Crucified One, as he died.

Resurrection is God's doing, God's work, God's way of being. Resurrection is God's protest against the finality of death. It is love staring down violence and laughter in the tomb. It is the reversal of death, the shattering of its hold on human beings' lives. It is our God of life who has the last word. The Resurrection of Jesus is God the Father's answer to anyone who kills, murders, causes the innocent to suffer, decrees death in war and ethnic cleansing, legalizes it as government controlled and sanctioned murder, anyone who considers other human beings expendable or collateral damage, or who thinks that killing a prophet or silencing someone who tells the truth renders him harmless, her cry mute.

The theologian J. Molthmann has written extensively on what the Resurrection of Jesus says about our God. Honed down to bare bones, it proclaims that God's graciousness is rooted and sourced in his own life and that His graciousness is now extended to all of us. Because of Jesus's resurrection, we are called, demanded even, to be analyzers of human history, especially the history of suffering, pain, horror, death, war, and violence, and to judge it and speak of it in light of Jesus's own death and resurrection. If we are followers of Jesus, then we must stand with God publicly in the world and take God's part, as Jesus did, by verbally and physically protesting with our very lives against the violence and suffering that are accepted, tolerated, and practiced in the world as inevitable. He writes in one of his Easter sermons:

> Death is an evil power now, in life's very midst. It is the economic death of the person we allow to starve; the political death of the people who are oppressed; the social death of the handicapped; the noisy death that strikes through bombs and torture, and the soundless death of the apathetic soul. Face the cross and protest against the finality of violence. Act with courage (Do this and remember me) and refuse to bend before the powers of darkness that use suffering and death as tools to retain power. Easter is the refusal to admit that anyone could be left for dead! (From personal notes)

These are staggering words, true words that announce resurrection as the most subversive act of God in human history and the most subversive belief we acknowledge before God and each other. We live defiant, trembling in fear still, but reliant on our God, who has raised Jesus from the dead. This is bedrock. This is where we stand as Christians. And we begin with this stance in the world when we rise from the waters of baptism, dripping with the oil of chrism, and gasp as we begin to sing the Alleluias with others who believe in this God of life, life everlasting, here and now.

The Resurrection is the culmination of the Father's liberating love for his beloved Son, who was obedient, knowing that speaking and doing the truth in love would cost his life. This is God's response to the cross, to all manner of execution, killing, and murder, brutal, legal, unjust, and not to be permitted among believers. The Resurrection reveals a defiant God who resists violence with powerful nonviolence and refuses to allow death to keep its grip on his child, on any child he has made. And by raising Jesus from the dead, he raised every story he ever told, every sermon he preached, every value he stood for, every preference for the poor and the outcast that he espoused. The Resurrection is confirmation of Jesus's words to his disciples at the last supper.

> The words that I say to you I do not speak on my own; but the Father who dwells in me does his works. Believe me that I am in the Father and the Father is in me; but if you do not, then believe me because of the works themselves. (John 14:10b–11)

But the lines that follow immediately shock us into the reality of resurrection life!

> Very truly, I tell you, the one who believes in me will also do the works that I do and, in fact, will do greater works than these, because I am going to the

Father. I will do whatever you ask in my name, so that the Father may be glorified in the Son. If in my name you ask me for anything, I will do it.

"If you love me, you will keep my commandments. And I will ask the Father, and he will give you another Advocate, to be with you forever. This is the Spirit of truth, whom the world cannot receive, because it neither sees him nor knows him. You know him, because he abides with you, and he will be in you.

"I will not leave you orphaned; I am coming to you. In a little while the world will no longer see me, but you will see me; because I live, you also will live. On that day you will know that I am in my Father, and you in me, and I in you. (John 14:12–20)

These words in Jesus's mouth, written for the community of the Beloved Disciple as many as seventy or more years after the death and resurrection of Jesus, both conceal and reveal Jesus's depths as the Truth of God, as the dying and rising One. But they also reveal and confirm that this affirmation by the Father of Jesus's life and death is now extended to all who believe and follow after him. We are baptized into Christ, bear his image upon our hearts and souls, and practice resurrection life in imitation of his own life, death, and being raised to glory.

We will begin our study by searching out the four Gospels and their many narratives of the Resurrection. Paul's letters and many of the hymns and prayers of the early church were written and devised early, but it is these stories that carry the heart of the message. There are two overwhelming realities to all of these stories: the empty tomb and the appearances of Jesus to individuals and groups of His followers. The stories span as much as seventy years of belief in the Christian community as its members sought so distill their experiences, their failures and strengths under persecution, the spread of the church and the power in the gospel proclamation of resurrection and Jesus, the Beloved Son of the Father, raised to life by the power of the Spirit, shared with us in baptism and Eucharist. The church became, in the words of a theologian, "the sacrament of the Risen Lord," the place where the Risen Lord's presence could be touched and tapped into and where this Presence transformed believers more and more into the image of their Crucified and Risen Lord.

The church kept looking back—as far back as the earlier testaments, gleaning from old stories new insights in light of their experience of the Christ who was alive! They remembered their own experience in light of the prophecies and promises of the ancient ones, the Psalms and Jesus's own words that they took to heart in deeper and truer ways with the gift of the Paraclete, who reminded them and taught them all that they needed to know to thrive in the grace of God. Their belief was proclaimed before it was inscribed in stories that held potent the shock of resurrection life for Jesus and his followers. The Acts of the Apostles and the letters carry short formulas of belief, but it is the stories that draw us into their experience and allow us to know for ourselves in the telling of the Good News what happened to them, as it is happening to us now.

The great theologian and preacher Raymond Brown wrote about what the timeline and process were as they proclaimed belief and then came to tell it in stories, so that those who came after them, those who weren't present in Jerusalem, could know the power of what had happened:

> Our Christian ancestors spoke about the Resurrection long before they wrote about it. The first believers proclaimed the truth by word of mouth in forceful slogans and exclamations: "The Lord was raised indeed, and has appeared to Simon [Peter]" (Luke 24:34). In Jerusalem in particular, biting challenges are recalled associating the Crucifixion and the Resurrection: "You crucified this Jesus . . . but God raised him up" (Acts 2:23–24; 4:10; 5:30–31; 10:39–40).
>
> Four steps are mentioned by Paul in a formula delivered to him from the earliest days of his coming to faith: "That Christ *died* . . . that he was *buried*, that he was *raised* on the third day according to the Scriptures, and that he *appeared* (1 Corinthians 15:3–5). What this sequence of events meant for Jews and Gentiles alike is explained by Paul: Jesus was "put to death for our trespasses and raised for our justification" (Romans 4:25).
>
> As vivid as these proclamations were, the story form proved to be a more effective way of conveying the full impact of the Resurrection. The association between the Crucifixion and the Resurrection needed to be fleshed out in a dramatic way so that those who were not present in Jerusalem could understand what God had done in making Jesus victorious over death. Consequently the Gospel stories are quite different from the brief formulas preserved for us from the early preaching. ["Jesus Is Risen! The Gospel Resurrection Narrative." *St. Anthony Messenger* (April 1994): 12]

This writer, exegete, preacher, teacher, and pastor spent nearly four decades researching and writing his opus magnus on the crucifixion narratives of the Gospels. Just weeks before he died, he was interviewed about what he was working on and writing next. When he was asked if he was going to write another book, similar to the gospel narratives of the Passion accounts, but this time on the Resurrection accounts, he said yes . . . and not really. He replied that he "planned on doing the research for that book, on the Resurrection narratives, face-to-face with God." He died within weeks of his words. But he wrote of the Resurrection often, and it was woven through all his writings as core to the understandings of any of the Scriptures.

So we will begin with the stories that have characteristics peculiar to themselves and extend that reality of resurrection and what it meant for the early church and how it transformed a group of terrified people into steadfast believers in a Crucified and Risen Lord. We will look at them in the order they were written—Mark, Matthew, Luke, and John—and it will be noticed that they build on each other, bits and pieces of one story becoming full-blown testaments in another gospel. Again it is the power of the Spirit in the church, inspiring the writers to gather and scribe what is necessary for each of the church communities to practice and pass on their faith to others.

These stories are familiar, and sometimes such familiarity precludes our hearing, really hearing, what is happening and what is being proclaimed: its ramifications and meaning for us today. Perhaps an incident that was shared with me will help us be open and slow to assume that we know what we are reading or to understand what we believe after long years as Christians, followers of the Crucified and Risen One.

Once upon a time, a young man was staying with friends while recuperating from surgery and cancer. He was grateful for his friends' hospitality and wanted to thank them, but had no money or resources. However, his friends had fish in an aquarium, not big, but big enough. They spent hours watching the fish, entranced. It soothed everyone and provided hours of conversation and company among them. But while they watched the fish, they didn't often clean the tank and the fish were beginning to look a bit seedy and move more slowly than fish should because of the crud that was accumulating in the tank. He decided that he could thank them for all they did for him by cleaning out the tank.

As soon as they left one morning for work, he set to work. The first problem was where to put the fish while he cleaned the tank. He decided on the bathtub on the same floor. It was an ancient variety, with great feet and large, long enough for someone six feet tall or more to stretch out in easily. He transported the fish, dumped them into their luxurious temporary quarters, and went to work cleaning their tank. It took hours, but finally there was fresh water, new algae, stones along the bottom, plants and stone pieces to swim through and play around. Back he went to the bathtub for the fish. And he was startled to find out what they were doing in their great tub.

Nothing! They weren't swimming its length and breadth. In fact, they were occupying the exact amount of space that they had left behind in their tank, maybe a quarter of the space they had in the tub to roam around in. They stayed enclosed in just that size and area. He was fascinated. He tried to get them to move out of their self-imposed prison. He ruffled the waters. No response. He poured their food way down at the opposite end. No response. He left a trail of food from their stationary place to the other end of the tub. No response. He created waves, with the waters splashing over the sides of the tub onto the floor. They stayed put. After trying everything he could think of, he gave up; they remained exactly in the area they had known in their tank. He took them back and dumped them into the clean tank and began to wonder and question himself. Hmm, do I live like those fish? Do I limit myself by my past experiences and knowledge, content to stay where I'm safe and it's known and begin to think that my small world is the world? Have I been moved up to a huge bathtub, but I'm still swimming around like I'm in a small tank? Bathtub! I don't live in a bathtub. I dwell in an ocean! Am I still living like I'm stuck in a fish tank?

I'd go a good deal further. By baptism, the waters of life, we dwell in the universe, the womb and heart of our God of Life. Do our lives reflect the vastness and power, the depth and horizons of God's vision and embrace, or are we content to swim around in a little space, no matter what grace and God's boundless love try to lure us out into? That is what the reality of resurrection does for us: it keeps moving us into deeper and deeper, cleaner and wider waters of life and freedom. But we must practice resurrection, alone and with others, to make sure that we are not shrinking God and life down to manageable areas and comfort zones that reveal only our fears, not the calling we have been given as baptized Christians: to live in the freedom of the children of God!

There is a grand old Irish prayer that can start us daily on our practice of resurrection life. It is attributed to St. Patrick and is found in old devotionals, but often chanted and prayed by both choirs and folks who start their days with it on their lips. It is a long prayer. Pieces of it are copied here to introduce it as a morning practice. Once you are familiar with it, it is easily remembered by singing it, making up your own melody as you go along. It falls naturally into music, the dance of resurrection while you go about your morning rituals.

I Arise This Day

I arise today
through a mighty strength, the invocation of the Trinity,
through belief in the Threeness,
through confession of the Oneness
towards the Creator.
I arise today in the power of the Incarnation of Christ with his Baptism,
I arise today in the power of His Crucifixion with His burial,
I arise today in the victory of His Resurrection with His Ascension,
I arise today by virtue of His coming on the Judgment day.
I arise today in the love of the seraphim,
in the obedience of the angels,
in the hope of resurrection and its sure reward,
in the prayers of the patriarchs and matriarchs,
in the predictions of the prophets,

in the preaching of the apostles,
in the faith of confessors,
in the purity of virgins,
in the deeds of righteous men and women.
I arise today by the power of Heaven, in the light of the sun,
I arise today in the brightness of the moon, and the splendour of fire,
I arise today in the flashing of lightning, and the swiftness of wind,
I arise today in the depths of the sea and the stability of earth, the
   compactness of rocks.
I arise today and bind myself today in
God's power to guide me, God's might to uphold me,
God's wisdom to teach me, God's eye to watch over me.
God's ear to hear me, God's Word to give me speech,
God's hand to guide me, God's way to lie before me,
God's shield to shelter me, God's Host to secure me,
against the snare of evil, and the seduction of vices,
against the lusts of nature, against anyone who would harm me,
whether far or near, whether the few or with many.
Christ with me, Christ before me,
Christ behind me, Christ within me,
Christ beneath me, Christ above me,
Christ at my right, Christ at my left,
Christ in the heart of everyone who thinks of me,
Christ in the mouth of everyone who speaks of me,
Christ in every eye that sees me,
Christ in every ear that hears me.
I arise today
in the Threeness of the One
in the Oneness of the Three, in the Trinity. Amen

2

Intimations: Stories That Prepare for Resurrection

Humankind cannot bear too much reality.

—T.S. Eliot, "Burnt Norton"

*T*he Resurrection narratives complete the Gospels. And yet the Gospels are written in retrospect, after the life, death, and resurrection of Jesus has been experienced and the gift of the Spirit has come to clothe the followers of Jesus from on high. The accounts of Matthew, Mark, Luke, and John are inspired by that same Spirit to enable the writers to see backward and present Jesus in such a way that the present is illuminated and a future opens up with the grace of many possibilities because of that one moment in all time: the Father raising Jesus from the dead in the power of the Spirit. Meaning shifts and changes. Eyes are opened, and you realize that before you saw everything blurred, if you saw at all. And oh, what you missed altogether! There is a haunting poem by the Spanish poet Antonio Machado (1875–1939) that speaks to this phenomenon:

> Wayfarer, the only way is your footsteps. There is no other.
> Wayfarer, there is no way, you make the way as you go.
> As you go, you make the way and stopping to look behind
> You see the path that your feet will travel again.
> Wayfarer, there is no way—only foam trails in the sea.

> (*Selected Poems*, 1982)

This can explain somewhat how the church first lived and told the stories of Jesus looking backward through the lens of the Resurrection that highlighted places they had overlooked entirely or misread. And while they struggled to follow in Jesus's footsteps after the Resurrection, the Spirit accompanied them, teaching them what they needed as they went. Jesus's death, resurrection, and ascension were the impetus for springing forward and the source of their interpretation of what came before these momentous events. And of course, this is the pattern of our own lives as well. Sheila Cassidy, a doctor who worked in Chile and was arrested for caring for victims without first ascertaining which side they were on and was tortured, has written:

> Much of our understanding of God's action in our lives is achieved in hindsight. When a particular crisis or event in our life has passed we cry out in astonishment like Jacob, "The Lord is in this place and I never knew it."

There are pivotal stories in the gospel accounts of Jesus concerning resurrection: the stories of Jesus raising the widow of Naim's only son from the dead; the raising of the daughter of Jarius from the dead; the raising of Lazarus, his friend. There are intimations that he is trying to share with his disciples what is coming—the Transfiguration accounts where he is seen standing between Moses and Elijah speaking of his Passover in Jerusalem. And there are statements about Jonah and the whale, the destruction of the temple and its being built up again in three days, along with the warning and prophetic sayings about the Son of Man, his rejection, and being handed over to death and rising on the third day. They appear enigmatic if they are not read looking back from the vantage point of the empty tomb and the Resurrection appearances that followed. There is a simple children's story that illustrates this for us.

Once upon a time, there was a young child who came home from school one day with the task of putting a huge puzzle of a world map together. The pieces were made of newspaper and the map was detailed and complex. He spent hours on it and was frustrated. It wouldn't come together. He just didn't know what it was supposed to look like when it was together and completed. He sat on the floor looking at all the pieces wanting to cry, but refusing to give up.

His mother appeared and said to him, "I can give you a clue that might help you out." "What?" he answered tersely. "There's a different picture on the other side of the pieces." The child's eyes lit up. "Really?" Quickly, he turned them all over and spread them all out again on the floor. But what was the other picture? His mother smiled and said, "It's a secret, and it looks like something you know best in all the world." And she walked away to leave him to his new task. The boy sat and looked and thought about her words and then between the bits and pieces on the floor and the certainty in his heart, he went to work. And within minutes, the puzzle started coming together. The picture was of people: a man and woman and many children, just like his own family. And he knew how to put them together. When his puzzle and his family were finished, he carefully rolled the paper and turned it over on the other side—

there was the map of the world, a world he did not as yet know, but had his whole life ahead of him to explore and visit and know as intimately as he did the people in his family.

It is a perfect story for trying to talk about specific pieces of the gospel stories that are intimations of what is coming. Just as someone put the world on one side and people on the other (which one came first?), so the community of believers finely crafted the Gospels in the same manner. They told the story of Jesus to be read, but there are other stories, inspired by the Spirit of Truth and Holiness, that are secrets hidden in the text, and they were put in along with the main thrust of the story. Each of the Gospels is filled with clues that alert us to the fact that there is always more going on than meets the eye. If you know the ending, it is easier to read and understand. And at the same time, when you begin to put the clues together, the secret world that is revealed is just that—another world that it will take lifetimes to discover and experience through the power of the Father, the Risen Lord, the Word and the Spirit in the community of believers. It is almost impossible to do on one's own. The community of believers is core to knowing what's underlying in the text and why it is in there, as a code, a language for our own living as a church and followers of the Risen Lord.

Now it is time to begin looking at some of these passages that enrich and give depth to the Resurrection accounts and afford us the road or map that we can use when we go back through the text again and again, year after year in the liturgical cycle, reading, preaching, and celebrating them in the Paschal Mystery of Word and sacraments. We will begin with the stories of those Jesus raised from the dead. These stories share—and in this diverge radically from the story of the Father raising Jesus from the dead—the stark fact that although these people have been raised from the dead and now live, they will all die again.

All three synoptic Gospels—Matthew, Mark, and Luke—tell the story of the raising of the daughter of Jarius from the dead. The story of the woman with the hemorrhage that is healed by touching the hem of Jesus's cloak is sandwiched between the beginning and the end of the story. It is found in Matthew 9:18–26, Mark 5:21–43, and Luke 8:40–56. In the first lines we meet the man who is the leader of a synagogue who comes to Jesus publicly while he is teaching and falls on his knees before him, begging him to come immediately and heal his daughter. In Matthew, the child is already dead. In the other two stories, she is near death. For the Jews, a person wasn't actually considered dead until he or she had been buried for three days, but in either case, time is of the utmost importance. This is a man with some power and standing in the community, but in the face of death, the death of someone he loves, he is helpless and distraught. Death levels us all. He prays, "My daughter has just died;

but come and lay your hand on her, and she will live" (Matt. 9:18). In Luke, we learn that she is his only daughter and that she is twelve years old, and he begs Jesus to come to his house. And in all the stories, Jesus turns from his teaching and goes with him immediately, with the crowd pressing around him and pushing from behind, curious to see what will happen.

Then comes the interruption in all the stories—that of the woman who for twelve years has been suffering from hemorrhages that drain her life and her savings, and she only gets worse with any cure she tries. Because her condition involves blood, she is seen and treated in the community as one who is dead, unclean, untouchable. Her life would have been strictly curtailed, and she would be unable to participate in any activity among people, including, sadly, prayer and worship in the synagogue. She is desperate, and she is adept at being invisible and disappearing into crowds. She thinks, if only I can touch his clothes, the fringes of his garment, then I will be healed. And in Mark we are told specifically that she has heard about Jesus—she sees him as a lifeline, as hope, as a shred of possibility for wellness, wholeness, and life. And in the instant that she touches his garment, she is made whole. She senses it and knows it in her body.

She is told, "Take heart, daughter; your faith has made you well" (Matt. 9:22). Mark extends these words: "Daughter, your faith has made you well; go in peace, and be healed of your disease" (Mark 5:34). Luke's version is very similar. Now this healing has been on the way to the place of death and it is taking up precious time. And at just this point of Jesus proclaiming peace and trust to the woman cured, messengers arrive to tell Jarius that his daughter is dead and there is no need to trouble the teacher any longer (Mark and Luke). But Jesus quickly turns to Jarius to reassure him and commands him, "Do not fear, only believe!" And they continue on to the house.

Now in Matthew, Jesus the teacher becomes even stronger and more decisive, and he commands the public mourners to stop their playing and dirges and go away for the girl is not dead, she is sleeping, and they laugh him to scorn. In Matthew the account of the raising is stark and unadorned: "he went in, took her by the hand and the girl got up" (Matt. 9:25); but in Mark and Luke, he takes with him, into the house, her mother and father and those who were with him, and in Luke they are named as his disciples Peter, James, and John, who are often witnesses to these amazing events of Jesus. In both Mark's and Luke's accounts, a heart-warming tenderness and regard for the parents and the child in the face of death afford us a glimpse of Jesus that is so human and so filled with the power of God. Listen to them both.

> [H]e went in to where the child was. He took her by the hand and said to her, "Talitha cum," which means, "Little girl, get up!" And immediately the girl got up and began to walk about (she was twelve years of age). At this

they were overcome with amazement. He strictly ordered them that no one should know this, and told them to give her something to eat." (Mark 5:40b–43)

But he took her by the hand and called out, "Child, get up!" Her spirit returned, and she got up at once. Then he directed them to give her something to eat. Her parents were astounded; but he ordered them to tell no one what had happened. (Luke 8:54–56)

In all the stories Jesus tells the people waiting around for the child to die, and those who tell Jarius that there's no need to bother the Teacher, since she's dead and that's obviously out of his power, to stop crying and weeping and to go away; he is ridiculed and scorned when he tells them that she is sleeping and not dead. There is a saying that fits appropriately here about truth.

All Truth passes through three stages.
First, it is ridiculed.
Second, it is violently opposed.
Third, it is accepted as being self-evident.
(Arthur Schopenhauer, nineteenth-century German philosopher)

And the story is about raising two people from the dead, from two differing kinds of death. The woman with the hemorrhages has been dead, made dead by her neighbors and community and Jewish law because of what is wrong with her. She has been accused of sin, belittled, exiled and never touched, shunned and excluded from all the basic human experiences of eating, praying, and speaking with anyone else. This is living death, being entombed in others' fear, insecurity, and self-righteousness. She's been dead for twelve years. And the young girl, who is twelve, who would have just come of age in the Jewish community, would have been considered a woman. The older woman has been condemned to death for as long as the young girl has been alive. Jesus raises them both to life. The older woman reaches out for life found in the person of Jesus—even in the clothes he wore—while all around him, even his followers in their blindness do not know that life is in their midst. And the young woman is brought to life by the entreaties, the prayers of her father who loves her. The nature of God is to give life when begged for in love for another. Dante Alighieri wrote of God, "The Infinite Goodness has such wide arms that it takes whatever turns to it." In the midst of the crowd curious about Jesus's words, his person, and his powers, there are only two, a desperate father and an exhausted woman, who seek and reach for the heart of Jesus's words, his person, and his power—life itself.

Was the child actually dead? For people who already believe in Jesus, it is not even a question. It is assumed that she is. For those seeking reasons, there aren't any. Brendan Kennelly once wrote, "I know it does not matter that I do not understand." Believing is either a quantum leap past reasons or a willed response to what cannot be explained. And there are some knowings that are only given after proof or reasoning is left aside. Meister Eckhart says, "The less theorizing you do about God, the more receptive you are to his inpouring." With these stories of Jesus raising from the dead another person who will die again, it is more important to look at the life that person is given and why it was crucial for others to see this life given, handed over. In all the stories, he takes the little girl by the hand and raises her up and commands her to live. And then instructs those around her to give her something to eat. At root, these are stories of baptism in the community, of being raised up to new life (and we will die again), and being fed in the presence of Jesus. And the exhortation not to tell anyone else is a hint about the mysteries of life and death, baptism and resurrection life, and the Eucharist that are cherished by only those who know them in their own persons and share them in the community that is the family of Jesus. These are all intimations about the meanings of the text, and they are all true, as are the ones that have not been found yet by the community. Again Meister Eckhart says, "Every single creature is full of God and is a book about God." And so is every single story and person and piece of Scripture that is the Word of God. It is given to us in the power of the Spirit for those who are baptized and confirmed in the Spirit, not so much for understanding, although that is there too, as for our conversion and transformation.

The stories question us. Whom do we love enough to beg and pray for in public as that person faces death, knowing that our position and reputation could be severely compromised? (And it cannot just be family, among believers.) "Do not fear. Only believe." These words of Jesus are commands. Are they the undercurrent of our lives and our responses to what happens around us in the world? Do we belong to a community made of family, of selected disciples who are publicly aligned with Jesus and those who are described as "those who were with him" (perhaps the woman just cured)? And do we rely on them, letting them in turn lift us up, calling us past our fear and deeper into belief. Miguel De Unamuno y Ingo wrote:

> I believe in God, in the same way in which I believe in my friends, because
> I feel the breath of his love, and his invisible, intangible hand, bringing me
> here, carrying me there, pressing upon me.

Do we live with this awareness of life, or like the crowd pressing around Jesus and even his "closest" disciples, have we still not sought deeper answers, prayed and practiced belief, and shared others' desperate pain that draws us into intimacy and knowledge with Jesus?

Have we known the surge of life within us, known gratitude for healing, forgiveness, and life, like the woman struggling so for twelve years, and risked everything, first perhaps in desperation and then consciously as followers in a new way of life? Do we follow those surges of life, rather than let life erode within us and in the world? Listen to this person's words:

> Sisters and brothers, the way of peace, justice, love is the only true way. Other things may appear to be true for a moment, but they are a mirage. . . . The resurrection means that those surges of life we feel, those dreams of a better world to which we would like to cling but are not quite certain we dare, those times when we walk the way of life on behalf of someone and feel our own life renewed within us are not illusion but reality. (Arie Brouwer, *Overcoming the Threat of Death*)

In light of Jesus's resurrection, we must read these stories with the eye and heart of belief and our baptisms, reading beyond and deeply into the text to find out what is the state of our own resurrection life, and letting the Scriptures ask us questions, probing into our fear and belief, commanding us to live. We must go way beyond the physical being brought back from the dead, because the child and the woman will die again. And though we have been baptized into the death and resurrection of Christ and have died and risen with him, we too will die again, and it is essential that we are practicing and growing in the art of living this new life in the presence of Christ. This is Ambrose's prayer.

> Lord Jesus Christ, you are for me medicine for when I am sick; you are my strength when I need help; you are life itself when I fear death; you are the way when I long for heaven; you are light when all is dark; you are my food when I need nourishment. Amen.

These stories and those that follow are all about our dying and rising in baptism and our lives and our deaths until we die again into the fullness of life in Christ.

THE RAISING OF THE WIDOW OF NAIM'S SON (LUKE 7:11–17)

> Widows and orphans are to be revered like the altar.
>
> —Didascalia Apostolorum, third century

This story appears only in Luke and reveals Jesus as a prophet in the tradition of Elijah and Elisha (whom Jesus himself has cited in reference to himself and what he is preaching earlier; Luke 4), who also raised people from the dead as a sign of the power of the Word of God in their mouth. With belief in the Resurrection, we see Jesus not only as a prophet of the tradition with the Word of God in his mouth, but we believe that Jesus is the Word of God made flesh, the very life of God. We listen to the story as believers, seeking to know how Jesus is trying to raise us to life and how and why we are to live this new life that we are given in baptism.

> Soon afterwards, he went to a town called Na'in, and his disciples and a large crowd went with him. As he approached the gate of the town, a man who had died was being carried out. He was his mother's only son, and she was a widow; and with her was a large crowd from the town. When the Lord saw her, he had compassion for her and said to her, "Do not weep." Then he came forward and touched the bier, and the bearers stood still. And he said, "Young man, I say to you, rise!" The dead man sat up and began to speak, and Jesus gave him to his mother. Fear seized all of them; and they glorified God saying, "A great prophet has risen among us!" and "God has looked favorably on his people." This word about him spread throughout Judea and all the surrounding country. (Luke 7:11–17)

Background can be essential to understanding, and the situation of widows without support from a family member at the time of Jesus was dire, literally life threatening. When her only son, her sole support and the one who would have given her a place in the community, dies, she herself is now in danger of dying. Those widows who found themselves without a family that would take them in and protect them became beggars, lived in the tombs outside villages and towns, or hired themselves out to soldiers. In every case, it was in reality being condemned to a life that was at best precarious and, at worst, a slow and lonely death. And Jesus sees her. That word "sees" for Jesus, and so for a Christian, says it all. He sees her grief and her loss and past that into a future that is deadening and without hope. She has no one. She is abandoned, without hope of any life after losing her only child. Jesus, who in the Gospel of Luke is himself the Suffering Servant, is compassion itself, knowing the pain of being human without being understood, accepted, or belonging to those who would literally live for you, so that you could live. And God in Jesus notices every small detail, every person in pain, everyone who suffers without kindness from others. A Chinese philosopher wrote, "Heaven's net is indeed vast. Though its meshes are wide, it misses nothing." And Jesus misses nothing. Or as Eckhart says, "The best name for God is compassion." And he will not let the community bury both of them. His words to her are blunt: "Do not weep!" She doesn't know it as yet, but she weeps in the presence of life and is bent in its shadow.

And he moves forward, into the crowd of mourners accompanying her and stops at the foot of the bier, touching it! Even the corpse bearers stop, accosted by this stranger who is unafraid of the reality of death and breaks the taboo and touches what carries death among us. His words are a command, "Young man, I say to you, rise!" What Jesus says always, everywhere in the face of death that will especially have consequences for others, contradicts death, stops it in its tracks, and does not allow it to destroy others' lives as well. One word: rise! And the body of the young man obeys. Jesus's word is imperious. It is not to be denied or ignored. It commands obedience. The young man sits up and begins speaking, and we read, he "gave him to his mother," a very tender phrase reminiscent of Elijah giving the widow who cares for him her child back from death. As once God gave her the gift of a child, a newborn life, now he gives her child back to her again. But as once she cared for him, now he, the child, is given to care for her, the widow. We are not told the reactions of the widow and her son. But one can surmise. And their life afterward? What would it be to know that you were brought back from the dead to care for one person? What would your reaction be to the person who summoned you back with a word: "Rise." How would you spend the rest of your life in response to that gift given again?

We are told the reaction of the crowd: fear seizes them all, and they glorify God, recognizing the work and the word of a prophet in their midst. This is the fear that can be the beginning of wisdom, that is on the verge of awe and worship. And they use a specific word in the next sentence to describe themselves as a crowd, a people in relation to God, with Jesus in their midst. "God has looked favorably on us people!" This is the same word used by the angel to describe Mary's relation to God as he comes to bring the gospel of the incarnation to her (Luke 1:30). This is the reality of the presence of the Word of God coming into the world to oppose death. This story takes us to the edge of life, to a place of fear, loss, insecurity, isolation, and lack of justice, providing the basic necessities of life for all rule. And those who follow the Word of Life must stop these realities and their impact on people dead in their tracks and bring the alternative of life and new relationships to these situations. And it begins with this exhortation by Hadewijch, a medieval mystic: "Be fervent in God, and let nothing grieve you, whatever you encounter." This is a command, in the same vein as "Do not weep!"

And what about us? What do we see when someone dies? Are we aware of those who are widowed, orphaned, left behind to fend for themselves? Do our churches and parishes tend to them as a first priority, making sure that they do not fall through the cracks of a society that is destructively individualistic and even makes a profit from funerals? Are we in opposition to and forcibly changing laws that impact single parents, widows, orphans, the elderly, and the sick negatively, leaving them with nothing when someone who is their sole support and love dies? Jesus is about making new relationships, realigning people so that life is served, especially in the face of death, which is inevitable, eventually. If this young man now lives to care for his widowed mother and is now a member of Jesus's community when he dies again, or his mother dies, there will be another family that will take them in, support and live with them. Are we the people of life, the followers of the Risen Prophet who "give people back to one another" in situations where there was no hope, no future, none of the basics of shelter, companionship, food, and relationship that are essential to survival and then real living?

And this is about baptism. All of us have been summoned by the Word of God back into life. We have stood on the threshold of the tomb, the baptismal pool, and stepped over it and gone down into the waters and heard the words "Rise to new life!" and that's when we can begin speaking, hesitantly, a whole new language of life that is not cramped and limited by death's clutch at our throat and our souls. Simone Weil writes, "God is rich in mercy. I know this wealth of his with the certainty of experience. I have touched it." We all have, in our baptisms, and we are all called to be that touch in a community dedicated to life, and especially to the lives of the poor, the widowed, and those left outside the gates of our cities to fend for themselves. The church in baptism is a community born of those outside the gates, at the borders and margins, on their way to the tomb and met on the way there by life itself. This is the Word that once commanded us to rise and now commands us again to live for others in their need, a gift of unforeseen life for those who need it the most, here and now. This is our daily baptismal resurrection life. How are we living it today?

THE RAISING OF LAZARUS (JOHN 11)

> I believe we were created for ecstasy. And redeemed for it, at considerable cost. Certain vagrant moments are, moreover, clues to the native structure and texture of things.
>
> —Daniel Berrigan

This story, more than any other, gives clues to the belief of the early church and teaches what baptism entailed. That is why it is told on the fifth Sunday of Lent every year when catechumens are preparing for baptism. For what happened to Lazarus is what they will experience at the Easter vigil when they are baptized: buried in the tomb, the waters of baptism, and drawn forth by the

Word of God into the new life of the community that "unbinds them and sets them free." This is the symbol and the story of how beloved disciples are made in the community of John, the community of the Beloved Disciple, never actually named, so that each person baptized into the death and resurrection of Jesus becomes that other disciple, the "one whom Jesus loved." It is our vocation from our baptismal day and it is the beginning of our life, hidden with Christ in God.

This is a story about another person raised from the dead who will die again, but it is also the paradigm of every person baptized and raised from the dead. It is our story. Lazarus is not his given name, but his baptismal name. It is our name. We are each and all the ones who have been brought back from the dead by Jesus to live now in a new relationship to him until we die once again and know the mystery of death in Christ and everlasting life. This story assumes that we are baptized or about to be baptized when we read it and it is structured with meanings from the baptismal liturgy. There is no limit to the understandings that are etched into this text by the Spirit of God. The limit of understanding is in us who do not put the text into practice and become Lazarus in our baptisms.

He is described first as a certain man who is ill, Lazarus of Bethany, the village of Mary and her sister Martha. Then he is described tenderly in a note sent by the sisters to Jesus as "he whom you love is ill." And then we are told that Jesus loved Martha and her sister and Lazarus. And in many translations when Jesus tells his disciples bluntly that he is dead, he says "our beloved Lazarus is dead." What is of essence is that he is the beloved of God, and what we are to remember is that each of us is that beloved of God, and no matter what happens, even death, we remain in that love. That is our primary identity, relationship, and meaning in life and in death. The poet William Butler Yeats writes, when he speaks of each of our souls, "No human soul is like any other human soul, and therefore the love of God for any human soul is infinite, for no other soul can satisfy the same need in God."

Even though Jesus loves all three of them dearly, he waits when he receives the message of Lazarus's illness and allows him to die. We must all die. There can be no escaping that, in life and in sacrament. If Lazarus is to be raised to new life, he must pass through death, and if we are to be raised to new life, we must die to ourselves and all that we were once, before being summoned into the presence of the Living God in our baptisms and given that life of God shared with us in the death and rising of Jesus. When he arrives in Bethany on the outskirts of Jerusalem (the cross is always shadowed in our deaths and baptisms), Lazarus has been buried in the tomb for four days. Jesus asks where they have laid him and goes to the tomb, deeply disturbed. It is a cave with a stone lying against it.

The steps in raising Lazarus from the dead are simple: first roll away the stone so that the glory of God can be revealed. Next, Jesus stands and prays out loud before all the people for their benefit.

So they took away the stone. And Jesus looked upward and said, "Father, I thank you for having heard me. I knew that you always hear me, but I have said this for the sake of the crowd standing here, so that they may believe that you sent me." When he had said this, he cried with a loud voice, "Lazarus, come out!" The dead man came out, his hands and feet bound with strips of cloth, and his face wrapped in a cloth. Jesus said to them, "Unbind him, and let him go" (John 11:41–44).

The voice of Jesus cries out and Lazarus is called by name and told to come out of the tomb. Most probably it is a stand-up tomb, and Lazarus is standing inside, wrapped in his burial shrouds. They can see him there, when the stone is rolled away from the entrance to the tomb. He falls out, bound hand and foot. And then Jesus orders those around him to go and unwrap him from the cords of death, uncover his face, stand him up, and turn him to face Jesus. And it is, of course, Mary and Martha his sisters, whom Jesus loves, who run and obey Jesus's words.

This is the ritual of baptism. Note all the similarities to the Resurrection stories of Jesus. He's been in the tomb for four days. He is really dead according to Jewish belief, and he is wrapped in his shrouds, like a mummy. Death holds him tightly in its grip. The stone is rolled away from the entrance to the tomb, and he is standing there before them all. Interestingly, there are baptismal fonts from the third and fourth century that are so narrow that only one person can stand in them, in stone up to one's waist or higher (painted on the vaults of ceilings in crypts of churches in Ravenna, Italy). And Jesus prays on behalf of the people, as the community prays to God for those who will be baptized and those called to the constant conversion of ever-deeper and more-demanding belief and practice of this new life beyond the hold of death. And he calls Lazarus by name, as we are baptized and named by God in public.

And Lazarus comes out. He obeys the Word of God made flesh in Jesus. That word is stronger than death, reaching past all death: sin, evil, injustice, violence, suffering, and physical death, loss, despair—everything that reeks and stinks of death, and it draws us back into the light and into life before God and all the people. But he is still bound by the strips and linen cloths, and he needs others to unbind him, stand him on his feet, and set him free. And each of us baptized into Christ needs to be unbound, untied from sin and evil, from death in all its forms with help from the community, stood on our feet, and with others learn to live in the freedom of the beloved children of God. Lazarus has been brought back from the dead, and John's community of the Beloved Disciple used this passage as the basis for the rite of baptism in their own churches.

All of them had known this story in their own bodies, hearts, minds, and souls as they became Christians, and at every Easter vigil, they enacted it again, unbinding and freeing the newly baptized, welcoming them into the embrace of the Risen Lord.

And later, Lazarus sits at table with Jesus, and Martha waits on him, and Mary anoints his feet in gratitude for what he has done for their brother and them. There is joy and exaltation, but in the midst of this, the decision is made to kill Jesus, and we are told in John that "the chief priests planned to put Lazarus to death as well, since it was on account of him that many of the Jews were deserting and were believing in Jesus" (John 12:10–11). And this was the reality of John's community. As people were baptized in the community of the Beloved Disciple and Christianity began to spread, those who were baptized, raised to new life, were persecuted and killed for their relationship to Jesus and for living with gratitude for what Jesus had done for them. This is our story, and we should spend all our lives seeking to understand its mysteries in our own lives. Our name is Lazarus, and our life begins at baptism.

Reading the Scriptures backward from the Resurrection and within the sacrament of baptism and within a community of believers together seeking to become the Body of Christ as witnesses in the world is difficult, a shift from reading them as individuals. But they are powerful. Thomas Merton writes:

> As a magnifying glass concentrates the rays of the sun into a little burning knot of heat that can set fire to a dry leaf or a piece of paper, so the mystery of Christ in the gospel concentrates the rays of God's light and fire to a point that sets fire to the human spirit.

JESUS'S THREE PREDICTIONS:
HIS PASSION, DEATH, AND RESURRECTION

> There are two kinds of Truth: small truth and great truth. You can recognize a small truth because its opposite is a falsehood. The opposite of a great truth is another great truth.
>
> (Niels Bohr, recipient of the 1922 Nobel Prize in Physics)

These predictions, warnings, foretellings, forebodings, reminders appear in all the Gospels, and they are first of all based on all the experiences and writings of the prophets of the earlier testament. Those who brought the Word of God to the people were always rejected, exiled, tortured, murdered, slandered, plotted against, ridiculed, and ignored. This is the history of prophets writ continuously, and Jesus speaks and walks within that tradition where all the prophets

die in Jerusalem before the leaders of the people, both political and religious, who conspire against the intrusion of the Word of God into their
carefully crafted plans that do not allow for God's design and will. What
proves the truthfulness of the prophet's words is either conversion of the
people or the suffering and death of the prophet, which accompanies the
coming to pass, the truthfulness, of their words in history. They always speak
of a God who is not easily manipulated to serve the interests of the powerful or the few in society, and God's Word always subverts reality, exposing it
at its roots as false and dehumanizing, empty of the grace and truth of God's
will. Recently Robert McAfee Brown wrote about this God of ours, "He's
not a 'safe' or a 'tame' God, securely lodged behind the bars of a distant
heaven; he has the most annoying manner of showing up when we least
want him; of confronting us in the strangest ways."

And again, they must be read backward and forward. The death and resurrection was reality steeped in belief and the ever-new experience of the Spirit's
wisdom of understanding given to the community that was knowing it again in
its own sufferings, rejection, martyrdom, and fervent hope in the final resurrection. It was present reality that was their history, their place of testing, and witness to what they believed and their personal and communal experience in relation to others: the Jews and the Romans. This helped to fashion how the
Gospels were written and what was emphasized and highlighted again and again.

Generally, the sayings come in threes, inserted in the Gospels at crucial
points where Jesus is being rejected by groups of people, the elders, the chief
priests, the Pharisees and scribes, the Sadducees, the people, and even his own
disciples. In Mark they begin at the half-way mark, in chapter 8, when he is
already being rejected by many of the leaders (it starts very early in Mark)
and is attempting to ascertain who his own disciples think he is instead of
what he has been trying to teach them. The people see him as a prophet in
the tradition of Elijah and John the Baptist, and Peter, speaking on behalf of
the others, tells him that he is the Messiah. They are thinking in simplistic
terms of some of the prophecies of the Old Testament that describe the Messiah as a political and religious leader who will regain the temple and power
in Jerusalem, freeing them from the hated Roman invaders who occupy their
land and their very temple. So when Peter answered Jesus saying, "You are
the Messiah," Jesus reacts strongly with the order not to tell anyone that
about him (Mark 8:28–30). And in the next line, he begins to try to teach
them (and us) the core, the hard stinging heart of who he really is and what
they can expect to happen to him (what in fact actually did happen to him).

Then he begins to teach them that the Son of Man must undergo great
suffering, and be rejected by the elders, the chief priests, and the scribes, and
be killed, and after three days, rise again. He says all this quite openly.

And with this first teaching of the cross, even Peter and his disciples balk and begin to reject him, ignoring much of what he says and the rising hatred around them and the plottings of those who find Jesus's words threatening, while the poor and those who are marginal to the religious community look to him as a savior—none of them understanding that he is prophet, the Word of God, the one who is to come, but not their version. In the very next lines, after turning on Peter and the disciples and calling them Satan, the one who hinders human beings from being the children of God, he says, "for you are setting your mind not on divine things but on human things" (Mark 8:33). He could just as easily be quoting the prophet Isaiah when he declares in the first person as Yahweh God himself, "For my thoughts are not your thoughts, nor are your ways my ways, says the Lord" (Isa. 55:8).

The second time this teaching is brought up is just in the next chapter. It always follows the same line, although small details are added in each text:

> [H]e was teaching his disciples, saying to them, "The Son of Man is to be betrayed into human hands, and they will kill him, and three days after being killed, he will rise again." But they did not understand what he was saying and were afraid to ask him. (Mark 9:31–32)

Their lack of understanding and their fear are starting to distance them from even asking what he means or how he knows these things. And then in the next chapter he speaks again, getting more and more specific. There is an intensity, a growing need for them to see what is already happening around them:

> They were on the road, going up to Jerusalem, and Jesus was walking ahead of them; they were amazed, and those who followed were afraid. He took the twelve aside again and began to tell them what was to happen to him, saying, "See, we are going up to Jerusalem, and the Son of Man will be handed over to the chief priests and the scribes, and they will condemn him to death; then they will hand him over to the Gentiles; they will mock him, and spit upon him, and flog him, and kill him; and after three days he will rise again." (Mark 10:32–34)

Jesus is being rejected by more and more people, individuals like the rich man who comes to him and walks away, the Pharisees who are constantly engaging him in debate for the sake of argument, rather than having any openness to what he is teaching, and his own disciples are panicking at the demands of the call to deny themselves, leave all to follow him, care for the poor, face persecution, and even the cross. Fear is beginning to seep in so deeply that they are blocking out whole pieces of what he is teaching and what is going on around them.

These tellings of the crucifixion, passion, death, and resurrection of Jesus are found in Matthew 16:21–26, 17:22–23, and 20:17–19. They are also in Luke 9:21–26, 9:43b–45, and 18:31–34. Some of these in Matthew and Luke are more specific calls to the cross and the cost of discipleship, urging his disciples to begin to empty themselves of their previous ideas and desires and deny themselves so that they can hear his words and follow in his way. And connected to this call to discipleship as a hard saying is the promise of judgment upon every human being according to their practice and actions and the judgment on all peoples and nations.

These sayings are a mixture of many things. They were in fact part of what Jesus was teaching before he went to Jerusalem and was killed. The level of rejection, hostility, anger, rage, and hate was building up because words were causing division between the poor and the masses of people hungry for hope and freedom and the leaders, who were disturbed at the rising of the people, afraid of what it would mean to the delicate balance of power they had in collusion with the Roman occupying forces. And while much of what Jesus was preaching was rooted firmly in the prophets and the law, there was also much that he was teaching that went beyond the law, questioning its outward practice and seeking always to go to the root and source of why it was written and how it affected people. He was questioning their belief and practices, and they were oftentimes coming up short and being exposed in hypocrisy. The few who were honestly seeking to hear him out were also too afraid to do it publicly.

Given the brutality of the Romans and the common practice of crucifixion for those who upset the status quo; incited the people; opposed their imposition of the law and truthfully confronted their violence and sacrilege, their lack of respect of worship; and those who openly broke rules of custom, crossing economic, religious, and political boundaries; all of these people posed threats not only to themselves, but to all associated with them, and to the leaders who were supposed to keep the people in line as the price for the small bit of power that they were still allowed to wield.

This was the actual passion and death of Jesus, in detail, and it was a vividly remembered fact that they had lived through. Whatever Jesus had said, it had come to this, and it was the reason for his execution. And now it was the reality that they had faced and had been facing for the thirty and more years since his death and resurrection. They had learned firsthand in their flesh and blood, their lives and relationships, that the preaching of the Crucified and Risen Lord resulted in rejection and discord, hatred and persecution, and martyrdom. The Gospels are statements of belief and catechetical texts, preparing people for baptism in the community and calling those baptized to live up to their vows and promises in a very hostile world that seeks to silence the gospel.

These exhortations and warnings and the reality personally known by all in the community were essential to the teachings and the preparation of catechumens and to the daily life of believers. Jesus's call to the cross and to suffering on behalf of the truth, the Word of God, and to persecution because of their generosity to the poor and their hospitality to outsiders, their inclusion and welcoming of the sinner, their overstepping of the customs and dividing lines elicited fear, anger, and persecution. Some of what is written in these sayings was actually Jesus's words, and some of what was written was the word of the Spirit in the evangelist's mouth because believers needed to hear it, take it into account, and take it to heart. And as the years followed the Resurrection, they grew in their understanding of what Jesus had said and what the Spirit taught them in the Word of God in the older testament, the older prophecies that were now attributed to Jesus and read in light of his words and death on the cross and his being raised from the dead. And the sacraments and the common life that practiced those sayings and teachings taught them more in detail what was required and what could and often was the reaction of others: the negative that caused persecution and distrust and the positive that brought new members into the believing community.

All these explanations deal with the descriptions of the rejection, crucifixion, and the death of Jesus, but do they apply to the actual saying of "after three days he will rise again"? This is a hard question and is the reason for the quote at the beginning of this section on small truths and large truths. Whether or not Jesus actually proclaimed his own resurrection from the dead is not what is a matter of belief. What is the matter for belief is that Jesus was raised from the dead by his Father in the power of the Spirit. And that mystery, that reality shocked his disciples, and it should continue to shock us every day of our lives, for it alters history and changes radically what it means to be human. The resurrection of Jesus is the largest truth of our faith, and paradoxically, the opposite of this great truth is another great truth. These words from an editorial in *Life* in 1956 put this clearly into focus:

> The resurrection cannot be tamed or tethered by any utilitarian test. It is a vast watershed in history, or it is nothing. It cannot be tested for truth; it is the test of lesser truths. No light can be thrown on it; its own light blinds the investigator. It does not compel belief; it resists it. But once accepted as fact, it tells more about the universe, about history, and about man's state and fate than all the mountains of other facts in the human accumulation.

The Resurrection is what demands a response from us, and the Resurrection is what our belief in Jesus is based upon as a community, a church. If Jesus knew about his resurrection prior to his death, then it becomes incredibly problematic to see him as fully human, facing all of life and death as other human beings do. The mystery of the Incarnation is that God became flesh in Jesus and that he is like us in all things but sin, and that means that he was not all knowing, with prescient knowledge of what was to happen. He was a believer in God, his beloved Father, and his prayer and relationship with his Father, God, in the power of the Spirit given to him in his baptism, drew him ever deeper into a knowledge of God that fashioned and transfigured him into all we know of God in human language and terms. He lived and died believing in the love of his Father and faithful to what he knew of God from his own rich Jewish tradition and Scriptures and what he learned from the fullness of the Spirit that was given to him in his baptism, his prayer, and his life. Because of this mystery of the Incarnation, many believe that Jesus did not know of his own resurrection prior to his death and these specific pieces were written into the text and put in the mouth of Jesus as core teaching that the Spirit had taught the believing, suffering, and obedient church of believers over the years after the death and resurrection of Jesus. They are given to us as grace, as comfort, as a source of transformation, as encouragement, as a reality check on our own lives and whether or not we are living the mystery of the cross, passion, and death of Jesus as we have been called to imitate it in our baptismal life. The Scriptures are God's present Word to us now, here to be formed in God's image in Jesus with his Spirit given to us in the sacraments and community. There are many other references to Jesus' passion and death, and allusions to the Resurrection, such as the ones found in the Transfiguration accounts, but they are too numerous to examine. We must painstakingly, daily and throughout the liturgical year, reflect on and study with our communities all these texts as they appear in the readings, reading them in the light and shadow of the Resurrection of Jesus and our own baptism into his passion, death, and resurrection. It is the Spirit that will enlighten us, give us understanding, and draw us more deeply into the mysteries that encompass our lives as followers of Christ. This was what was known in the early church as the time of the *mystogyia,* which began after baptism and never really ended, because the mysteries pervaded all of life and taught the new believer how to perceive all of life, all history in its details and large horizons from the vantage point of belief in the Resurrection, the depth of the eye of God, and the judgment of the Trinity. No matter what age we are, or how long we have been baptized, or how much we have studied the Scriptures and the rites of the sacraments, or more importantly lived them, we know next to nothing. In the end (and at the beginning), it is love that teaches us, the love of God in the person of Jesus Christ risen from the dead, the love of the Father that includes us in that life of resurrection, and the love of the Spirit that transforms and transfigures our lives into the pattern of Jesus's own life. Pedro Arrupe, former superior general of the Society of Jesus, writes of what this love can do to us, without limit:

Nothing is more practical than finding God, than falling in love in a quite absolute, final way. What you are in love with, what seizes your imagination, will affect everything. It will decide what will get you out of bed in the morning, what you will do with your evening, how you spend your weekends, what you read, whom you know, what breaks your heart, and what amazes you with joy and gratitude. Fall in love, stay in love and it will decide everything.

It is a story to linger over, full of mystery and unanswered questions that hopefully will lead us, in the words of C. S. Lewis, "further up and further in" to the mystery of the passion, death, and resurrection of Jesus as it is proclaimed in our own lives. There are inherent truths in stories that cannot be learned in books and lectures. Rational and historical inquiry can be helpful, but it cannot penetrate the breadth of symbols and meanings in a story. This is Nikos Kazantzakis's tale of St. Francis and his response to a novice who wants a book to explain things.

> "Listen my child," he said. "Each year at Easter I used to watch Christ's resurrection. All the faithful would gather around His tomb and weep, weep inconsolably, beating on the ground to make it open. And behold! In the midst of our lamentations the tombstone crumbled to pieces and Christ sprang from the earth and ascended to heaven. Smiling at us and waving a white banner. There was only one year I did not see Him resurrected. That year a theologian of consequence, a graduate of the University of Bologna, came to us. He mounted the pulpit in church and began to elucidate the Resurrection for hours on end. He explained and explained until our heads began to swim; and that year the tombstone did not crumble, and, I swear to you, no one saw the Resurrection.

This mystery lives in us, in our communities worldwide, as it lives in the text and the telling of the Scriptures and in the ways we struggle to appropriate them so that they become a revelation in our lives, for others to read. And it is this mystery of the cross and resurrection of Jesus seeded in us in our baptisms that gives people the courage to stand up for life, for justice and truth, facing the cross and knowing that their own tombs beckon when they speak out and stand in solidarity with those who suffer because of the truth and because they are poor, yet believe that Jesus the Crucified and Risen One stands and lives in communion with them. Julia Esquivel is a Guatemalan poet who has been described as someone who writes "a hope so indomitable, so improbable in the face of the reign of evil, that one can only name it resurrection hope" (book jacket notes by Rosemary Reuther). Her poem "Threatened with Resurrection" speaks of bearing the cross and believing in the resurrection of Jesus, who walks and lives with the people of Guatemala, suffering with them and urging them on with his presence and his gospel. Here are selections of it to close this chapter. They can have the same impact, the same questioning, the same nervousness and fear that Jesus's words about the cross had on his disciples.

They Have Threatened Us with Resurrection

There is something here within us
which doesn't let us sleep,
which doesn't let us rest,
which doesn't stop pounding
deep inside,
it is the silent, warm weeping
of Indian women without their husbands,
it is the sad gaze of the children
fixed there beyond memory,
in the very pupil of our eyes
which during sleep,
though closed, keep watch
with each contraction
of the heart,
in every awakening. . . .
What keeps us from sleeping
is that they have threatened us with Resurrection!
Because at each nightfall
though exhausted from the endless inventory
of killings since 1954,
yet we continue to love life.
They have threatened us with Resurrection
because we have felt their inert bodies
and their souls penetrated ours
doubly fortified.
Because in this marathon of Hope,
there are always others to relieve us
in bearing the courage necessary
to arrive at the goal
which lies beyond death.
They have threatened us with Resurrection
because they do not know life (poor things!).
That is the whirlwind
which does not let us sleep,
the reason why asleep, we keep watch,
and awake, we dream. . . .

Accompany us then on this vigil
and you will know what it is to dream!
You will then know
how marvelous it is
to live threatened with Resurrection!
To dream awake,
to keep watch asleep,
to live while dying
and to already know oneself
resurrected!

(In *Threatened with Resurrection/Amenazado de Resurreccion:
Prayers and Poems from an Exiled Guatemalan*. Elgin, Ill., Brethren Press, 1982)

May we live so threatened and "already know ourselves resurrected," as disturbing as that might be today as it was two thousand years ago for Jesus's first disciples.

➳ *3* ➳

Mark's Account: Mark 16:1–8

> After death something new begins, over which all powers of the
> world of death have no more might.
>
> —Dietrich Bonhoeffer, *The Mystery of Easter*

Mark's Gospel is the first chronologically of the three synoptics that we have
and was probably written by or around 60 to 70 A.D. Each of the Gospels is a
belief statement of a particular community of believers. It is a bedrock source
of ethics, morality, and practice of faith that has been and is being lived in relation to and with others in the Body of Christ in the world. These Gospels
were written for believers who were having difficulties living according to the
belief they professed by their baptism in a culture and history that resisted this
Good News of God and persecuted Christians. And yet, in the face of martyrdom and the struggle to live out their baptismal vows, these communities
sought ways to pass on to those who came to belief the riches of the life, death,
and resurrection of Jesus. In a sense the Gospels were written for the "ear" in
community, for use in liturgical settings, calling for conversion singularly and
exhorting and deepening the faith life of the community. They sought to make
conscious, visible, and incarnate the Body of Christ living and active now as
this community of believers, witnessing to the world the presence of the Risen
Lord among them.

Mark's Gospel is written for the church in Rome, caught in the early 60s
A.D. in a web of fear, politics, persecution, and growth. Both Peter and Paul
have been martyred, and the church's base has moved from Jerusalem to Rome,
the seat of the power of the Roman Empire. The long shadow of violence,
might, and power is cast over the small Christian community as it struggles to
live out the teachings of Jesus. How are they to live out the Resurrection daily
in their lives in this political and nationalistic context?

Mark's church had lived and struggled with Jesus's words, life, crucifixion, and death for more than thirty years and knew the Resurrection to be the source and meaning of its life, strength, and courage. How could its members tell the story of how the Spirit revealed to them over these decades what the Resurrection meant for them and what it could mean for others who came to believe? Each of the gospel writers would attempt to do this for his own community as the church grew in the context of history, in relation to the Jews, the Gentiles, the Roman Empire, and the experience of both stable and missionary foundations. The text of the Gospels contained intimations, concealed and hinted at in Jesus's stories and works, that would come to fruition in the culminating account of the Resurrection.

Two points will become hinges for all the narratives: the discovery and reality of the empty tomb and Jesus's appearances to those who believe after the discovery of the empty tomb. Mark's Gospel presents this initial story of the empty tomb, but there is no account given of appearances to the disciples and believers. The original ending was verse 8 in chapter 16. Then there was another ending added that tells the story of an appearance to Mary of Magdala (verses 9–11), then two further, very short accounts of his appearance on a road in the country and later to the eleven disciples while they are at table, when he chides them for not believing those who had seen him (verses 12–14). Finally, much later, the ending we have now was added (verses 15–20), exhorting the disciples to go out and proclaim the Good News to all creation, accompanied by signs. Then, he is taken up from their sight, and they go out and preach. But originally, Mark's Gospel ends abruptly at 16:8, and we will look at Mark's resurrection account as though that is all there is in order to appreciate what Mark was trying to say about the empty tomb.

Each narrative of resurrection builds on the entire text that precedes it, bringing into sharp focus the heart of the message of that gospel. Here Raymond Brown succinctly describes what Mark is attempting to do with these eight lines, pulling together all that has come before in Jesus's ministry, preaching, and death:

> *Only through suffering will the disciples reach fuller understanding.* Throughout the Gospel Mark emphasizes how difficult it was for those who followed Jesus to believe in him fully because they did not understand that suffering and rejection were an essential part of the identity of God's Son. In the great trial of Jesus' passion the male disciples have all failed and run away—an experience reflecting fear and shameful weakness. But their pain leads to light. After they have suffered and failed, Jesus will appear to them in Galilee. (Mark 14:27–28)

The women followers of Jesus, spared the Gethsemane trial where the disciples fell asleep and fled, looked on from a distance at the Crucifixion.

They too must experience the difficulty of faith; even after they are told of the Resurrection, they do not automatically become proclaimers of Jesus' victory. Rather they flee in silence and fear. (Mark 16:8)
—["Jesus Is Risen! The Gospel Resurrection Narrative."
St. Anthony Messenger (April 1994):]

These themes of the rejection, crucifixion, and death of Jesus have been steadfastly ignored, and even pushed away, by Jesus's disciples, beginning with Peter in Mark 8, where Peter takes Jesus aside after a proclamation of his coming sufferings and "protests strongly" (CCB) or "begins to remonstrate with him" (NAB). This provokes Jesus's strong words to Peter and the other disciples: "Get behind me, Satan! You are thinking not as God does, but as people do" (Mark 8:33b). Consistently, the disciples do not understand what Jesus is doing or saying, and they more often than not resist Jesus's words and grow full of fear as Jesus incurs more and more resistance on his way to Jerusalem.

In Mark's account of the crucifixion and passion of Jesus, Jesus dies utterly alone and without support of his followers or friends. "Even the men who were crucified with Jesus insulted him" (Mark 15:32b). When Jesus dies, it is the Roman soldier standing guard at the cross who declares, "Truly, this man was the Son of God." And we are told that "there were also women looking on from a distance; among them were Mary Magdalene, Mary the mother of James the younger and Joses, and Salome. These used to follow him and provided for him when he was in Galilee; and there were many other women who had come up with him to Jerusalem" (Mark 15:39b–41). In older translations, the distance mentioned is amended to "a safe distance."

Jesus dies the evening before the Sabbath. It is told that Joseph of Arimathea goes to Pilate and "boldly" (after the fact of death) asks for the body of Jesus. It is he who removes the body from the cross, prepares it hastily for burial, puts it into a tomb cut out of the rock, and rolls a stone across the entrance. The two Marys "take note of where the body had been laid." Jesus is dead and buried. It is over and done with and everyone goes back to his or her life, back to the Sabbath celebrations with grief, fear, and despair.

Now it is time to go with the women to the tomb and find it empty. If the torturous death of Jesus by public execution on the cross was devastating to his followers, the shock of finding the tomb empty would have been even more so. But before we listen to the text of Mark, let us listen to a children's story from Asia. There are a number of versions of it available as a children's book, but this is the way I have been told it and I call it "Li Po and the Flower Pot."

Once upon a time there was a good emperor who sought justice for his people, keeping peace on his borders and making sure that all his people were never hungry. He was loved and cherished by his people, but there was a great sadness in his life that was a source of fear and uneasiness for the people. He had no heir. His wife had died, and they had had no children. Finally, one day after much consultation with his advisors, he decided on a plan for choosing a suitable heir, someone he would adopt as his own son, who would then be trained to be emperor in his place when he died. It would ease the fears of the people.

He summoned all his people together, telling them to bring their children with them, all the boys and girls who were five years old. They were assembled and listened in amazement to what their emperor intended to do. Each child was given a seed and told to treat it with great care. They were to go home and plant it and nurture it and care for it and see what it would become. In a few months' time, all the children were to return with their flower pots and what had grown under their care, and the emperor would look at all of them and choose from among them the most beautiful. The child whose pot he would choose would be adopted as his own child and would grow up to be emperor in his place, hopefully caring for his people as carefully as the child had once tended the seed given to his or her care. The children took their seeds home, planted them, and waited to see what they would be.

One of the children, Li Po, loved plants and gardening, as did his father and grandfather before him. He was so excited about the prospect of finding out what the seed would be. He carefully picked a small pot, with good drainage, and filled it with his best soil. Once the plant appeared, he planned to change the soil and the size of the pot to encourage the growth of that particular flower or bush. He picked the best place in the garden for sun and shade and waited. Every morning it was the first thing he did: carefully check the pot to see if his seed had broken through the dirt and was beginning to emerge. For weeks he waited and watched. Nothing appeared. He began to worry. Was it the right soil? Had he watered it too much? Was it getting enough or too much light?

After almost a month he was near tears, because there was nothing growing in his pot. He went to his father and asked him what he thought was wrong. His father questioned him, but he answered all the questions truthfully and his father didn't know what could be wrong with the plant either. His father counseled patience, because some seeds took longer than others to sprout—perhaps it was a tree and not a flower or a bush. That was it, Li Po decided. He had a tree, and it would take longer for it to appear. But time went by, and there was nothing. As the day approached for them to bring their pots before the emperor, Li Po was upset and fearful. If he appeared before the emperor with nothing the emperor might be very angry that he had not treated his gift with respect. He was tempted to take a seed out of his garden and replant it in his pot; then, he'd have something to bring with the other children before the emperor. At the very last minute he told his father and was ashamed of what he was going to do. His father encouraged him and said, "You did your best and that is all you can bring before the emperor."

The day arrived, and Li Po dressed in his best clothes, which had been cleaned for him, and he took his small pot that only seemed to have dirt in it and nothing else and went to the pavilion with all the other children. As they all gathered, he was even more nervous and anxious. The other children had magnificent flowers, pots filled with blooms, each more gorgeous than the other: peonies, chrysanthemums, a persimmon, flowers and plants he did not recognize. They were all beautiful, and he had nothing. The emperor appeared, and Li Po shrank behind some other children, hoping that the emperor wouldn't notice him and his empty pot. But the emperor was being very careful, going to each child in turn, complimenting them on their flowers and plants, asking them questions about how they had known what it was and how to care for it, listening to their answers, smiling and putting his hand on their heads, bending before them.

And though he was dreading being seen, eventually the emperor got to him, and he found himself standing before the emperor, his head bowed, his face crimson, hoping that he wouldn't be asked why he had nothing to show the emperor. It seemed that the emperor stood before him forever. He could see his shadow where it fell at his feet. Finally, he raised his eyes and found the emperor looking at him very intently. And he was asked, "Where is your flower? Didn't you plant your seed?" And fumbling for words, Li Po blurted out his story. He told the emperor how he had carefully planted it, choosing the pot, the soil, the place in his garden for sunlight, watering it, watching it, changing pots, back and forth, everything, but nothing happened. The tears were running down his face, and he was afraid and humiliated. He had disappointed the emperor. But after awhile he realized that the emperor wasn't angry. In fact he was smiling, beaming at him. He stopped telling his story, and the emperor spoke. He turned to his people and solemnly and loudly declared in public: "Here is my new son! Here is the child who will be your emperor!" The people were stunned and silent.

The emperor continued. "I gave to each of your children a seed. But I do not know how all these flowers and plants grew from those seeds that your children have brought before me. For all the seeds were dead. Nothing could grow from them. Yet only this child, Li Po, planted and tended his seed, and in spite of nothing appearing, brought it back to me and told me the truth—that all he had for all his work was an empty pot. This child tells the truth no matter what might happen, and this child will be my child and emperor." No mention was made of how the others all came to have flowers, and the people cheered (though they were ashamed too), and Li Po became the emperor's son, moving into the pavilion with his own family and grew up strong and true, careful of his people as he was of his seeds and plants, and became emperor. They say that while he lived there was peace and prosperity, no one was hungry, and flowers grew everywhere in the country.

The empty pot and what appears to be nothing, what appears to be dead, is the source ultimately of truth, of the future, and of power for a whole people. The empty tomb of Jesus the Crucified One portends power, life beyond imagining, and hope for the future for his followers. But entering this tomb and living with the fear and loss of everything is not easy. It wasn't for the women and the disciples of Jesus then, and it isn't for us, his followers today. The scene of Mark's Resurrection account is preceded by fear: fear of Pilate, fear of crucifixion and violence, fear of death, and the fear that all is lost. But instead of the story being over, the story is just beginning!

This is the gospel of the Lord according to Mark. Let us listen and be attentive!

> When the Sabbath was over, Mary Magdalene, and Mary the mother of James, and Salome bought spices, so that they might go and anoint him. And very early on the first day of the week, when the sun had risen, they went to the tomb. They had been saying to one another, "Who will roll away the stone for us from the entrance to the tomb?" When they looked up, they saw that the stone, which was very large, had already been rolled back. As they entered the tomb, they saw a young man, dressed in a white robe, sitting on the right side; and they were alarmed. But he said to them, "Do not be alarmed; you are looking for Jesus of Nazareth, who was crucified. He has been raised; he is not here. Look, there is the place they laid him. But go, and tell his disciples and Peter that he is going ahead of you to Galilee; there you will see him, just as he told you." So they went out and fled from the tomb, for terror and amazement had seized them; and they said nothing to anyone, for they were afraid. (Mark 16:1–8 NRS)

As with all the gospel texts, each phrase and line is layered. The first phrase sets the passage in religious and liturgical time: "when the Sabbath was over," which would make it as late as ten in the evening. Jesus has been dead and buried, and his followers and all the Jews in Jerusalem went to celebrate the rituals of keeping holy the Sabbath, with rest from all labor, the lighting of the candles to welcome the Shekinah, the presence of God with the people in exile, the meals, prayers, chanting of psalms and blessings, the telling of God's history with his people. This was the day that belonged to God alone. Traditionally, not even the name of someone who had died would have been spoken, and grief would not have been expressed. This was the day of the Lord of Creation and the Lord of the Exodus.

Next, we are introduced to the three women. In the eastern church, there are many icons called "The Myrrhbearing Women," which go back to at least 230 A.D. For the Orthodox, the sepulcher, the tomb, is called "the source of life." John Chrysostom in his Paschal Homily declares, "Forgiveness has shown forth from the grave!" Some of the women, Mary of Magdala among them, had watched to see where Jesus was buried, but did not take part in that ritual. In the story, it is Joseph of Arimathea who does what is required for the body of Jesus. This detail serves to deepen the shame of the disciples, who in fear were not present and did not even honor the body of their Lord in death. The women were bearing herbs, spices, and myrrh, which would be used to venerate the body, but also to cover the stench of decomposition, which would have been unbearable in the tomb. Traditionally, the mixture of myrrh and aloes was about a hundred-pound weight.

Who are these women? Mary of Magdala is mentioned by name in all four of the gospel accounts. The others differ significantly. Here is Mary, the mother of James, sometimes called James the Lesser. Earlier at the burial, she is Mary, the mother of Joset. She could be the mother of the other James Alpheus, one of the apostles (not the mother of James and John, Jesus's cousins). And there is Salome, whom we know nothing at all about, except her name, which has been remembered in the tradition. Before Jesus goes into Jerusalem in Mark's Gospel, he is anointed in Bethany at the house of Simon the Leper by a woman who brings an alabaster jar of expensive perfume made of pure nard. She breaks it and pours it over Jesus's head, ritually anointing him in honor, acknowledgement, and respect as kings, priests, and prophets were publicly anointing in the presence of the people. The worth of the perfume was astounding—equivalent to a year's wages! She is criticized, but Jesus defends her, saying, "She has done what she could; she has anointed my body beforehand for its burial. Truly, I tell you, wherever the Good News is proclaimed in the whole world, what she has done will be told in remembrance of her" (Mark 14:3–9). Is one of these women she who had anointed him beforehand? We do not know, but the story is told of her and of them. These myrrhbearing women reveal much to us. In *Resurrection Narratives of the Synoptic Gospels*, Herman Hendrickx writes:

> By this verse Mark seems to affirm three things: firstly, the reality of Jesus' death; secondly, the attachment of the women to Jesus; thirdly, that they did not expect anything like a resurrection. They are described as fulfilling a duty out of devotion and are not at all expecting the divine action, which, in fact, has already taken place. (p. 4)

The Sabbath is over. They have obeyed the requirements of the law and have waited to mourn, waited to grieve. They are going to wail and keen the death of a loved one, and they go to perform a corporal work of mercy. Within Judaism the anointing of a body for burial was the highest corporal work of mercy, because it made those who performed it unclean themselves. Further, to anoint the body of a condemned criminal, especially one who had been crucified, was seen as beyond the limit of service, for many Jews believed that such a one was abandoned even by God, so horrible was the public punishment.

And again, we are given more details about time. "Very early on the first day of the week, when the sun had risen" to be precise. The first day of the week—what day is that? For the Jews, the Sabbath is the seventh day, the fullness of the week's time, in imitation of the Creator who rested on the seventh day. This would be the eighth day, a day that would open up a new time, a new era, that would inaugurate a new creation. It is now called Sunday, originally the Day of the Son. In the Orthodox liturgy, the Greek word for Sunday (which in Russian also means "resurrection") is *Kyriake hemera*, meaning "the day of the Lord." This refers to the first day, or the "Unique Day," which is Holy Pascha. This day is the day upon which all time hinges, the before and after of the Resurrection. Michel Quenot describes it in *The Resurrection and the Icon* thus:

> St. Justin writes: "We all gather on the day of the sun because it is the first day, on which God, by giving substance to the darkness and to matter, created the world, and on that same day, Jesus Christ our Savior rose from the dead." (First Apology, 67:7)
>
> "Yesterday I was buried with Thee, O Christ. Today I arise with Thee in Thy Resurrection" (Paschal Matins, Ode 3). The Eighth Day, the "Unique Day" without end is not merely a promise; it has already begun: "Therefore if anyone is in Christ, he is a new creation; the old has passed away, behold, the new has come." (2 Cor. 5:17)
>
> Having appeared at the end of the first creation, man [and woman] stand at the beginning of the second, since the world is transfigured through [them]. And while the first creation marks the beginning of time, the second enables one to depart from it and attain to the light of the never setting Sun. (pp. 92–93)

As we pore over these texts line by line we must remember that they are not primarily historical renderings of what actually did happen. They are about theology, about belief and liturgy, about sacraments and about the presence of the Risen Lord in the community of believers. And all the Resurrection texts are steeped in the experience and practice of the rites of baptism. At the Easter vigil, the first reading of the long night that precedes the Easter proclamation of the Resurrection is the account of creation in Genesis. And on that first day of the week, "God said: 'Let there be light;' and there was light" (Gen. 1:3). This is the beginning of a new creation, a new world and time. All has been redeemed, transformed, and shifted toward the glory of God. God has already done this marvelous thing of raising Jesus from the dead. Now, it is about to be proclaimed and heard for the first time.

Their journey from wherever they were staying in Jerusalem to the outskirts of the town would have been a sorrowful one. They would have been remembering all that had happened to them and to Jesus during the long hours of the Sabbath, and now they are up and about, doing what needs to be done, if not for Jesus's body, for their one sense of having done something for the one they had loved in life. And on the way all that they seem to talk about is the "stone"—it was a large one. Some translations say over and over again that it was "huge." Are they attempting to do something nearly impossible? Joseph of Arimathea had rolled the stone across the entrance to the tomb, couldn't three women who might be carrying a hundred pounds of materials between them be able to unwedge the stone from its place? Again the account is not just about facts, but about theology. The tomb from the earliest days of Christianity is the baptismal font, and there are huge impediments to approaching the sacrament and vowing belief in this Jesus of Nazareth who was crucified. Mark's entire gospel repeats again and again that even his disciples were reluctant to look at what was required of Jesus's followers. It is central in their thoughts and what they share with one another: the obstacle, the large and looming reality of death and what they have lost in the person of Jesus and his relationships with them. For all of us there are huge stones in our life, and they often seem to be stumbling blocks for any possibility of new life, of freedom, or of hope in the future. The early Christian community faced huge problems of persecution, infighting, exclusion from the Jewish community, the coming to grips with their own betrayals of Jesus and their refusal to listen to what he said when they found it too hard to imagine or bear. And to their surprise, when they get there—the stone has been moved! The Resurrection is already a reality. God has raised Jesus from the dead. All obstacles, anything that might keep us from participating in the new life of freedom and the love of God given to us in Jesus, have been removed. All of history, our personal lives, our community experiences have been radically altered in the rolling away of the stone and a tomb that stands glaringly empty! But the women are in for even more of a shock.

The passive verb describing the stone "being rolled" away indicates in other parts of Scripture that the action was done by God or someone sent by God. The story keeps slowly, inexorably moving toward the announcement, the central line of what is to be revealed—all of Mark's Gospel has been leading up to this and the tension mounts and mounts. The women enter the tomb (remember baptism) and "they saw a young man sitting on the right side, dressed in a white robe; and they were amazed." Now whom do they see? Herman Hendrickx explains one possible option (remembering that all of the options can be true and what we need to hear and take to heart in our lives).

> "[T]he young man" is a representation of the risen Christ because he represents the believer who through baptism participates in the resurrection of Christ. Lately, it has been said that the "young man," who acts as a messenger, is not just the baptized Christian in general. It is the newly baptized

Christian in Mark's community, or even that community itself, including Mark. It is the Markan community, rather than the risen Christ, which delivers the message.

Secondly, the position of the young man now becomes clear. In Mk. 12:36 and 14:62 Christ is referred to as sitting at the right hand of God. The same state is promised to the Markan community by the position of the young man.

Thirdly, the white robe is that worn in heaven (Rev. 6:11; 7:9, 13, 14), and the phrase "clothed" (*peribeblemenos*) is also repeatedly found in the heavenly context (Rev. 7:9, 13). (p. 7)

All that! And perhaps even more! This is Mark's community and their proclamation of belief, the essence of which they would have been teaching and proclaiming to new believers and stating for themselves in a creedal faith statement. The catechumens to be baptized were dressed in white garments that they were to bring unsullied to their place in heaven where they would be judged worthy to sit at the right hand of God. This is the believer who witnesses to the Resurrection.

Often people want to know if this is Mark himself. The only time we see Mark in his own gospel, he is, like the apostles, not shown in a very positive light. It is the night of betrayal in the garden. Judas has marked Jesus with a kiss, and he has been seized by the soldiers. We are told, "A young man was following him, wearing nothing but a linen cloth. They took hold of him, but he left the linen cloth in their hands and ran off naked" (Mark 14:51). This, traditionally, has been Mark. It has been thought in the past that this young man in the tomb is Mark also, but Mark now proclaiming in his gospel and community his steadfast belief in Jesus, from whom he once ran, suffering with in fear. Perhaps. And there are many who think it is an angel who interprets for the women what has happened, the Resurrection, and at the same time announces (as angels are wont to do) what is now transpiring in the world.

The description of the women's reaction to the presence in the tomb of this young man who does not have the body of Jesus has been translated variously as amazed, disturbed, alarmed. It is a rare Greek verb (*ekthambeisthai*) that is used only in Mark (in both Mark 9:15 and 14:33). The first use is in chapter 9 just after the Transfiguration when Jesus has described his coming sufferings as the Son of Man and the people react to Jesus when they see him arguing with the teachers of the law. The second time is even more powerful. It is used to describe Jesus's own feelings in the garden of Gethsemane when he takes Peter, James, and John with him to pray, and he "becomes filled with fear and distress; he said to them, 'My soul is full of sorrow, even to death.'" It is an incredibly strong reaction as Jesus tries to come to terms with his own destruction and execution. It is awe in the face of the unknown and mysterious, but it is also outright fear.

This reaction is akin to many other uses of the word when it means "disturbed," such as the waters of the Red Sea being disturbed before they were parted and the people passed through—the reading of Exodus 14:15–15:1 from the Easter vigil. It is also akin to the description of Mary in the first chapter of Luke when she hears Gabriel addressing her with the words, "Greetings favored one! The Lord is with you." Mary was deeply troubled at his words (Luke 1:28–29). In Matthew's Gospel, it is Herod who is described as "frightened, and all Jerusalem with him" on hearing the wise men describe the rising of the newborn king of the Jews' star in the East (Matt. 2:3). This kind of disturbance, this fear, shifts and alters the course of events and peoples' lives radically and powerfully. And the women are right there on the edge of such fear and awe and disturbance.

The young man has their undivided attention, and what he speaks and proclaims aloud now is the core of the message that is to be heard and taken to heart. This is what believers stake their lives on and are willing to go to death clinging to as Truth.

> Do not be amazed, alarmed, disturbed, filled with fear; you seek Jesus of Nazareth, who was crucified. He has risen, he is not here; see the place where they laid him. But go, tell his disciples and Peter that he is going ahead of you to Galilee; there you will see him, just as he told you.

His words are a series of commands: Do not be afraid. See, look here at the place of his burial and where his body was laid. Go, tell his disciples and people, speak words that will thrust the community into the future and send them back to Galilee. That is where he is—out ahead of you, and you will see him there! This is the core of Mark's faith statement about Jesus. This is what is essential for baptism: to believe in Jesus of Nazareth and all that entails, that he was crucified, but he was raised by God and now is the Risen One. This is a liturgical formula, not so much directed at the women per se, but at all believers. He is not here! Look where he once was. The young man points out the obvious to the women: the tomb is empty. There is no body! And then he goes on to tell them where the Body of Jesus can be found—in Galilee. He goes before them, the message echoing Jesus's words to his disciples earlier that he goes before them and they are to follow, but so often they have refused. Specifically, on the night he is betrayed while still with them on the Mount of Olives, singing songs after the last supper, he told them, "You will all become deserters and fall away; for it is written: 'I will strike the Shepherd and the sheep will be scattered.' But after I am raised up, I will go before you to Galilee" (Mark 14:27–28). These words are a warning to all the disciples, and then he tells Peter specifically that he will betray him that night. The gospel text is all of a piece—the women are commanded to go and tell the disciples and Peter, that order delivered in the same words that Jesus spoke before his crucifixion and death.

This command is startling because of one detail, the ordering of to whom they are to tell the message—first to the disciples and then to Peter. Peter, of course, usually comes first, but even the message, the *kerygma*, of resurrection belief reveals Peter's status and his sin in three times refusing to acknowledge any connection to Jesus the night that he is condemned to death. Peter is singled out because of his denial that the church in all those years was very conscious of having had to deal with the leader being the one who most loudly and adamantly denied even knowing Jesus in public because of his fear. Fear is laced through, under, and around the text and in the people at the tomb, those hiding out in the city, and all believers who seek Jesus the Crucified One in the midst of their society, culture, and history. The proclamation of the Good News is about laying down one's fear and standing up for what one believes in the face of situations that evoke massive, paralyzing, debilitating fear.

The Risen Lord is the shepherd of his sheep, and as once they were scattered, he will now gather them again and lead them to peaceful and plentiful pastures. But you won't find this Risen Lord "here." Where is here? It is a tomb, a place of carnage and death, rotting flesh, decomposition, grieving, and ends. The tomb is traditionally in a garden on the outskirts of the city of Jerusalem, both the city of peace and the city that kills the prophets. You won't find the crucified and Risen One here—not in any place of death, wealth, power, and influence. You won't find him where religious power is codified and in collusion with economic and political power or where violence is a part of religion and life, where lies, false witness, and interpretations of the law that destroy peoples' lives and souls are given as the law of God. You will not find him in palaces and governments and hierarchical systems that lay burdens on the backs and hearts of the poor, practice the death penalty, and torture and rule harshly with hate and arrogance, in the name of religion. We are told where he is found—out there in Galilee. In a word, the women and the disciples and Peter and all peoples are told to go home, go back to Galilee where they came from, when they were called to be "fishers of folk" in the beginning of Jesus's preaching and as they traveled with him in his ministry as he made his way to Jerusalem and the cross and the Resurrection.

Galilee? Far from the centers of religious, economic, and political power, even far from the scribes and Pharisees, Sadducees, base of education, erudition of the law, and practice of the temple liturgy of sacrifice, tithing, and prayer. Galilee is the backwater of Israel, rural and close by the borders of pagan territories where Samaritans and Gentiles lived and had commerce with Jews of somewhat dubious obedience to the law. But Galilee was lush and fertile, the breadbasket of the country, which produced crops that literally could feed an army—Caesar's army. That was why Israel was occupied territory, the Israelites oppressed and treated as slaves in their own country. Caesar needed the food harvested in the northern region of the country for his army and expansion of his realm. The people were taxed and taxed and taxed again, as well as robbed of their food to keep Caesar in power. Galilee was the crossroads where empire dominated, slave and free met, where other nations did business and traveled back and forth to Jerusalem and Rome and the ten cities. Go back there— that's where you'll find him. Another way of saying it: Jesus the Crucified and Risen One is loose out there in the world at large! And he's waiting for you to turn around and come back to him!

The women now have their commission, the words of unbelievable good news, a proclamation of life, new life that cannot be snuffed out by death or hate or contained by any tomb. The unbelievable is reality! The Word has been given forth to them. Now that they have heard it, they must go and obey. But their reaction is the exact opposite:

> And they went out and fled from the tomb; for trembling and astonishment
> had come upon them; and they said nothing to anyone, for they were afraid.

Say those words forcefully out loud and then end the reading with the words "This is the end of the gospel of the Lord!" It is shocking. It is over. Everything falls flat. The response is, Huh? Is that all there is? What happened? If they didn't say anything, how did the church get here? It appears on initial reading that Mark didn't exactly know how to end his gospel! The women are described in the end, just as the male disciples were, as fearful, disobedient. They flee instead of following. These are the last words of the story. Sadness. They do what the men have done. They had seen, heard, walked with him, touched him, seen the awe and anger he evoked in others, denied him, kept their distance, and eaten with him, and now they add their silence to the thundering betrayal. They too are frightened thoroughly.

But is that the end? The text reads, "They said nothing to anyone." It is awesome in groups and also very funny that people react to that line immediately. What do you mean they said nothing to anyone? And then someone invariably asks, "Who's anyone?" And that's crucial. They say nothing to anyone who had not been with them since Galilee, to anyone who betrayed him, was part of his torture and death, to anyone who had not been a part of their company, anyone who was just a stranger, part of the crowd of the last few days. But they did go to the others, frightened and fearful as they were, to Peter, who denied him three times, to the scattered and shattered followers, and they did go home, back to Galilee. Galilee is about ninety miles from Jerusalem, along some of the roughest terrain imaginable: down from the city to the Dead Sea, through the wilderness, then slowly back to the north where the Jordan River finds its source in the Sea of Galilee and the land turns green and fertile again.

So they went home: the eleven male disciples, the twelve or so female disciples, perhaps many of the seventy-two disciples who came up with him to Jerusalem, perhaps a hundred or so people. They walk the ninety miles back, and they walk their way through their fears. How? They talk their way home. They tell the stories of Jesus, their encounters with him. They retell his stories, the parables and experiences of healing and forgiving and share their excitement, their memories—their hopes rise again. They discover more than just their personal beliefs or thoughts about him. They talk of the Word of God made flesh that walked with them, called them to life and insisted again and again that there was suffering involved in being his disciple because the reaction to the truth is often resistance, rejection, persecution, and pain inflicted by those who are afraid of losing what they have on those who are afraid for many of the same reasons. On that road back to Galilee they became a believing community, sharing the Word and their faith together, realizing that the way upon which they had walked with Jesus of Nazareth was, of its very nature, a way of conflict, challenge, and conversion, one that demanded breaking off from the corrupt social order and injustice tolerated and accompanying Jesus, who allied himself with the poor, the leper, the outcast, even the Gentile and sinner.

Mark's Gospel is primarily a primer for apprenticeship to discipleship, to the cross and the way that calls them to "let them deny themselves and take up their cross and follow me. For those who want to save their life will lose it, and those who lose their life for my sake and for the sake of the gospel, will save it" (Mark 8:34–35). In the end of the story is found its beginning, and the story has been trying to say the same thing over and over again in different ways for the first fifteen chapters, and the returning disciples (like us) have been ignoring it every step of the way. Their return is their repentance and their starting over again.

Perhaps Mark knew exactly what he was doing! His gospel doesn't end, it returns to the beginning, to the words that open his account of the gospel: "This is the beginning of the Good News of Jesus Christ, the Son of God." And it immediately goes back, way back to the Book of Isaiah the Prophet, leapfrogs forward to John the Baptist in the desert, with all the people from Judea and the city of Jerusalem coming out to hear him, and then to Jesus of Nazareth. John baptizes Jesus and what follows is monumental in import.

And just as he was coming up out of the water, he saw the heavens torn apart and the Spirit descending like a dove on him. And a voice came from heaven, "You are my Son, the Beloved, with you I am well pleased." (Mark 1:10–11)

Did we miss that initially? Who Jesus is? Jesus Christ, Son of God (the words the soldier in the service of Rome spoke at the cross of the Crucified One)? That this Jesus of Nazareth is in the long tradition, the line of the prophets, Isaiah and John the Baptizer, and that it is Jesus's baptism that reveals to him and to others who he actually is: the Son, the Beloved, the Chosen One, filled with the Spirit of God—did we miss that too? Like the disciples, did we hear only what we wanted to hear, interpreting the story from our vantage point and what we were looking for? Did we miss Jesus entirely? How much was lost on us because we refused to obey, to follow, to suffer, to deny ourselves, to know that rejection and crucifixion was part of the way? So it is time to start again, and again, and again, and to go back to the beginning, this time in a community that has known the Resurrection and has been commanded to go looking for Jesus now, there, everywhere, but especially at all the crossroads of the world.

This was a community trapped between the violence of the Roman Empire and the violence of the Jews who were pushing the Christians, many of whom were still Jews, though more and more Gentiles were coming into the church to fight with them against the Romans to preserve and protect the Temple in Jerusalem. They were in conflict with local and far-flung authorities, and they were on the way. And it was on the way—on the way home that they learned who they were, because they learned who Jesus truly was: from Nazareth, the Crucified One, who had been raised from the dead.

This is Mark's community that year after year celebrated the Paschal mystery in liturgy, in gospel, in the sacraments of baptism, confirmation, and Eucharist. They followed Jesus's words and life in their own lives, and intensely brought new Christians into their company, baptizing them in the font, the tomb, and drawing them out and up to new life in the freedom of the children of God, with Jesus, the Beloved Son, the Chosen One of God the Father. And year after year, they learned more and were steeped more deeply in the way and in the mystery of Jesus's baptism and passover from death to life and their own passover, which began in baptism. Mark's Gospel is written in a circle, a circle that spirals in on itself, going deeper and ever deeper into the gospel, forming those baptized into the Body of Christ, crucified and risen from the dead in the world. Raymond Brown says it pastorally, gathering all those early believers in with all of us who are more contemporary believers.

People may say that they believe firmly in the risen Christ, but they must realize existentially in their own lives that the one they are following is none other than Jesus the Nazarene who was *crucified*. Mark who has been somber in describing discipleship throughout the passion remains somber about the requirements of discipleship after the resurrection. (p. 17)

This is resurrection, totally out of the world's imagining. The stone has been rolled away, and Jesus has been raised, not by anything we do or could do, but by the power of God. The words in Greek are in the perfect tense and the passive voice. As Ched Myers writes:

But how? Not by our muscle, nor by our technology, nor by any of our Promethean schemes. The verb here (in Greek, apokekulistai) expresses the perfect tense and the passive voice—the grammar of divine action. This stone has been moved by an ulterior leverage, by a force from beyond the bounds of the story and history, with the power to regenerate both. It is a gift from outside the constraints of natural or civic law and order, from the One who is unobligated to the state and its cosmologies, radically free yet bound in Passion to us. [*Sojourners* (April 1994): 23]

Now, how about us? What does Mark's Resurrection story tell us today about what Jesus's resurrection means and how it happens for us, what it asks of us. First of all, do we face death? Are we about visiting the tombs and burial places of others, literally those who have died speaking the truth, silenced by governments, nations, organizations, sometimes even the church itself? Many historians and Jews of today condemn the church for its silence, except for rare individuals, in speaking out against the Nazis and the concentration camps and for not publicly using its power in the world on behalf of the Jews and thus colluding in the Holocaust and the death of so many. More recently, many people who have worked with both East Timor and with Tibet decry the church's lack of response and reluctance, for fear of offending Indonesia and China and perhaps jeopardizing the church's position in these countries in the future, to speak out forcibly on behalf of people suffering and being persecuted.

Do we tell the truth and confront failure in discipleship in individuals and in groups, as the proclamation of Mark does with singling out Peter and in revealing the shocking lack of faithfulness within the entire community at the conspiracy, arrest, false witness, torture, and the legal punishment by death penalty of their master? Are we really disciples now, as a church, or have we all betrayed the Crucified One in our midst again, and yet again?

Even more powerful is the statement, "I know you seek Jesus of Nazareth, the Crucified One!" Is the Crucified One the source of our spiritualities, the one who benefits from our resources in life and in death, the center of our prayer, our liturgies, and our ethical and moral decisions as individual baptized Christians and as communities of belief? Are we known for the company we keep: the poor, those condemned to death, legally but inhumanly, those tortured and imprisoned, those excluded from civil rights and from entrance into or residence in our countries? Are we afraid of the homeless, those who do not speak our language, are not of our race and religion, and do we adamantly deny that we have any connection to them at all, cursing them so that we are not associated with them in any way? The Crucified One is in our midst, hungry, bombed, imprisoned, stuck on welfare, and lost in demeaning situations of underemployment, dangerous neighborhoods and schools, without health insurance or medical care. As Christians baptized into the waters that make us the children of God, called to live in freedom from fear, how large are our hearts and how extended are our families?

In Mark's account, the Resurrection is an accomplished fact long before the women get to the tomb, but their going sets in motion the revelation of God's power active in history and sets them up for hearing the proclamation of Easter life and the destruction of death forever. It begins with three of them (though there will be more in other stories) attempting to do a corporal work of mercy—preparing the body for burial of a condemned prisoner of the state, abandoned even by God, according to the cultural and religious belief of the day. And it has already been done by another—Joseph of Arimathea, not even a disciple! And there's that stone—a huge one that stands in the way of their inadequate expressions of grief and devotion and their need to do something for the one they loved. This is, amazingly enough, exactly how we discover and set in motion the reality and power of resurrection in our lives today in our world. We must grieve the Crucified One, the Body of Christ in the world and begin, simply, in threes and more to do the corporal works of mercy, even in the face of great stones and obstacles to our feeble attempts to do what others who are not even of our company often have already done before us. In the face of death, violence, torture, the death penalty, hate, rage, the destruction of other human beings individually and as groups of religious people and nations, we must not let our fear deter us from mercy, from taking care of the bodies of those caught in the grip of death. We must go forth, after we have worshipped, into the tombs and cities and their outskirts to make sure that all those who have suffered, even killed, are treated with respect and honor.

It sounds like a lifestyle of trying to do the impossible on a regular basis in response to what happens in the world. And that's exactly what it is, and out of that response of compassion and mercy and grief at the sin and destruction of other human beings, we will uncover the power and presence of God already at work before we even suspect that life is abounding and the seeds of resurrection are wild and growing free. But we must enter the tomb and see and hear before we can know resurrection or begin to believe and live this life that defies death and overcomes it with tenderness and the power of love.

We must delve into our baptisms, our initial entrance into the tomb, our descent into the waters of life where we are drawn into the community of life, mercy, forgiveness, truth telling, and love in obedience to the Word of God. We have to live the Paschal mystery each year with attentiveness and intensity, renewing our commitment to our promises and vows as Christians personally and, in public at church and weekly, through the Sunday liturgy and Scriptures, enter again and again into the story of Mark's Gospel—the primer on discipleship— and look this time, this year, at the call to embrace the cross, deny ourselves, help one another, and not rely on our own resources and power to be a follower of Jesus.

We have to go home again and again, as the first followers did, and learn to stop fleeing in fear from the truth and the reality of being a disciple in the world. We have to keep going back to the beginning of the gospel and tell it, share it with others, listening to their faith, their failures and insights and their experience of Jesus of Nazareth, the Son of God, the Crucified One, the Son of man, the Risen Lord, stretching our individual belief into the belief of the community. We need to let others tell us what we have rejected out of hand from the Scriptures because it did not fit our agendas and caused us anxiety. We need to face our own denials of Jesus and their effects on the rest of the community.

We have to walk and talk our way through our fears, which have caused us to disobey the Word of the Lord, to betray our faith, to be caught in collusion with governments, economic policies, national agendas, and those with power. We have to make sure that our religion and its practice, our faith, and our standing up for it are not limited to tombs, churches, and places where it is accepted and taken for granted as what dominates and controls society. We have to go to Galilee, the cities, the crossroads of commerce, where people of other races, nations, religions, and cultures live and interact with them, in the marketplace and the nation-state and the world court, where people are crucified and where Jesus the Risen One dwells. Without this community that travels the way together, the way of Jesus, the way of the Word, the way of the Cross, we will not be able to see that He goes before us, even as he told us he would. They covered ninety miles in a week, maybe ten days of hard travel, before they could even see that they had missed him in their past—all of them had missed him. We, like the men and women of the early church, were told to go back to the margins, the edges of society and the heart of the world, and begin again to come after Him and become fishers of other men and women in the tradition of the prophets, those now called to be the beloved children of God.

Like the Markan community, we must be reminded, in the text and among one another, that belief is not sufficient, nor are words nor statements nor intent. We must practice what we believe, live what we profess, and walk the way of the cross in the world, with the company that breaks open the Scriptures together. And it is here that Jesus walks before us in life, in suffering, and in death, straight into the tomb and out again into resurrection light. This walk begins for each of us and all of us in our baptisms, our walking into the tomb and the waters of life, and up and out into the world at large with the company of disciples who follow Jesus of Nazareth, the Crucified and Risen One, wherever and everywhere he goes. The story isn't over—it is just beginning!

Suffering and death change life irrevocably. As Rachel Naomi Remen says, "Our vulnerability is our wakeup call. People can be in a constant state of mourning for the way things used to be, or they can develop a deep appreciation of what they have now" ["Making Peace with Fear." *AARP* (May/June 2002): 65]. All of us live with varying degrees and states of fear. Some we agonize with alone, and others we share with our families, our ethnic and religious groups, or a whole nation. The fear of pain and suffering that is unnecessary, violent, and inflicted by others and the fear of death, especially a death that is unexpected, organized, planned, and executed by those with power over those without power, whether it is sudden or experienced as a slow process of disintegration, are as universal and human as all peoples. And all fears are fed by insecurity, failure to look at the truth, or failure to confess to one's participation in evil and injustice. It is fed by others who deliberately ignore larger issues and view the problem as people, as individuals who must be stopped, eliminated, and terminated for the good of all.

In a short piece called "Beyond John Wayne," Harold S. Kushner, the Jewish rabbi who wrote *When Bad Things Happen to Good People,* writes about God, about fear and insecurity, and about reality in this last year. When questioned about why God could let such terrible things happen he responds.

> Before the events of last fall, we had this fantasy that we could take care of everything with American intelligence, American know-how, American resources. Since then, we've learned something about our vulnerability. My aphorism is: Our awareness of God starts where self-sufficiency ends. We pray for health and peace, family and justice, because we cannot achieve them on our own.
>
> . . .
>
> God's promise was never that life would be fair. God's promise was that we won't have to confront the pain and the unfairness alone. The 23rd Psalm doesn't say: "In the valley of the shadow of death, I will fear no evil because there is no evil in the world." It doesn't say, "I will fear no evil

because people get what they deserve and I'm a good person." It says, "I will fear no evil because Thou are with me." Accepting our vulnerability is the beginning of wisdom. (p. 80)

A Buddhist practitioner looks at fear and breaks it down into six components according to the Buddha's comment: "Not apart from relinquishing all, do I see any safety for human beings." He describes behaviors that result from letting fear control and rule us when we feel that our lives as we perceived them have been altered or threatened:

> When concerns about survival, safety, or identity resonate strongly with ba-
> sic fears, we experience terror. It is not a comfortable experience.
>   Fear is a reactive mechanism that operates when our identity (including
> the identity of being a physical entity) is threatened. It works to erode or
> dissipate attention. We move into one of the six realms and react: destroy
> the threat or seek revenge (hell being); grasp at safety and security (hungry
> ghost); focus on survival (animal); pursue pleasure as compensation (hu-
> man); vie for superiority (titan); or protect status and position (god). Because
> we are less present to what is actually taking place, our actions are corre-
> spondingly less appropriate and less effective. We go to sleep in our beliefs
> and ignore the consequences of maintaining them. ["Taking Fear Apart."
> *Tricycle* (Winter 2002): 23]

These comments deal with fear from traditions that source our own or are very different from ours, but they are helpful in speaking about our fears in very human ways. They are good preparation for looking at our fears before we look at them in light of our own religion and belief in the Risen Lord, alive and dwelling in the world. We believe as Christians that this fear, any fear we have as individuals and as church or nation, is cast out by love, simply by love. And that love is a person, Jesus the Crucified One, raised from the dead by his loving Father in the power of the Spirit. Our fears are best faced in the light of truth with others of our company as we walk through them and talk through them. Our fears are laid to rest, or blunted and banked down as they are looked at with the Spirit and others seeking in the Scriptures to hear the Word of God present and living in our midst now, going before us and sharing with us the Father's power over death in our baptisms and Christian life.

There is a marvelous story from the Hasidic tradition called "The Fragrance of Paradise" that reminds us of all that we have looked at in Mark's account of the Resurrection as the culmination of his gospel. And it adds an ingredient that can sometimes be missed or overlooked when we live in a climate of fear, anxiety, and loneliness in the face of what the world and others can do to us.

Once upon a time there was a wise rabbi who tried very hard to be a good rabbi, a good preacher, and a model for his people, and who even aspired to be holy before God, blessed be His name. Each Sabbath as the day ended he reluctantly turned from rejoicing in and celebrating the presence of Hashem (God) with his people and immediately picked up the Torah scrolls and looked at what the portion, the reading, would be for the following week and began preparation for his next Sabbath sermon. This was the pattern of his life, living from Sabbath to Sabbath, feeding on the Torah and seeking to share all that he could with his people so that their lives would be richer, more filled with meaning, especially in the face of so much hardship, poverty, suffering, and persecution.

When things were especially hard and he drifted as he studied the Torah portion, he would always go back to a story he had been told by his father, grandfather, and elders before him. Even his mother would whisper it to him when he was young and too tired to stay at his books and study of the Scriptures. It was a simple story, more a memory that you could spin off as you wished to or needed to. It seemed that Paradise—Gan Eden—wasn't anything like most descriptions of it. The piece that he loved most and would hold to his heart most was that on Sabbath afternoons in Paradise, all the sages, the patriarchs and matriarchs, judges, kings, and prophets would gather together and study the Torah portion for the week to come. Ah, he thought, if only once I could sit in on that group and listen as they shared their insights and knowledge across the centuries: King David, Myriam, Deborah, Moses, Isaiah, Abraham, Rachel, Jeremiah—all the characters he was so familiar with that he thought of them as old friends, revered ones, of course.

Well, one day as he sat in his study as the Sabbath was coming to an end, he had a visitor. Stunned, he knew immediately who it was: it was the prophet Elijah come to bring him a message. Elijah smiled at him and said not to be afraid for God, blessed be His name, was well pleased with his rabbi and had sent Elijah to bring him a gift. A gift? "Yes," replied Elijah. "What would you like?" "I can have anything?" he asked. "Yes." Instantaneously, he knew exactly what he wanted. "I want to visit Paradise for a Sabbath afternoon and be a part of all those who have gone before us in faith while they study the Torah portion for this week." Done! He found himself at the gates, and Elijah waved him on in.

He was overjoyed, nervous, and anxious, but he entered and Paradise took him by surprise. It far exceeded anything he'd ever heard or dreamed of. But what struck him most was that Paradise smelled heavenly. It had a fragrance that he couldn't put his finger on, familiar, strange, strong, lush, sweet. What was it? Honey, rich flowers, herbs—the scent was so unique and singular and as he walked further into the Garden of Eden, it grew stronger. It was in or on everything. Quickly he found the group of prophets and kings, judges, singers, leaders, and poets of his people and slipped in among them as they studied the Torah. The time sped by, as they argued, told stories, anecdotes, pieces of personal experience, what God, blessed be His name, had said and meant to them! But as engaging as the discussion was, he kept drifting off. That smell, that scent, was intoxicating, freeing, overwhelming. He was lost in it, tantalized, wondering what it was.

Then suddenly, as though he had just been there a few minutes, Elijah appeared at his side. It was time to go. He was reluctant and had the feeling that the prophet would have to tear him away. He pulled back and asked, "That scent, that smell—I had no idea that Paradise smelled so good. Could I, may I take some of it back with me to earth?" Elijah answered him, "Of course, as much as you like." And he wanted it all. Then Elijah added, "but whatever you take now, will of course be taken out of your portion in the world to come." He was brokenhearted. As much as that scent touched him, even healed him somehow, he didn't want to lose even a small portion of his time in Paradise. And so he sadly said he would take none and was as ready as he'd ever be to leave—now that he had had a taste—a whiff of Paradise on a Sabbath afternoon.

He was back in his study and Elijah was gone and the sun was going down. He wanted to be disconsolate, cast down, but he couldn't. He had been to Paradise and studied with the great teachers and holy ones of his tribe. But that smell? He stood up and breathed in—that was it! He was sure of it. Oh, it wasn't as strong by any means as it was there, but it was that scent. He went from room to room trying to discover where it was. He walked, stopped and sniffed, breathing deeply, trying to pinpoint it. He couldn't. It eluded him. Hours later, in the dark, he collapsed in his chair exhausted. Without thinking he raised his hand to rub his tired eyes and there it was! It was on his sleeve. He had walked through the gardens and his long caftan, with its voluminous sleeves, had dragged on the ground, gotten caught in the bushes, brushed the flowers, and been saturated with the air. It was caught in his robe. Carefully he removed it and wrapped his Torah scrolls in it. Now the scent of Paradise would be with him always.

For a long time he did not tell anyone about the visit of Elijah and his visit to Eden, afraid that people wouldn't believe him or would think him proud. But daily he would do his devotions and study near the scrolls wrapped in his robe. And the scent filled him with peace, with hope and courage, with a sense of freedom and wild passion for God and justice. One day a woman came distraught at the death of her child, and he instinctively brought her into his study and had her sit near the scrolls. He told her to be still and breathe deeply, and within minutes she had calmed and wept, but was ready to go back to her family, trusting in God. After that, they came, more and more every day—the poor and the hungry, those who had lost loved ones, those who had loved ones imprisoned, those struggling with despair and anger, hate, and fear. And they sat quietly near the scrolls and the robe and often the rabbi would read to them a portion of the Scripture and they would leave, in peace, with courage, healed, freed from the domination of their fears.

The years went by and the rabbi died, leaving his robe and the scrolls wrapped in them to his followers and family. And they died. Somewhere someone threw out the robe and the scrolls were buried in the ground, as a person is buried, as is the custom among the Jewish people, and the scent was lost. Or was it? Those who tell the story say that the scent of Paradise is found in every Torah scroll, in the sound of the words, the touch of the letters on the page, among those who gather to listen and take to heart the words of God. And the scent, the fragrance of Paradise, seeps into the world, deeper, truer, stronger whenever and wherever the Word of God is proclaimed and studied, shared and taken into peoples' hearts.

Mark's story of the Resurrection, the first and the simplest, reminds us of the power of this story. It is in the words of the Scripture, in the shared Word of God in the company of believers, as they walk and talk their way through their fears, along the way of the cross and the Good News, that the scent and fragrance of resurrection, new life, and the freedom of the children of God are always found. This is where we begin, over and over again, with the words "After the Sabbath was over," for Jesus the Crucified has been raised and he goes before us. Come, let us follow him ever more closely.

4

Matthew 28

No one ever made more trouble
Than the "gentle Jesus, meek and mild."

—James J. Gillis

Matthew's account of the Resurrection makes a quantum leap away from the simplicity and shock of Mark's story of the empty tomb, which commands believers to obey and they will see the Risen Lord, but has no account of that actually happening. Matthew's community is a world away from Mark. The church was growing, surprisingly, expanding out into the Gentile world. The community, which had originally been primarily Jewish, had been exiled from its Jewish roots, the practice, study, and prayer of the synagogues, and shunned culturally, familially, and economically because its members had refused to fight the Romans to protect the temple in Jerusalem. And the temple was destroyed by the Romans in 70 A.D. Matthew's Gospel is written after this event (between 70 and 80 A.D.) that changed forever the relationship between the followers of Jesus who became Christians and the Jewish community. Animosity, hatred, and anger became the gulf between them. The fledgling community of believers found itself between a rock and a hard place: persecuted by the Romans and equally so by the Jewish communities, while often quarrelling among themselves as to who they were and how they were to act. But the gospel situates the believing community right in the midst of international and local politics and religious intrigues and collusion with mutual enemies for immediate gains.

We begin with a story to situate ourselves in Matthew's Gospel and to see where we stand and how we read the text. The basis of this story was sent to me by a friend, Beto Caravassas, ofm. I call it "Do You See What I See?"

69

Once upon a time a father decided to send his young son off on vacation. The family was very wealthy, and he wanted his son to experience poverty firsthand so that he would know what he was to avoid in his life. For two weeks the boy was shipped off to his poorer relations in the countryside. The time elapsed, and the father came to pick up his son, whom he found healthy, thriving, and running around the yard with his cousins, dogs, chickens, and an assortment of animals. Once in the car, they headed for home, and the father began to question his son on what he had learned from his time with his poor cousins. "Well," he began, "how was your vacation?" "Oh, Dad," the son said, "it was so so good. I learned so much. You were right to send me, even though I didn't want to go at first." The father got right to the point: "Did you see how poor people can be?" And the boy responded, "Oh yes, I see now."

The father continued probing. "What did you see and learn?" His son answered, "Oh, first I saw that I have a dog at home, but they have four! And cats, pigs, hens, chickens, and rabbits to play with. And we have a swimming pool that's pretty big, but, Dad, they have a stream, almost a little river. It goes on and on, with snakes, fish, turtles, and mud. We went wading, swimming, fishing, and just exploring." And he continued on with his list: "We have a really big lawn with a fence around it, but they have hills, and you can see farther. I'd run up and down, and there was always more to see off there in the distance. We have lamps around our patio, but they have stars! The stars—I never knew there were so many. I learned their names and how they got there, how far away they are, and one of the best things was to lay in the grass at night and just look at them looking down at me. And, Dad, you and Mom have parties where you bring in people to fix the food and play music, but last night they had a party for me since I was going away, and everybody brought food. After we ate, we all sat around, and people told stories and sang, and we danced and laughed. And then we were all so tired from working all day that we just all laid around and were quiet. We looked at the stars and then just before we all went to bed, grandma said, 'Isn't God good to us! Isn't the world he made just gorgeous!'

"Dad, I learned so much. I don't know how to thank you. Now I know exactly what I want to be—I don't want to grow up to be poor like us, I want to be poor like them!" The father was speechless. The rest of the ride home he was silent and the boy chattered on and on about his new way of seeing things.

Some folks really like this story, and others do not like it at all. It rather simplistically and clearly points out to us that most of life and our choices depend on how we perceive things and what our point of view is when we look at events, circumstances, and people. And that one's point of view can alter just about everything substantially. The questions arise, Who's poor? What kind of poor do you want to be? The lesson the father intended to teach his son back-fired, and now he can either learn from his son, or angered and frustrated, try to reteach his son a thing or two. The story digs into us and questions us about our values and about with whom we stand, whom we consider rich and poor, whom we want to be like, and to whom we belong. These questions are important because they define for us how we see reality. My Nana used to say, "Position in life is everything, dear. Make sure you're where you want to be, in the right place."

This story posits us before the gospel narrative of Matthew and asks us what point of reference we will use, with whom we stand as we read the gospel. And there are generally three points of view: the soldiers and the Roman Empire, the leaders of the Sanhedrin and priests, or the disciples. To look at Matthew's story of the Resurrection, we have to look at what comes before and what comes after, both in the gospel and, more immediately, preceding the burial of Jesus.

A note before we begin. Matthew's story is dramatically different from Mark's, and sometimes that poses problems for people. There are more than a dozen accounts of the Resurrection. Remember, this is mystery par excellence and whatever it is, it happened to many people, often at the same time, and the understanding of the meaning of what happened to them grew and deepened over time. The gift of the Spirit, the Paraclete, that would lead the followers of Jesus to all truth, taught the church what it was and how it was to be in the world. As time progressed, the church knew more and more about who Jesus was and what they were called to be. The power of the Risen Lord and the gift of the Spirit in the community formed it in history, in liturgy, and in the believers' work and witness in the world.

A Scripture teacher once told me years ago that it is a startling truth that the farther you get from the actual historical person of Jesus and his time, the more the church knows about Jesus and understands more deeply the truth of the Scriptures. This idea takes some getting used to, but it clarifies things too. We, as believers in Jesus in the years following 2000, know more of the truth of Jesus the Risen Lord and his Word because we have been the recipients of more than two thousand years of faith, of life lived in the power of the Spirit and the Word in our midst. The power of the presence of the Risen Lord is not static, but dynamic, and growing ever stronger as the kingdom on earth comes more into its fullness in time and place. It is an awesome thought that calls us to responsibility and gratefulness for having been given this gift from those who have gone before us in faith. It is our privilege and inheritance, which we must be sure to pass on to those who come after us, in forms that are ever richer, more expressive and inclusive of others.

Someone once said that Matthew is gentler than Mark as he tells his story, but more forceful because of what he adds that brackets the story. Matthew's Gospel begins and ends with violence, corruption, lies, and deceit. In the beginning of the gospel, when Jesus is born in Bethlehem, his coming into the world is situated in history; specifically, we are told that Herod is king in Jerusalem and wise men come from the East inquiring about the child to be born who will be "king of the Jews." This is not exactly auspicious news for the existing king, who is notorious for his conniving, killing, and brutal arrogance. Herod is disturbed, but crafty and designing. He gets all the information he can out of the unwitting wise men and uses the scribes and chief priests of the people to find out what the Scriptures and the prophecies say about this one who is to come. He is adept at using anyone and all the resources of his kingdom for his own gain and agenda, and he has no intention at all of letting this child, dangerous or not, live. When the wise men go home by another route, and Herod realizes he has been tricked, he is furious and his anger is translated into deadly killing. He uses both the religious knowledge and the information from the wise men and calculates how to kill the child by commanding the slaughter of all the boy children in and around Bethlehem two years of age and younger (Matt. 2:1–12, 16–18).

The birth of this child, who was promised as the shepherd "who will rule my people Israel" (Matt. 2:6b), sets in motion murder, disturbance in the king and in all the city, and the grieving of families who have lost their innocent children just because they were associated with this child by place and time. It is a horrifying beginning that warns upfront that this child is dangerous to all existing powers, nations, and authorities, religious, civil, and national.

There are the intimations too that this child already has set in motion the stars and is reordering the universe. With the arrival of those from the East seeking to do homage, there is the hint that the child's destiny has ramifications for the entire world. On a more personal level, even the story announcing Mary's pregnancy and his coming, told from the point of view of Joseph, has ominous foreshadowings. Joseph initially decides not to "expose her to public disgrace, planned to dismiss her quietly" (Matt. 1:19). The exposure could have meant that she and the unborn child would be stoned to death according to the law that was sometimes carried out, and dismissing her or putting her away quietly would mean exiling her from the town, having her child on her own, and living as a servant, slave, or prostitute if she had no distant family to take her in with them and cover her shame. Joseph changes his heart and does not obey the law, but the story is shadowed by killing, by evil, and by law that can destroy rather than give life. This background is the opening bracket of Matthew's Gospel.

The closing bracket is what happens immediately before the burial of Jesus and after the Resurrection itself. This is the unique piece that Matthew contributes to the growing tradition surrounding the Resurrection. Once again, Raymond Brown sums up this addition pointedly:

> *An attempt to block the resurrection of Jesus.* Even more dramatically, in Matthew 27:62–66; 28:4, 11–15 we are told of a scheme to frustrate the Resurrection by getting Pilate's soldiers to guard Jesus' tomb. One of the tragic elements in Matthew's Christian experience is a hostile relationship between synagogue authorities and Christian believers. That is reflected from start to finish in Matthew's Gospel.
>
> At the very beginning of his Gospel, Matthew portrayed King Herod, the chief priests and the scribes plotting to destroy the newly born Messiah (2:3–5, 16–18, 20); but God frustrated them. So now at the end of the Gospel, Matthew portrays the prefect Pilate, the chief priests and the Pharisees plotting against Jesus. Once more God intervenes to frustrate them. Though the polemic attitude behind this story should not be imitated, Matthew reminds us that the Christian proclamation of the gospel will not be without struggle. (p. 14)

This story of the Resurrection includes many more of the historical and political overtones of the actual experience of Matthew's Christians and the persecution and exile they knew as a direct result of the practice of their faith and the reactions it caused in both the Jewish and the Roman circles of power. The ending of the gospel sets up a structure that includes three points of view, two in collusion with each other to some degree, and the opposing one, that of the disciples. The pattern it follows is structured right into the text itself. In chapter 27, beginning with verses 57–61, we have the actual burial of Jesus, which follows almost the exact pattern of Mark's with Joseph of Arimathea requesting the body from Pilate and attending to the arrangements, watched at a distance now by Mary Magdalene and the other Mary, who sit opposite the tomb, watching. This detail of Joseph of Arimathea parallels the good Joseph of the birth stories that cares for the child as his own and takes both mother and child into his care in the face of the law, threats, and actual danger to them. Matthew's Jesus lives from before his birth under the shadow of the sword of violence and power disturbed by his very presence in the world.

Verses 55–61 tell of the burial, with Joseph of Arimathea, who has now developed into a disciple of Jesus, attending to the body, with Mary of Magdala and the other Mary watching.

Verses 62–66 tell the story of the plot to discredit the Resurrection before it happens, just in case it happens, by both the Sanhedrin and Pilate in collusion. It is calculated and indicative of how religious and political leaders individually and in their spheres of power often act together against the truth of a person and an event.

> The next day, that is, after the day of Preparation, the chief priests and the Pharisees gathered before Pilate and said, "Sir, we remember what that impostor said while he was still alive. "After three days I will rise again." Therefore command the tomb to be made secure until the third day; otherwise his disciples may go and steal him away, and tell the people, "He has been raised from the dead" and the last deception would be worse than the first." Pilate said to them, "You have a guard of soldiers; go, make it as secure as you can." So they went with the guard and made the tomb secure by sealing the stone. (NRS)

The conspiracy is set in motion. Even dead, this preacher disturbs them, and they are afraid of any untoward possibility, or "what if," and they do not want to take any chances. The language itself provokes a climate of deceit as they refer to Jesus as "that imposter," quoting his own words, as they often did in the gospel, attempting to trap him so that they could arrest him. The second deception (of the disciples stealing his body and saying he had been raised) would be worse than the first, the first being Jesus himself and all that he spoke of and stood up for in his life and teaching. The chief priests and the Pharisees gather before Pilate, just as Herod gathered the teachers of the law and the priests when he wanted information about the child to be born. This has the overtones of a plot and is used in the gospel and in Acts to speak about those who are opposed not only to the teachings of Jesus, but to anyone preaching about Jesus (see Acts 4). The entire perspective is malevolent and hostile, both to Jesus and to his disciples.

The hostility of these Jewish leaders (not the people) is nothing in comparison to the power and the perceived threat that Jesus might be, dead, or worse, alive, to Rome. Pilate gives them their guard and orders that the tomb be made "secure." This is tantamount to saying that Rome will stop anyone from getting into the tomb. The seal of Rome would be applied to it, threatening in itself, as though the police had sealed or cordoned off a crime scene and was not allowing anyone to pass. The verb used is significant:

> The verb "to secure" (*asphalizein*) is used three times in this pericope (Matt. 27:64, 65, 66) and should therefore be given due attention. The only other usage in the New Testament is found in Acts 16:24, stating that Paul's and Silas' feet were "fastened" or "secured" in the stocks. It is part of a "liberation miracle" (Acts 16:22–35) narrating Paul's imprisonment and miraculous liberation at Philippi. No matter how much the authorities "secured" Paul and Silas, God's powerful intervention set them free. So here, no matter how much the authorities made the sepulcher secure, God's interven-

tion would not be foiled. If the disciples preached that "he was risen from the dead," it was certainly not because the authorities did not take the necessary precautions.

. . .

> After receiving the go-signal from Pilate, the Jewish authorities took all the necessary steps: the stone was sealed and the guard was set. The entrance of the rock tombs was closed by a great round stone. It was sealed by putting slime or wax on and into the joint between the stone and the rock and impressing a seal into the wax. The scene reminds us of Dan. 6:17, "A stone was brought and laid upon the mouth of the den, and the king sealed it with his own signet and with the signet of his lords, that nothing might be changed concerning Daniel." In the early Church, Daniel's escape from the den of lions was considered a type of Jesus' resurrection, but we cannot determine with certainty whether Matthew already did so. (Hendrickx, pp. 27–28)

Certainly this seems like a lot of concentration on what actually precedes the Resurrection, but Matthew is concerned that his listeners know where they stand—and so we need to know were we stand too. The whole Resurrection account in Matthew is a triptych that begins with the disciples (Joseph, the two Marys), then jumps to the leaders of the Jews and Romans who are in opposition to Jesus; then moves to the heart, which is the Resurrection itself and the proclamation; then goes back to the leaders, and once again to the disciples, who this time actually see Jesus as they leave the tomb, and then to many of the disciples as they are commissioned in Galilee.

Everything swirls around the actual tomb and grave of Jesus. The setup is important as it reveals the sharp distinction between those who oppose Jesus and those who obey Jesus. From the beginning of the account we are giving hints that a decision is involved, and it impacts people today. Reginald Fuller, a New Testament exegete, adds this interesting piece of information:

> The opening phrase is curiously worded, in a way that obscures the fact that the "next day," the day after the Preparation, was actually the sabbath! The chief priests and Pharisees sought an interview with Pilate (v.62), obtained permission for a guard, sealed the tomb, and placed the guard—all on the sabbath. . . our suspicions at least are aroused. (p. 72)

Jesus has been dead and is now buried in the tomb. It is cross quiet. The tomb is duly sealed and guarded. It is dead quiet. The dead body of Jesus is secure in the custody of the Roman Empire, for society, the people, must be protected from his lies and who he claimed to be, as well as from his disciples' lies and from the theft of his body by his disciples. It is deadly still, and the stage is set for resurrection.

None of the gospel writers ever speak about the actual resurrection. Their narratives are about the proclamation of the Resurrection after it has happened. It is as though you cannot speak about what actually happened. That is the domain of God the Father in the power of the Spirit who raised Jesus from the dead. It is indescribable, hidden, and concealed in God alone. Easter morning is when the disciples discover what God has done in the night, and the world begins to cope with the radical altering of history and life. Alice Meynell (1847–1922) wrote a poem that speaks of this, playing with the images of sound and quiet, as does Matthew's Gospel.

Easter Night

All night had shout of men and cry
Of woeful women filled his way;
Until that noon of sombre sky
On Friday, clamour and display
Smote him; no solitude had he,
No silence, since Gethsemane.
Public was Death; but Power, but Might,
But Life again, but Victory,
Were husted within the dead of night,
The shuttered dark, the secrecy.
And all alone, alone, alone,
He rose again behind the stone.

(In *The Poet's Christ: An Anthology of Poetry about Jesus,*
compiled by David Winter. London: Lion Publishing, 1998, p. 117)

And now we come to the tomb with the women while it is still dark and the story is catastrophically different from Mark's telling. There is no way to be prepared for what has happened—the Resurrection—and the way it will be proclaimed to those who come to the tomb.

After the sabbath, as the first day of the week was dawning, Mary Magdalene and the other Mary went to see the tomb. And suddenly there was a great earthquake; for an angel of the Lord, descending from heaven, came and rolled back the stone and sat on it. His appearance was like lightening, and his clothing white as snow. For fear of him the guards shook and became like dead men. But the angel said to the women, "Do not be afraid; I know that you are looking for Jesus who was crucified. He is not here; for he has been raised, as he said. Come, see the place where he lay. Then go quickly and tell his disciples, 'He has been raised from the dead, and indeed he is going ahead of you to Galilee; there you will see him.' This is my message for you." So they left the tomb quickly with fear and great joy, and ran to tell his disciples. (Matt. 28:1–8)

This is the announcement and as Matthew has had recourse to from the beginning, it is done in the style of the birth announcements when the angel comes to Joseph to proclaim what has happened: Mary is pregnant and is going to give birth to a son (Matt. 1:20). And then twice more Joseph is warned in dreams by angels to flee and take the child and his mother, and then commanded only to return when it is safe, and Herod is dead. Now there is an angel in full glory, accompanied by the earth's shuddering and quaking. It is all light, and God's reality shakes all the earth to its very foundations. This description echoes what happened at Jesus's death on the cross earlier (Matt. 27:51–54), when the earth quaked, the curtain of the temple was torn, the graves were opened, and many bodies raised, and those who saw were in awe. This is God's glory reflecting on the earth as it did in the Exodus (19:18) and when Elijah was visited by God (1 Kings 19:11–12).

And now those who sought to guard the tomb, to take custody of the body of Jesus, shake like the earth and fall down like dead men. The angel rolls away the stone from the tomb, breaking the seal of Rome as if it were child's play, revealing that the tomb is already empty! Then he sits on the stone, as though enthroned, shining in glory. The stone becomes a pulpit, and this is the first Easter morning sermon delivered with power from heaven itself. And the actual words are almost identical to those of the young man in Mark, though the sense of their power is heightened with the closing line: "This is my message to you." Just as the angel proclaimed to Joseph the fact of the Incarnation already in motion and commanded Joseph to obey, now the angel proclaims the Resurrection and commands the women to obey his words and "go quickly and tell his disciples."

There are small details that change: there are only two women now, and they are the same who watched the tomb while Joseph was burying the body. And now they go to "see" the tomb. Again, we must ask ourselves what was in their hearts that early early morning after the Sabbath rest? Elizabeth McAlister, who knows a few things about tombs and prisons herself, writes in a reflection on this story:

> Imagine the feelings of these women. It is a terrible moment, swirling with apathy, betrayal, overwhelming odds, oppression, and senseless suffering. Jesus had promised so much—where is it now? It seems so long ago.
>
> The weight of the powers of this world and their inertia (or worse) forces us to concede that the world can't be transformed! It is also a bitter journey for these women. . . . But the tomb is sealed shut by a huge boulder. Put there by the authorities to certify Jesus' defeat, the stone serves also to ensure the women's separation from him. They aren't even granted the presence of his corpse to comfort them in their ritual of mourning. It is the final ignominy.

> But then there's an earthquake, an angel, guards frozen in fear! This is the
> kairos moment, an aperture of hope that the story might have a future after
> all. Like the tomb, the story has been reopened. . . . Is it possible that not
> even the imperial death grip and sealed barricade could put an end to the
> journey? They are too frightened to think, too joyful to stand still. What is
> this all about?
>
> Amazingly, it is an invitation to follow him again. Resume the way. And
> resume it, knowing what the consequences may be. . . . From within the old
> human being, guarded and barricaded and securely sealed, a new person is
> emerging. ("Resurrection Ironies." *The Other Side* (May/June 1999): 25)

In an instant the world shifts. They are wrenched from their misery and grieving and thrown into life, pushed back into the world they have found so dis-
tressing, so violent, and so destructive of their hopes, their ideals, and most especially of the one they so loved and had begun to follow. And they are
instructed to tell the disciples (there is no separation of Peter from the group).
But now their reaction is different. They are obedient and leave the tomb
(which they do not seem to have entered; they only looked and saw what the
angel pointed out) and "go quickly with fear and great joy to tell the disciples."
They are running into a future that is wide open before them. All is undone.
He is alive. He is raised. Jesus kept faith with his Father, and his Father has kept
faith with him. Now Jesus keeps faith with those who betrayed him in the past.
His disciples have shifted—now they obey. And now, in the act of obedience,
they run right into him! He is already coming toward them.

> Suddenly Jesus met them and said, "Greetings!" And they came to him, took
> hold of his feet, and worshipped him. Then Jesus said to them, "Do not be
> afraid; go and tell my brothers to go to Galilee; there they will see me."
> (Matt. 28:9–10)

This is where Matthew parts company with Mark and adds to the tradition, so that we actually see the appearance of Jesus, the Risen Lord, when they
leave the environs of the empty tomb. It is he who approaches them and
speaks. The word used here is "Greetings," but perhaps other translations say it
more aptly: "He greeted them" (NAB), which in the Jewish tradition would
be the words, "Peace be with you! Shalom!" His first words risen from the dead
to his friends in awe, shock, fear, and worship. For that is what they do. They
do him homage, bending, approaching him as a servant would a master, as a
slave or a lord would a king, "taking hold of his feet" in reverence and affec-
tion. And Jesus continues with the phrase he has told them over and over again
throughout his time with them, "Do not be afraid." But there is one massive
change in the words when he repeats what the angel had told them. He says,
"Go and tell my brothers to go to Galilee." My brothers—there is a world of

mercy conjured in that simple shift of what they are to him, how close they are: not disciples, but brothers and sisters. God mercifully raised Jesus from the dead, and Jesus mercifully calls us all brothers and sisters: all of us are included in his words and gift of forgiveness. His very presence as Risen Lord draws us back closer than before we failed and refused to testify to our faith in him. And off they go again, running to find his brothers and sisters.

Now the action splits in two directions. The women go off to find the disciples and tell the disciples to go back to Galilee; meanwhile, the soldiers, who have revived, set off to go into the city and find those who hired them and tell them what has happened. The split between those who believe and those who oppose widens.

> While they were going, some of the guard went into the city and told the chief priests everything that had happened. After the priests had assembled with the elders, they devised a plan to give a large sum of money to the soldiers, telling them, "You must say, 'His disciples came by night and stole him away while we were asleep.'" If this comes to the governor's ears, we will satisfy him and keep you out of trouble." So they took the money and did as they were directed. And this story is still told among the Jews to this day. (Matt. 28:11–15)

There is much written on why this forms the backdrop to Matthew's Resurrection account. Historically, there was tension between the two communities, and many Jews did refuse to believe that Jesus had been raised from the dead, and stories did circulate about the disciples stealing the body. Partially, the story serves an apologetic function, defending the tradition of the empty tomb as valid. The reality of the empty tomb does not prove the raising of Jesus from the dead, but it is a focal point for the pronouncement of that belief to the community. At the time Matthew's Gospel was composed, the Pharisees were a major obstacle and the source of persecution of the community. The angel sitting on the stone, with the soldiers as though dead, connotes ancient images of judgment and apocalyptic power signaling the end of what was history and the start of what is new and liberating. The Resurrection is a judgment on all power and authority. This theme will continue when the disciples meet Jesus in Galilee.

The soldiers are struck with fear that either makes them faint, or they are cowering in the presence of some source of power. Again, even if the story is not about the actual occurrence, the writer is attempting to reveal truth about the source of power of God and how the Resurrection affects history and other kinds of power. In the Orthodox Church, the Easter liturgy speaks of the stone, the grave, and the soldiers partially as judgment, but also as invitation to belief and exhortation to look again.

The empty tomb is an invitation to seek the living Christ elsewhere, it is a reminder of the angel's words: "He is risen as he said" (Matt. 28:6). The Scriptures have been confirmed and enlightened by the light of the tomb that reveals their meaning. Hence the insistence, at the very heart of the liturgy, on eliminating every trace of doubt:

O ye blind unbelievers, deceivers and transgressors, who disbelieved Christ's arising as though it were a lie: What do you see that is unbelievable? That Christ, Who raised up the dead is risen?

O ye enemies of Christ, though ye disbelieve, ask your soldiers what they suffered. Whose hand rolled away the stone of the sepulchre?

. . .

The stone itself crieth, the seals call out; when ye placed them, ye appointed a watch to guard the tomb. Truly Christ is risen, and He liveth unto the ages.

. . .

The soldiers are struck by fear at the sight of the angel and not of the Risen One. Could they have otherwise accepted to spread the lie that the body had been removed by thieves? All those who recognized the divinity of Christ confessed Him to their death. Thus, when the centurion, Longinus, and his soldiers were present at Golgotha, saw the earthquake and what took place, they were filled with awe, and said, "Truly this was the Son of God!" (Matt. 27:54) ("Sunday of the Myrrhbearing Women," Matins, Ode 8, tone 2, quoted in Quenot, pp. 96–97)

Here we are reminded that even among soldiers there were those who believed and those who opposed. The Resurrection demands a response—yes or no—and the narrative highlights how those choices affected the early community.

Now Matthew continues with the tradition that is peculiar to his own church that has already become truth, as he writes it and as across the ages of history it has continued to be accomplished. The women see him and obey him and pass on to his Easter family the injunction to go to Galilee. And there, they do see him for the last time, together.

Now the eleven disciples went to Galilee, to the mountain to which Jesus had directed them. When they saw him, they worshiped him; but some doubted. And Jesus came and said to them, "All authority in heaven and on earth has been given to me. Go therefore and make disciples of all nations, baptizing them in the name of the Father, and of the Son, and of the Holy Spirit, and teaching them to obey everything that I have commanded you. And remember, I am with you always, to the end of the age." (Matt. 28:16–20)

The disciples meet Jesus on a mountain, a familiar place in Matthew's stories, whether it is the Sermon on the Mount (Matt. 5), where they learn the

New Covenantal law and what constitutes the new holiness code among his people, or the Mount of the Transfiguration, where they glimpse the power of God shining through him as he prays and is seen with Moses and Elijah, the liberator and law giver and the fiery prophet, the disturber of Israel, speaking about his passover—his coming crucifixion and death in Jerusalem (Matt. 17:1–8). And in the very beginning when the Spirit drives Jesus into the desert, he is tempted by Satan; in the final temptation, he is taken to a high mountain and showed all the kingdoms of the world in a single glance, and they are laid out like bait before him. Satan—the name means "what hinders"—tells him that he can have all this power and splendor because it belongs to him, and he can give it to whomever he chooses, if Jesus will only fall down and worship him. Satan is ordered to leave him, and even Satan obeys that command (Matt. 4:1–11).

Now it is a mountain in Galilee where he began his teaching, healing, and forgiving ministry. The disciples see him, and they worship, but some also doubt him. As in the beginning, they worship as those who came from the East, bowed down in worship before the child. But belief isn't instantaneous upon seeing the Risen Lord. Raymond Brown explains this dilemma with hopefulness: "the doubt would remind the readers, that even after the resurrection, faith is not a facile response. It might also encourage them that Jesus is not repelled by doubt, for he now comes close to the disciples to speak. Doubting or not, they have worshipped him, and he responds to them" (p. 35). There is more of comfort and Jesus's care for his "brothers" in the text than might be immediately apparent.

> We are told in 28:17 that when the disciples "saw" the Risen Jesus some experienced doubts about his reality or identity. By introducing the apologetic problem of doubt at this point, Matthew is preparing to reassure his church in the following verses that Jesus truly appeared to the eleven and convinced them of his identity as the Risen Lord. In 28:18, therefore, Jesus "comes near" (*proselthon*) and reassuringly "talks with" (*elalesen*) the disciples, thereby overcoming the uncertainty. (Perry, p. 75)

And when he speaks, it is profoundly powerful. He is not just the teacher, or the master and Lord. He is more than they could imagine and what they must grow into believing as a community together. And they will mature in their faith by obeying the commission that he gives them. "All authority in heaven and on earth has been given to me." He is the Lord of heaven and earth. His power, his kingdom, is over all. This is authority and power that shatter the seals of Rome, stun an army if need be, and will seep into the whole world with an alternative to the world's power with which Satan tempted him at the beginning and by which we are all tempted still. The world's power is found in money, prestige, arrogance, military might, technology, mass production, reputation, fear, bullying, weapons, violence, and consolidated power that destroys and feeds on the blood of people in war, forced labor, poverty, starvation, and inequality to keep going.

The Risen One's power is very different. His power is to make disciples from every corner of the earth. To stir the hearts of people everywhere to freedom, liberation, the living of the beatitudes, and the belief that God the Father is the God of life, justice, mercy, and love and that His power is stronger than sin, evil, injustice, and hate. Earlier Jesus prayed aloud to his Father:

> All things have been handed over to me by my Father; and no one knows the Son except the Father and no one knows the Father except the Son and anyone to whom the Son chooses to reveal him.
>
> Come to me, all you that are weary and are carrying heavy burdens, and I will give you rest. Take my yoke upon you, and learn from me; for I am gentle and humble in heart, and you will find rest for your souls. For my yoke is easy and my burden is light. (Matt. 11:27–30)

This is what the disciples are learning, slowly, painfully, in fits and starts. It is the power and authority of love, of nonviolence—meekness and gentleness, being humble of heart, relying on the power of God, not their own sources of power as the world does. This is the power of the cross—the yoke that Jesus bore to his death and the community that yokes together his followers so that they can do things they could not conceive of doing alone. This too is the yoke that binds them together in the joy of the Resurrection. In the movie *Zorba the Greek,* toward the end when Zorba loses everything, he grabs his Englishman friend, puts his arms over his shoulder, and draws him into a rhythmic powerful dance. That too is the yoke of Christians who know the dance of resurrection and the freedom from death's hard grip.

And in that power and authority, Jesus sends his followers forth out into the world to do three things: make disciples, baptize them in the name of the Trinity, and teach them all that they have been commanded to obey and practice. This was already the practice of Matthew's church that was spreading through the Greek and Roman Empires. Disciples were being formed in the catechumenate and baptized. This is the first mention of the Trinitarian formula used in baptism—acknowledgment that it was already the practice and the awareness of the church of the Father, the Son, and the Spirit as one. These three works of witnessing to Jesus would make the church a reality. Making disciples is prebaptismal catechesis, baptismal and then postbaptismal teachings that eventually were referred to as the *mystogyia,* the sharing of the mysteries with those who had been initiated in the Trinity, into Jesus's relationship with the Father in the power of the Spirit at baptism. Matthew's Gospel was conceived as a new Torah, with Jesus as the new Moses, and so his emphasis is on teaching. And the disciples, who were learning to obey all that Jesus had commanded them, were, in turn, to make disciples. The primary form of teaching, it is intimated, will be modeling the behavior of Jesus as he taught in his discourses and his parables about the Kingdom of God. This is an unconditional obligation of disciples: the obligation to obey the Word of God and put it into practice so that they truly are "mother, brother and sister" to Jesus.

And the last line completes the giving of power: "Remember! I am with you always, to the end of the ages." This is both a promise of enduring presence and a declaration of what is an already existing reality—since the beginning at the Incarnation. When the angel appears to Joseph, he is told what to name the child to be born of Mary: "name him Jesus, for he will save his people from their sins." And all this fulfills the prophecy of Isaiah, that of the one to come: "they shall name him Emmanuel, which means 'God is with us'" (Matt. 1:21–23). In a sense these farewell words to his family are not a farewell, but an assurance that he is always with them, with us. They will always be able to draw strength from his risen presence and power, which will sustain them through hardship, persecution, dark and hard times, and even through their own infighting and failures. We, like the disciples, are to go out into the whole world, but not in the way of the world. We are to resist temptations, as Jesus did with Satan in the desert, and, instead, we are to follow the way of the new Torah, the law of the New Covenant of the Spirit, until all is complete, fulfilled, and the kingdom comes "on earth as it is in heaven."

Jesus repeats four times the word "all": "all authority is given to me. Go and make disciples of all nations . . . teach them to obey all I have commanded you and I will be with you all days." This is sweeping, all-inclusive of geography, peoples, time, histories, cultures, languages, of a new world altogether—the Kingdom of God. This summons to go fans out from heaven and earth's authority, to all the nations, beginning with Israel, as Jesus himself did, then specifically, the proclamation is given to the women who are sent to the men, who are sent to the ends of the earth to the end of time. This command is given to all who are baptized in the name of the Father, the Son, and the Spirit, to each and all of us. This is the ultimate act of obedience and submission, of trust and devotion: to be witnesses in the world by being disciples and letting everyone see our faith as it is practiced in liturgy, teaching, and the bringing of the kingdom into every corner of the world. Just as Matthew's Gospel begins with a genealogy that goes all the way back in time to Abraham, now those born of the Risen One are to spring forward throughout all time.

Someone once said that Stephen Austin didn't like preachers at all. The capital of Texas is named after him. He swore that "one preacher could stir up more trouble that a dozen horse thieves." Matthew's Gospel reminds us that it is the role of a disciple of Jesus to stir up trouble by playing an active, resistant role in the struggle of good and evil, by resisting the ways of the world and its power bases—economic, religious, nationalistic, politic, military—which are most often in direct opposition to the ways of the Kingdom of God and the way of discipleship. And sometimes, others who wouldn't think of themselves as disciples do more to bring discipleship and the kingdom into the world than those designated as such. Leonardo Boff writes:

> Whenever people seek the good, justice, humanitarian love, solidarity, communion and understanding between people . . . there we can say with all certainty that the Resurrection One is present, because the cause for which he lived, suffered, was tried, and executed is being carried forward. (*Catholic Worker* 1978)

We who are baptized in the name of the communion of the Trinity and summoned to live our discipleship in such a way that we invite the whole world into the mystery of our relationship with the Risen Lord as his brothers and sisters stand before the empty tomb and on the mountain, worshipping and doubting. Ken Untener, the bishop of Saginaw, Michigan, puts out small books for the season of the year for study and reflection on the Scriptures for his people. In his "Little White Book" for Easter 2002, Untener reflects on this portion of the gospel:

> Matthew does not describe what the Risen Jesus looks like. He gives only the disciples' reactions. Their first reaction is to "worship" Jesus. This word takes us back to the beginning of Matthew's gospel. When the Magi finally found Jesus, their first act was to worship him. Now after abandoning Jesus at his arrest, the final act of the disciples is to worship him.
>
> But they also had some doubts. Matthew is teaching us that disciples of the Lord will always be caught between worship and doubt. The truths of our faith are never mathematical certainties. Inevitability, from time to time, for just a millisecond, doubts flit across our mind. Matthew is encouraging us. Don't panic because doubts come. Faith doesn't come from us. It comes from God. And God's gifts don't wear out. Need your faith strengthened? Talk to the Lord about it. (From reflection for Monday, third week of Easter)

For each of us the appearance of the Risen Lord must become rooted in our prayer. This is the only way we can live as disciples in a world that resists the gospel and opposes us. Everything depends on our point of view: we have our choices—from the point of view of the powers of the world, from the point of view of those in religion, of our own and others who are in collusion with the world's authority, and from the point of view of discipleship. We must worship to assuage the doubts, and there are many in our world and church today. Maria Boulding in her marvelous little book that is dense with insights writes about prayer in the Easter Christ:

> "This is what the Lord asks of you," says the prophet Micah, "only this, to act justly, to love tenderly and to walk humbly with your God." The common experience of spiritual failure in the sense described can be a means used by the Lord to wean us from our own limited ideas about the way our life and prayer ought to go. We are forced to pray from a position of disillusion and bafflement, and this can lead us into the heart of Christ's paschal mystery. The real cross we are asked to carry is to believe that Jesus is Lord of every situation in our lives, and in particular that he is Lord of our prayer. From within our situation we have to listen to his word. (*Marked for Life: Prayer in the Easter Christ*, 14)

We must be worshipping disciples, allowing the Risen Lord to use even our doubts as a catalyst for belief, for both ourselves and others, just as the empty tomb was a catalyst for belief for those who looked for the Crucified One, went to the tomb to see, and watched, even from a distance, when he died, or weren't there at all. The Risen Lord is the Lord of history, all history, which is more often than not the history of violence, of war, of the slaughter of the innocents, ethnic cleansings, racial hatred, extension of territory, and the arrogance of power that works in collusion with anyone who will serve its ends.

And we must choose where we stand and what we see from that vantage point, Matthew asserts in his account of the Resurrection. A remarkable story has been told these past few years about a group of women called the Women in Black. They are Israeli Jews who meet at the wall in Jerusalem (all that is left of the temple that was destroyed in 70 A.D.). They meet every Friday, the Sabbath evening, and pray. They begin by singing Kaddish for all the Israelis killed in the fighting in Israel that week. When they are finished, they pause and read all the names. Then, they turn again to face the wall and sing Kaddish again, this time for all the Palestinians killed in the fighting that week, and they turn when they are finished and once again recite the litany of the names of those killed.

Often they are harassed, taunted, cursed, and physically abused. Jews throw stones, mud, garbage, food at them, insulting them as they pray for all the people killed in the violence and hatred. One of the leaders is a diminutive woman, and yet she commands authority dressed in her black chador. This is the dress of the Palestinian women, but the Jewish women all wear it at the wall to pray in solidarity with all those who mourn and grieve their dead loved ones.

On one Sabbath evening, a man was more violent than usual and pulled the veil from her face, spit at her, and cursed her, saying, "How can you pray for our enemies, those pigs?" He continued with a stream of abuse. Finally, when he stopped, she replied quietly, "I once thought like you do about the Palestinians. Eleven years ago, my young daughter, my only beautiful daughter, was killed in a suicide bomb attack, and all I wanted to do was hate, to kill, to make someone pay for my pain and grief, my loss. But my hate did not help or change anything, and I slowly began to realize that if I hated and killed that I was just like whoever killed my daughter without even knowing her. I realized then that the Palestinians are not our enemies. No one is our enemy. There are only two kinds of people in the world . . . only two! There are those who seek war and violence. And there are those who seek peace. I decided I am one of those who seek peace." And she looked him directly in the eye and quietly asked him, "And you, sir, which one are you? Do you seek war and violence? Or are you one of those who seek peace?"

The story is staggering. There are only two kinds of people in the world. In Matthew's Gospel there are three points of view. Here that number is reduced to two: Do we make disciples of all nations who universally teach peace, reconciliation, the beatitudes, the communion of God with all of us as brothers and sisters and a world where life, and only life, is served, no other authority or power on earth? Or do we oppose the authority of the Risen Lord by serving the powers of the world that Satan delegates and teaches? In Matthean terms, are we alive in Christ or are we living, but like the dead, like the soldiers at the tomb?

Seamus Heaney's poem "From the Republic of Conscience" questions all people along these lines. These are the first and last pieces from it.

> 1. When I landed in the republic of conscience
> It was so noiseless when the engines stopped
> I could hear a curlew high above the runway.
> At immigration, the clerk was an old man
> Who produced a wallet from his homespun coat
> And showed me a photograph of my grandfather.
> The woman in customs asked me to declare
> The words of our traditional cures and charms
> To heal dumbness and avert the evil eye.
> No porters. No interpreter. No taxi.
> You carried your own burden and very soon
> Your symptoms of creeping privilege disappeared.
> . . .
>
> 3. I came back from that frugal republic
> with my two arms the one length, the customs
> woman having insisted my allowance was myself.
> The old man rose and gazed into my face
> And said that was official recognition

That I was now a dual citizen.
He therefore desired me when I got home
To consider myself a representative
And to speak on their behalf in my own tongue.
Their embassies, he said, were everywhere
But operated independently
And no ambassador would ever be relieved.

(In *Opened Ground: Selected Poems 1966–1996*)

We are ambassadors of the Risen Lord, followers of the Crucified One, and so dual citizens no matter where we dwell or what countries we visit. Our lives, our words, our example as disciples are our only currency, and all the world looks to us for hope, for life and justice and forgiveness, the mercy of our God, who in Jesus calls us all brothers and sisters and in the Spirit sends us out to speak on their behalf in our own tongue. And we will never be relieved of our duties and our God is with us always, even to the end of the ages. Alleluia. Alleluia. Alleluia.

Luke's Account: Luke 24

PART 1: THE TOMB, LUKE 24:1–12

Looking is what saves us.

—Simone Weil

We begin by going to the tomb, by facing the emptiness and loss, by doing what we can in the face of death, a death that was violent, calculated, and brutal. For many of us, this beginning piece of Luke's account is not very familiar. It is the second part, that of the encounter on the road to Emmaus, that we hear about so often, but this is the prelude, or the preface, if you will, for the unfolding of that story. This is the setup and is crucial for understanding Luke's intricate design and fitting all the pieces together. Literally, the word "preface" means "to stand before the face of someone," or "to stand in the presence of someone," and to stand before God's holy face in the person of his beloved Son, Jesus, the Risen One, we must begin back at the tomb and go looking for the face of the One so marred by crucifixion. Jesus is dead and Joseph of Arimathea has procured the body from Pilate, wrapped it in linen cloths, although hurriedly, and buried it in a tomb where no one had lain before. The women, not named, are described as those "who had come with him from Galilee followed, and they saw the tomb and how his body was laid. Then they returned, and prepared spices and ointments. On the sabbath they rested according to the commandment" (Luke 23:55–56).

It was the Sabbath, the full day from eventide when the first star rises in the heavens until that star rises again the following day, and it belongs wholly to God. They want to prepare the body fittingly for burial, but it must wait. It must wait on the commandment, on the Word of God given to Moses and remembered and honored by all who believe in the God who led them out of bondage, accompanied them in the desert wanderings for forty years, and led them into a land of hope that they could call home, where they could worship their God in freedom. It is during this waiting time in the dark of the tomb that God does the work of resurrection, the work of vanquishing death forever. All the accounts of the burial of Jesus are somber, laced through with the silence of grief, the shock that violence does to one's soul, even experienced vicariously in the body of another who is loved. They are written as though they are dirges, laments hidden in the silences and spaces between the words. And the transition period of that seemingly lost day would be filled with familiar rituals of lighting candles to welcome the Spirit of Yahweh in exile with the people, and shared meals, offerings that would guarantee that the poor also could celebrate and honor the law and rest from their labors, and with the prayers: psalms, ancient stories of hope and promises still to be fulfilled. The name of the one mourned and grieved over would not be spoken aloud, for it was the day that belonged to the honor of God and grief was not allowed to intrude. It would cast its shadow long and it would seep into the hearts of those who worshipped, but it would be a lingering presence rather than a grief observed and spoken about among others in pain.

Jesus is dead and buried. The sentence has such finality to it. It is an ending, and those words must be felt and known in our deepest places. We believe that death does not have this final word, but it must be spoken and it must grasp us in a deathly hold for the wild power of what God has done for us in Jesus to be experienced and known in our hearts. This is prelude for sensing the power of what will happen to our bodies and how we are to face death now in our lives and in the world around us. Our culture feeds on death, in wars, hundreds of billions of dollars for weapons of destruction, the stockpiling of missiles, and allocations for new nuclear weapons even as we have storehouses that could turn the entire planet into a huge tomb hundreds of times over. Jails, prisons, detention centers, juvenile facilities, welfare programs, all are institutional tombs as we spend four times as much building new prison systems than we do schools and hospitals. Oddly or aptly enough, the huge sprawling Manhattan county jail is nicknamed "the Tombs." Once there, you might as well be dead, all hope gone. The place reeks of despair, hopelessness, endless night, rage, and sorrow. You disappear into the Tombs and even the inmates quote the line to visitors as a warning, "Abandon all hope, you who enter here." Jesus, a condemned and executed criminal, according to the existing capital-punishment laws, all nice and legal, has been dealt with appropriately and is buried. Case closed. They assumed they broke him, instilled terror in his followers that would deter them from obeying him, and stilled his voice that gave hope to the many who lived in darkness in the midst of their struggles to survive a life of slavery, oppression, poverty, and misery. But the God of life, the God of Abraham and Hagar, of Isaac and Ishmael, of Jacob, Rachel, and Leah, and the matriarchs and patriarchs, prophets, kings, and people, has never tolerated death or allowed it to have the last word. The whole story has been one of interference and refusal. The pun on the word "interference" is intended. What we bury, our God redeems: whether it is hopes and a life for his people or a whole nation destroyed and exiled in Babylon. In the dark of night while his people observe the Sabbath once again, God is making a new thing. God is beating back death and disarming its power and hold over human beings.

Luke's account begins, sounding like the ones who wrote in testimony and belief before him:

> But on the first day of the week, at early dawn, they came to the tomb, taking the spices that they had prepared. They found the stone rolled away from the tomb, but when they went in, they did not find the body. (Luke 24:1–2)

In these two lines there is a realm of possibility, of surprise, of fear and mystery. As soon as the requirements of the Sabbath laws have been fulfilled, the women move out to do the corporal work of mercy, the act of last kindness of preparing the body for endless decomposure and return to the earth. They would still be held in the grip of shock and the exhaustion that grief takes as a toll on body and soul. It would have seemed a lifetime since they prepared the materials for wrapping the body in the time-honored ways, and they are getting on with their lives. They find the stone rolled away, and they enter the tomb. This is the same kind of finding as the "finding of a treasure in a field, a pearl of great price," though they are unaware of that at the moment. They enter the tomb. The entering is the beginning of knowing. It is the doorway, the threshold to the just kingdom of peace opening out before us and seeping ever more truly into the world. For us, this entering into the tomb is our baptism, being buried with Christ, and our immersion and rising from its waters begins our rising from the dead into new life hidden with Christ in God.

And the encounters with hope begin now:

> While they were perplexed about this, suddenly two men in dazzling clothes stood beside them. The women were terrified and bowed their faces to the ground, but the men said to them, "Why do you look for the living among the dead? He is not here, but has risen. Remember how he told you, while he was still in Galilee, that the Son of Man must be handed over to sinners, and be crucified, and on the third day rise again." Then they remembered his words. (Luke 24:4–8)

This is the proclamation of resurrection, the beginning of the story for Luke's community of believers, and it starts by remembering. This is the word that characterizes this whole chapter and story. Remember! This word is not about what is gone, dead and buried in the past, but about what lives, is present and seeded with life here and now. Remember, in its most simple and strongest meaning, is "to put back together again as it was in the beginning," and the word is used in many cultures among storytellers to begin the old stories ritually. It is a summons, a command to be attentive, to reorient yourself in the community, in your history and place in the universe. It pulls all the past into the present moment and summons the future to be imagined and made in its light. It is a long, long word reaching backward and forward.

There is a short marvelous story by Urs Banerter that pulls this word and its meaning together for us. The story has no title, and as it was told to me, a Frenchman tells the tale.

> I was fourteen years old and on Sunday afternoons after dinner I'd go walking. My walk always ended in the same place, in a small garden on a bench near the church. I'd sit and look and see what I could see. One day I watched while a blackbird, a crow or a raven, one of that tribe, sat in an elderberry bush and ate the berries. I was fascinated and watched for a long time. Just as I was about to leave, it flew up, finished with its afternoon snack, and sat on the nearby cemetery wall on the other side of the garden and began cleaning the seeds off its beak by rubbing it back and forth on the stones.
>
> After being away from home for forty years, I returned and on an afternoon retraced my steps of that old familiar walk, back to the garden near the church and my stone bench. I sat and to my utter surprise found an elderberry bush now growing out of the cemetery wall! I investigated and found its roots in the crumbling mortar and stones right in the wall. Those seeds over time had split the stones of the wall and opened it so wide that I could get my whole hand in there, along with the roots of the elderberry bush. With a piece of mortar that had broken away, I wrote on the wall, "The work of a blackbird!"

The work of a blackbird—this opening of the tomb and the dawning of resurrection upon the world is the work of our God. The women are confused, disoriented, and there is the sense that they are stumbling about, and then they are terrified at the sight of angels and dazzling clothes, and the natural response to such extraordinary light is to fall down with their faces to the ground. It is instinctual, protective and submissive. But the message from God is filled with clarity, light, and opens their minds. This is a new question being posed by the evangelist: "Why do you look for the living among the dead?" In the other accounts the women were told not to fear because the messengers knew that they were seeking the Crucified One and that he was not there. Now his name is changed. He is the Son of Man, the title that Jesus himself often used to teach his disciples that he was, in the tradition of the prophets, specifically this figure found in the Book of Daniel, who is the fullness of being human, yet suffused with the light of the Divine, coming in power to judge all the living and the dead with justice. And what gives him this right to judge is what he has suffered and endured as a human being who was innocent of any wrongdoing or evil. This is the one in the prophecies and found again and again in Jesus's warnings and attempt to get them to see him in a larger view of their own histories and belief rather than in terms of their peculiar wants and sight. And when the words are spoken aloud, the women remember. It comes back. It seeps into their minds and hearts. It is reseeded in them, and a shoot sprouts up as though laced with a good dose of fertilizer or a long dose of light. And once they remember, they move out of the tomb and into the light of day, into the future, and run to tell the story with it fresh in their minds.

> Then they remembered his words, and returning from the tomb, they told all this to the eleven and to all the rest. Now it was Mary Magdalene, Joanna, Mary the mother of James, and the other women with them who told this to the apostles. But these words seemed to them an idle tale, and they did not believe them. But Peter got up and ran to the tomb; stooping and looking in, he saw the linen cloths by themselves; then he went home, amazed at what had happened. (Luke 24:8–12)

Now we have some names: Mary of Magdala, who appears in all the accounts, Joanna, who had earlier been named as one who had been with Jesus since the beginning of his ministry in Galilee (along with Susanna and many others; Luke 8:1–3), and Mary the mother of James, presumably the other apostle James the Lesser, or son of Alphaeus (Luke 6:15). There are at least six women named in the first three accounts, so far. And when they remember, they set off to tell the story to the eleven—a hint that they are still gathered together, probably having celebrated the Sabbath together the day before. But they are not believed. That word "but"—Luke's chapter begins with that word—serves as a bridge between the burial of Jesus and the discovery of the empty tomb, but, sadly, here it serves to break that bridge and cut that rope, that lifeline of hope to the community. An idle, an empty tale. The tomb, the deadness and despair hold them so tightly they cannot breach its darkness with even a shaft of light and angels' pronouncements. Peter though does go running off to check it out. What he finds is an empty tomb. Only an echo of the women's words and he goes home, back to the upper room, amazed, but obviously confused, and still wallowing in his grief, guilt, and despair, more singularly than the others, perhaps because of his public betrayals and disowning of his Lord in the moment when he needed a friend, a disciple, anyone who would stand with him as he stood facing his death.

This is Luke's introduction to the marvel of resurrection, of Jesus, the Son of man, crucified and risen from the dead. Now we abruptly shift to another location, later in the day, as though this were a documentary film adding pieces to the puzzle of where the body is and who this Jesus, crucified, dead, buried, and now risen and alive, is.

PART 2: ON THE WAY

The mouth tastes food, the heart tastes words.

—Hmong proverb

The story of the Resurrection and the appearances of Jesus to his disciples begins to multiply like the food he was wont to spread around among his disciples, friends, and crowds who flocked to listen to his stories on hillsides and in deserted places. Whatever resurrection is, it demands numerous tellings, experiences, and encounters by many who believed in him, who sought his words, and now knew without a doubt that he was dead and their dreams of another life were shattered and gone. Life had to go on, if only on a level of mere survival, and the pieces had to be picked up, and some semblance of normality regained. Grief initially paralyzes, but then the routine of life carries us temporarily, until other levels of sorrow can be absorbed and lived through.

Raymond Brown again compares similarities and differences in the three accounts:

> Like Matthew, Luke follows Mark in the basic story of the empty tomb, but then goes his own way in the appearances he reports. While Matthew recounts an appearance of Jesus in Jerusalem to two women, Luke recounts at length (24:13–35) the appearance of Jesus to two male disciples on the road from Jerusalem to Emmaus. (p. 14)

This is a good place to start looking at the story and hearing it, and chewing on it and digesting it, for it is as much about eating as it is about seeing, hearing, and recognizing—putting the pieces together and finding out that what they are seeking is a person alive and with them all ways, everywhere. But to begin with, I would humbly disagree with the assertion that the appearance is to two male disciples. We are told that "one of them, whose name was Cleopas," is the one who does the talking. The other is silent, a companion traveler and listener to the stranger's stories. But in John's Gospel, we are told that there were a number of people "standing near the cross of Jesus." They are named: "his mother, and his mother's sister, Mary the wife of Clopas and Mary Magdalene" (John 19:25b) The spelling is different, but it is significantly similar. Could this other person be Mary of Clopas, Mary, the mother of Jesus's sister, Cleopas's wife? Was she one of the women unnamed, but with the women who came to anoint the body of Jesus earlier in the morning at the tomb, and one of those who came to tell the "idle tale" of angels and of there being no body, and the amazing statement that "he was alive"? These two could be Jesus' aunt and uncle on his mother's side of the family. It makes sense and ties pieces together more intimately. This is a family affair, and it impacts all existing relationships, as well as shattering the plans of those who think they make history and decide the course of nations, playing at being god in their decisions of who lives and who dies.

The two of them are on the road, on the way, one gets the impression, home. They are leaving Jerusalem, leaving the harrowing events of the last days behind them. They are running away from the violence, the collusion of their leaders with the Romans to destroy someone they had trusted and hoped in; running away from their life with their teacher, Jesus, whom they had followed, perhaps as one of his seventy-two disciples. But it is over, and it is time to go home and go back to their old way of living. And as they go their way, they are discussing all that has happened, trying to put their lives back together again in some sort of order, seeking meaning from it all, and then, they are joined by a stranger making the same journey. It is a long walk, about seven miles one way. If you walk without much energy or with leaden hearts and broken dreams, you can walk a mile in about thirty minutes. The trip would take them about three and a half hours, probably after the midday meal and the heat of the day. Jesus joins up with them, but they do not see him for who he is; he's just a stranger on the way.

> While they were talking and discussing, Jesus himself came near and went with them, but their eyes were kept from recognizing him. And he said to them, "What are you discussing with each other while you walk along?" They stood still, looking sad. Then one of them, whose name was Cleopas, answered him, "Are you the only stranger in Jerusalem who does not know the things that have taken place there in these days?" He asked them, "What things?" They replied, "The things about Jesus of Nazareth, who was a prophet mighty in deed and word before God and all the people, and how our chief priests and leaders handed him over to be condemned to death and crucified him. But we had hoped that he was the one to redeem Israel. Yes, and besides all this, it is now the third day since these things took place. Moreover, some women of our group astounded us. They were at the tomb early this morning, and when they did not find his body there, they came

> back and told us that they had indeed seen a vision of angels who said that
> he was alive. Some of those who were with us went to the tomb and found
> it just as the women had said; but they did not see him. (Luke 24:15–24)

Ah, here we have the first half of the story, or the story without the Resurrection, the story without grace and truth, without the God of Jesus telling the story. This is what those who followed Jesus believed before he was raised from the dead. It is the basics: he is Jesus of Nazareth (as in Mark's account), but now he is seen to be a prophet, mighty in deed and word, before God and all the people. This is Luke's version of Jesus, who heals the sick, the crippled, the lepers, and the blind, even raises Jairus's daughter from the dead and gives the widow of Naim her only son back from the dead. This is Jesus who utters the blessings and woes of the sermon on the plain and tells marvelous stories of forgiveness, reconciliation, while eating with sinners and feasting with those who needed mercy and compassion just to survive in a community that is harsh and stingy. And this is Jesus as the Suffering Servant, turning toward the Jerusalem that killed the prophets and setting his face toward suffering and death.

But the line that sums it all up—the why of the return home, the turning away from all that has happened, the violence of Jesus's death at the hands of their own leaders and the Romans in collusion—is slipped in with their own loss: "But we had hoped that he was the one to redeem Israel." That is the crux of the matter. It is the hinge on which the door either opens or closes, and they had decided to close it. They have lost hope, lost heart, lost any vision of freedom, and this is the reason they are "restrained from recognizing him," as many translations describe their inability to see Jesus for who he is when he joins them on the way. Discouraged, disheartened, despairing, grieving, they are sightless with hurt and anger.

Even with the empty tomb and the women's story of angels, light, memories jogged with Jesus's words while he was alive, and a possibility that there might be life, they choose still to walk away from it, to disbelieve, to sink into their grief and despair. Since they "did not see him," they stopped looking. And some just up and left town. It is behind them now.

They aren't alone, these two disciples. We have all walked that road all too often, not seeing who is with us, not seeing any meaning in what's going on around us, afraid of the violence and darkness loose in our world, running away from reality without hope, giving in to our despair. Rachel Naomi Remens tells a delightful, childish, and telling vignette of her own life that reveals us to ourselves and sheds light on why we do this, why we read stories and interpret them and our God and our lives from such a pollyannaish point of view, refusing to look at reality or let grace transform and redeem our lives. This comes from a version I heard on tape, as I remember it, most apropos for this chapter on remembering the crucial stuff, even if we do not like it or want to include it in our lives and stories.

When she was little, she remembers, her father gave her mother a huge jigsaw puzzle for her birthday. It was set up on a card table in the living room and not just her parents, but the many visitors who came to the apartment would invariably stop on their way into the kitchen and stand over it and work on it awhile before going in for coffee and conversation. But no one thought to explain to her what exactly it was, or what they were trying to do. So one morning when there wasn't anyone around, she dragged a chair over to the table and stood on it and looked at what this thing was. It disturbed her. All she could see was bits and pieces of cardboard that were scattered all over the table. Oh, there were some that seemed to form a square that would eventually hold them all but it didn't make any sense. Some pieces were light, white, pale blues, streaks of pink and gold, but there seemed to be many more dark pieces, grays, blacks, with lines and figures she couldn't quite make out. She didn't like so many dark ones. So, looking around to make sure no one was watching she took a handful of the ugly ones, as she thought of them, climbed down from the chair and hid them under the cushions on the sofa.

As the days and evenings passed and more and more visitors came to the apartment to work on the puzzle, she would almost daily in the mornings take more pieces away and squirrel them away in the sofa. People became more and more frustrated at why they couldn't seem to get the puzzle to come together; there were patches and pieces missing everywhere. One day her mother noticed that she was peering up at the table with the puzzle and looking very grim, and suddenly her mother realized that it was probably Rachel who was behind the impossibility of the puzzle making any sense. She was kind and asked her what she was looking at, and then she realized that Rachel didn't know what this thing was at all. She lifted her up on the chair and looked at the puzzle with her, asking her what she felt about it. Rachel was slow to answer, but finally said that she didn't like it. It was ugly and filled with so much darkness. Her mother asked, with some cajoling, dragging it out of her, "Rachel, what have you been doing?" And Rachel climbed down off the chair and went over to the sofa, dragging the cushions off and revealing probably a hundred pieces shoved into their hiding place. Her mother gathered them up and put them on the table. She propped up the cover of the box with the picture of the puzzle completed in front of them and started putting the missing pieces in their places. It went quickly, surprisingly, because she was now so familiar with the puzzle, having struggled with it for weeks on end, without the missing pieces.

Rachel stood on her chair mesmerized and delighted as she watched her mother's hands fly across the card table making this gorgeous picture of the sun coming up in the early, early morning on a beach. It was sand and water and sky, all shadowed, but now the sun's beams and streaks of gold and pink began to spread across the landscape and transform what was meaningless and dark into a place and time that was filled with light. Rachel clapped her hands when it was finished. And then they talked. She said she'd taken the pieces because they were dark and ugly and they made her afraid, and her mother explained that it was the dark ones that gave depth and meaning to the picture, highlighting the colors and drawing out the sunrise across the sand dunes, the water lapping the beach, and the sky coming out of the night. And it was then, she said, that she first learned that it is the dark times, the hard places, the ugly pieces of our lives that give depth and meaning to our stories. It is precisely through the suffering, the losses, the pain, even death and illness, and facing them in our own lives or in the lives of those we love, that we come to see a larger picture, something that contains the dark and the light, giving vision and hope beyond what immediately looks grim and foreboding to us. She learned with a jigsaw puzzle when she was young. And yet as we grow older and life begins to take its toll on us, and evil and injustice, violence and despair can creep in and take over even in religion, when we decide there is no meaning and we want only to run away and make all that is ugly go away, we can resort to such a childish reaction to life. Even as adults, we tend to ignore or hide the dark pieces in our lives and in our ideas and images of God, of the struggle to be whole and to make meaning. This is Jesus's way of putting all the pieces together, over long histories and traditions, in the lives of his people Israel, in his own life, and those of his disciples, and of all people for all times. The pieces of the cross, of suffering and death, rejection and betrayal and sin must be included, or the presence of the pieces of light, of resurrection, forgiveness, love that is stronger than death, friendship and intimacy with God in Jesus, the gift of the Spirit of life will not have meaning, and depth will not be able to surge into our lives when it is essential and needed to survive with grace as believers in Jesus, the Crucified and Risen One among us. We will not be able to get the picture, the whole picture, which is the Scriptures' story, God's Word revealed to us, especially in the Word made flesh in Jesus.

But now it is Jesus who begins to tell the story, his story, from a stranger's point of view—from God's point of view. It is the long story, the whole story, the story told with heart and passion and truthfulness. It is the story he had been telling all along, but they (and we) just did not want to hear it, couldn't bear to hear it, did not understand it, and so rejected it. And oh, what a story it is!

Then he said to them: "Oh, how foolish you are and how slow of heart to believe all that the prophets have declared! Was it not necessary that the Messiah should suffer these things and then enter into his glory?" Then beginning with Moses and all the prophets, he interpreted to them the things about himself in all the scriptures.

As they came near the village to which they were going, he walked ahead as if he were going on. But they urged him strongly saying, "Stay with us, because it is almost evening and the day is now nearly over." So he went in to stay with them. (Luke 24:25–29)

We are told in just three lines what Jesus took more than three to four hours to tell them? If only we had those stories and interpretations! But we are told first and foremost that the two of them, all the disciples, we today, are still foolish, slow of heart to believe what has been declared and written. Other versions are much blunter and hardly complimentary—the disciples are described as stupid and stubborn of heart. We have had the Scriptures, the ancient stories of liberation and promise, the Exodus, and all the law and the prophets from Moses and Miriam, through Elijah and Elisha, Jeremiah, Isaiah, Amos and Hosea, Ezekiel, Joel, Micah, so many of them telling of the suffering of the people, the call to conversion of heart, of wild hope in one who would come who would be the presence of justice and mercy among the people, summoning them to live in such light that they would become a signal to the nations. All would stream toward them because they would recognize the presence of God with this people because of the way they related to one another and lived in truth, justice, and peace. And the harder pieces of constant rejection, of the slaying of the prophets and their torture and exile, and that the one to come would only be followed, even waited for by a remnant who turned and turned and turned to God again and again, that this beloved of God would be cast off, humiliated, dishonored, handed over to those who would make him the laughing stock of the nations and mar him beyond any recognition of humanity, resembling more a worm than a man. They should have seen it, read it, taken it to heart, reflected upon it, struggled with it, rather than just ignoring those parts, rejecting them out of hand, and continuing to want to make the story nicer, easier, less powerful, less true, the way they wanted it to read and end. We should learn from their ways that our ways are not God's ways and our thoughts are not God's thoughts (thank God), and that the story is unbelievably good and without parallel in any culture or among any people or other religion. So, slowly, thoroughly, painstakingly, he takes them on a pilgrimage, tells them the stories, goes back over the lay of the land and the history, retelling it with his eye for detail, his meaning and intent, his long vision of seeing and understanding how his God makes all things new, redeems everything that we destroy, and remakes all that we unmake into grace and truth.

What hours they must have been with him! No wonder the time passes so quickly, and before they know it, they are at their intended destination. But they do not want him to leave. They do not want to lose him. Jesus is moving on, but they press him to stay, and he obliges them and comes in, keeping them company still.

They heard a most amazing story, strings of stories told from the Spirit of God's singular point of view, against the horizon of hope and God's passionate, undying, suffering love for his children, all the nations and peoples of the world that he made and keeps in his hand and shared all things with, even his beloved child to come among us, living and dying with us, even being killed among us. What happened to Jesus is all part of the fulfillment of the stories, the Scriptures, the Word of God revealed in the past, and now made known in the flesh of Jesus, the Son of Man, crucified and risen from the dead, the Risen One among us. This legacy of Luke's account, begun with the angels' words to the women, "Remember!" and then Jesus's own retelling of the Scriptures in relation to him, reminding them of the richness of their tradition and the steadfastness of the Word of God that has been reliable through all times and circumstances right up to the present day and that it will continue, becomes the heart of Luke's Gospel, and it becomes the foundation of the early church community in Acts. The presence of the Risen Lord is being intimately, imperatively tied to the Scriptures told, heard, and interpreted in community as normative for understanding Jesus, Christian life, in following him through life, into death and the tomb, and rising with him to freedom as the beloved children of God. It has become the practice, the way of life, the Christian's way of the cross, and their way to Jesus's God to tell all these stories going back to Moses and coming up to the present day, interpreting them from Jesus's Word, both in his words and deeds in the newer testament, but in the Word made flesh in the community of believers, called the liturgy of the Word, the work of his people, constituting the foundation of worship, and giving wisdom and enduring grace to individuals and communities in the church, no matter what happens in history and to them personally. It is up to us to dig into the Scriptures and retell the stories, struggle with all the hard parts and look at our own lives, our sins and failures, our violence and collusion with evil, our histories and cultures, our communities and church, and interpret our lives with the eye and heart of the Crucified and Risen Son of man judging, guiding, questioning us, and oftentimes telling us that we are stupid, slow of heart, foolish, and stubborn, missing even the power of resurrection because our stories and our version of who God might be have little to do with the original story, unbelievable except by faith and the practice of telling the story and making it come true in us. Incarnation, life, crucifixion, and death, resurrection and ascension, the gifting of the Spirit of Jesus into our hearts and the preaching of the Good

News of forgiveness and the power to make holy and redeem everything by the power of the Father, the beloved Son, the Spirit walking with us and seeking always to draw us back into walking, not our way, but the way of the cross and the way of resurrection, together and with God. This is the heart of the Emmaus story: the words, the companionship and the presence, unknown, unrecognized, and yet hungered after, and once it is known, not wanting to let it out of sight for even a moment.

But the tale has an ending no one could have expected, although it was hinted at all along in Jesus' life and in many of the tales that Luke tells in his good news. Jesus went in and stayed with them.

> So he went in to stay with them. When he was at the table with them, he took bread, blessed and broke it, and gave it to them. Then their eyes were opened, and they recognized him; and he vanished from their sight. They said to each other, "Were not our hearts burning within us while he was talking to us on the road, while he was opening the scriptures to us?" (Luke 24:29–32)

Jesus has stories to tell that will surprise them yet again. He sits down to eat the evening meal, supper, with them. And he begins to act out a story that had become his trademark, his characteristic way of being with people all during his life. Whenever he had taught the disciples and the crowds, whenever he had spent hours and days with them, healing and supporting, encouraging and listening to the ills and pains of the people, he always fed them and wouldn't think of letting them go home hungry. It was a way of teaching his followers that, with him, word and bread, presence and passion, community and communion were somehow all one in him, with God.

From the beginning he was connected with food: born in Bethlehem ("house of bread"), laid in a manger, a feeding trough for animals, tempted to make stones into bread, but living on other food from his Father and exhorting us to live on every word that came forth from the mouth of God (Luke 2, 4:4). And he compared himself to Elijah and the widow of Zarephat and a continuous supply of meal, provided for an outsider when Israel refused the Word of God (Luke 4:24 ff.). But the stories of the feeding, the feedings of huge masses of people hungering for hope, for justice and life and for bread are his mark, his signature among them. He feeds five thousand, not counting the women and the children (so about 25,000 to 30,000, a new exodus in the desert), and fills them with leftovers enough to fill twelve baskets (all the tribes of believers in the covenant). He used the same pattern and followed the same ritual: "And taking the five loaves and the two fish, he looked up to heaven, and blessed and broke them, and gave them to the disciples to set before the crowd" (Luke 9:16).

He always did have a fondness for telling stories and then eating with his listeners! And on the night before he died, betrayed and abandoned by his friends, he sat down to table with them and performed that same ritual intimately with them, breaking up the pieces of the ritual, making bread his body, wine his blood and his presence among them forever. Once again his words were noteworthy and not to be forgotten: "Do this in remembrance of me." But these words could just as surely be translated, "Do this and remember me!" Remember, the words and the bread are bound together, just as truly as we are bound together with Jesus when we do this remembering of all that he said and did. We are put back together with him in the telling and the taking, the blessing, the breaking, and the sharing with others—both the story and the food for body, heart, and soul on the way.

Oddly enough there is no mention of their actually eating the bread that Jesus broke and gave to them, because they recognize him in the breaking of the bread, the tearing apart of what they are to eat, and in the instant of recognition, he vanishes from their sight. They had been eating for hours, feasting on his words, his stories, his presence and companionship. Even though he had taken the Scriptures and his life and torn them apart, broken them up in bits and pieces so they could eat them, even the hard parts and the tough pieces, they were full. They turn to each other, and they know they have been brought back to life, their hopes and dreams, immeasurably small, are now magnified beyond belief or expression. First, on the way, telling his story from the strange vantage point of God's intent and design and imagination, he stirred their hearts to fire; he planted fire in their bones and stoked the ashes of their burnt-out and dead lives. His word brought them life. The sound of his voice and the gift of understanding the Scriptures, and the presence of the fire of the Spirit of God loose in the world in the person of the Risen One, have altered the story so significantly that all previous plans and stories fade. With burning hearts, they have been raised, and so, running, they can turn back, go back to the place they first heard the words, the hope, and first met the Word made flesh.

PART 3: THE RETURN TO JERUSALEM

What is carved on rocks will wear away in time,
What is told from mouth to mouth will live forever.

—Vietnamese saying

Seven miles out, and now, a much faster seven miles back. Some people laughingly say that this is the first 10K run, and they are sure that the two of them, no matter their age, made the trip back in record time! Running not on adrenalin alone, but on the fire of God, the energy of the Spirit, and the hope that everything was different now, and oh, what a story they had to tell to the others!

> That same hour they got up and returned to Jerusalem; and they found the eleven and their companions gathered together. They were saying, "The Lord has risen indeed, and he has appeared to Simon!" Then they told what had happened on the road, and how he had been made known to them in the breaking of the bread. (Luke 24:33–35)

The story grows! And by leaps and bounds! Their companions and the other disciples already have their stories to tell, even Simon! That story isn't recorded, although it is mentioned in passing here. What would that story be like and how would Simon, his name before he met Jesus, tell that story of his encounter with the Risen Lord after having last seen him in the court of the high priest on the night he was betrayed by Judas, by Simon, and by all the others. That story, too, each of us and all of us must learn to tell: how we sinned and lied, betrayed and backed away from association with Jesus, and how he came to us again, sought us out, and in just that action, forgave us and called us back. Those stories are crucial to the understanding of resurrection. They are stories hidden in the telling of the story of Jesus, the Crucified One, risen from the dead, reconciling all of us to the Father in the Spirit. But they are eager to share their own unique experience, and it is told, probably back and forth with each of them starting and finishing each others' sentences, until the whole group has heard of this marvelous thing: Jesus teaching, telling the Scriptures, interpreting them, and then taking the bread, blessing and breaking it, and giving it to them to give away—does it dawn on them yet that this is the story of Jesus's life and our life to come as disciples? We are to tell the stories, and like a pelican or a mother bird, break them up in pieces so that others new to them can digest them, and then take, bless, break, and share the bread, our lives, with one another, so that all are full and all are satisfied and have enough to live on, feasting in the kingdom of the bread of hope and the wine of freedom and joy with the Risen Lord.

Usually this is where the story of Emmaus ends, with this line of their coming to recognize him, their eyes no longer restrained; in the action of Jesus's feeding them, the story is over. This is the way it is told on the Third Sunday of Easter and whenever it is used for a description of liturgy, and yet it is not a natural way to break the line, to stop the story. It continues amazingly: the telling summons the actual presence of the teller, the person of the Risen Lord!

> While they were talking about this, Jesus himself stood among them and said to them, "Peace be with you." They were startled and terrified, and thought that they were seeing a ghost. He said to them, "Why are you

frightened, and why do doubts arise in your hearts? Look at my hands and my feet; see that it is I myself. Touch me and see; for a ghost does not have flesh and bones as you see that I have." And when he had said this, he showed them his hands and his feet. While in their joy they were disbelieving and still wondering, he said to them, "Have you anything here to eat?" They gave him a piece of broiled fish, and he took it and ate it in their presence. (Luke 24:36–43)

The line that is as powerful and instructive for the community of disciples as that line, "he had been made known to them in the breaking of the bread," is the line that announces, While they were talking about this, Jesus himself stood among them and said to them, 'Peace be with you.'" Just as Jesus's breaking of the bread caused them to recognize his presence among them for hours while he opened their minds and stirred their hearts back to life on the road, now our telling of the stories, literally, telling of how we encounter and come to recognize Jesus in the breaking of bread and Word in our lives and in the larger history of the world community, we summon the presence of the Risen Lord among us! The telling of the story, our revealing of the Good News of death and resurrection in our lives and Jesus's brings him to stand among us. It is a circle. Jesus draws out the disciples on the road to talk about their lives and belief, and lack of it, and where their faith finds a dead end, and then he tells the story—opens the Scriptures, reveals the Word of God to them, raising them from the dead by his Word in the tradition of the Scripture. That telling and breaking of the word enables them to see, opens their eyes to his presence in the breaking of the bread, and then he vanishes. They return to tell the story to others, who tell more stories, and in the telling, the presence comes again, in the person of the Risen Lord, whose first words to his gathered community are "Peace be with you." The peace of the Risen Lord is summoned by our telling the stories of the Scripture and letting that story rewrite our own lives and futures. The peace of Christ comes to the community as we announce the Good News to one another.

But they are shocked, afraid, and they think they're seeing a ghost. This resurrection from the dead takes some getting used to by everyone. He tries to reassure them. Other translations are closer to "get a grip, get a hold of yourselves!" And Jesus is so human, so careful of them, letting them see him, touch him, get used to him, asking for dinner and eating a broiled fish while they watch so that they know he is alive—he is flesh and bone and heart. He shows them his wounds, his hands and feet. He is the Crucified and Risen One among them. The world has done their worst to him, and he has come through and is alive! They have no reason to fear. They are beginning to get it, to let the joy rise in their souls, but they are doubting, fearful, and disbelieving. Their hearts are full, chock full of all sorts of emotions and feelings and stutterings of doubt, halfhearted belief, and the shock of what this could mean. He is here, among them, and God in his infinite mercy and tenderness says, "Touch me and see!"

But he has more to say, more stories to tell. This is the way he will stay with them, dwell with them, be in their midst always, as strength, as knowledge and understanding, as presence and hope, as Word made flesh. They can touch and see him in his Words.

> Then he said to them, "These are my words that I spoke to you while I was still with you—that everything written about me in the law of Moses, the prophets, and the psalms must be fulfilled. Then he opened their minds to understand the scriptures, and he said to them, "Thus it is written, that the Messiah is to suffer and rise from the dead on the third day, and that repentance and forgiveness of sins is to be proclaimed in his name to all the nations, beginning from Jerusalem. You are witnesses of these things. And see, I am sending upon you what my Father promised; so stay here in the city until you are clothed with power from on high." (Luke 24:44–49)

Now this is the proclamation of who Jesus is and what believers in Luke's community attest to in their baptism and witness with their lives, and it is put in the mouth of Jesus. In Mark it was in the mouth of the angel, or Mark himself, in the tomb. In Matthew it was in the mouth of the angel seated upon the stone rolled away from the tomb, and later in Jesus's mouth while he is standing on the hill where he sent them into the world. Luke now has Jesus among his gathered friends, eating with them, letting them touch and see him, showing them his wounds and teaching them, interpreting the Scriptures with them, and opening their minds to understanding. And it all revolves around the issue of suffering and death and how they are seamless pieces of who the Messiah was promised to be and how he was to live and die, among them. The cross is integral to who Jesus was and is and will be—the Father raising Jesus from the dead in the Spirit fulfills Jesus's life and death, and it will be the same for us, in the promise of God. We have God's word on it. This is the pattern of a believer's life and the community's own ritual of celebrating and growing in belief and understanding—opening the Scriptures together as we share our lives, and then breaking the bread. The presence of the Risen Lord is found in both, or in three experiences: the breaking open of the Scriptures with Jesus, the breaking of the bread with Jesus, and the breaking open of our lives and stories, the good and the hard, with Jesus. This is who we are and where we come to see Jesus for who he is and where our hearts are stirred to fire so that we can burn out in the passion of truth telling, and once we have known this Jesus as the forgiveness of God, we can go forth to preach the Good News of forgiveness and repentance to all the earth. We are witnesses of the Word and the bread and community in the Risen Lord. We are sacrament, the presence of the Risen Lord for the world to see, and come to understand, take heart from, and come back to life, joining us in the story to save the earth from suffering and death, from sin and evil, from despair and violence, and from our own warped and bent versions of the story.

Luke is prefacing his story of the early church and its formation in Acts, where he will have the major leaders, Peter, Stephen, Paul, and the other disciples, as preachers and witnesses to the words of Jesus. Each of them will emphasize the Scriptures as the place to begin to recognize and see the meaning of Jesus and find him present in the church. The church begins almost immediately to read and interpret the Scriptures as anticipating what did happen to Jesus and explaining why it happened and how the story has been radically altered in the life, death, crucifixion, and resurrection of Jesus. The story moves out from Jerusalem into the world and history. From here on out, all must be interpreted in light of the name of Jesus, the forgiveness of Jesus, and the meaning of suffering and death that Jesus lived, seen from the eyes of resurrection. And in the tradition of the prophets, Jesus ends by promising another gift, the Spirit that is described as clothing them with power from on high—in essence making them prophets, preachers and teachers, healers, listeners, and those who forgive because he is present still with them. Now it is time for him to leave them and leave the story and its final ending, with all its intricacies, contraries, complexities, and communities, to us.

> Then he led them out as far as Bethany, and lifting up his hands, he blessed them. While he was blessing them, he withdrew from them and was carried up to heaven. And they worshiped him, and returned to Jerusalem with great joy; and they were continually in the temple blessing God. (Luke 24:50–53)

He is still leading them on the way, going before them. And his last action among them is what he is singularly known by in Luke: he blesses them, as he blessed bread and wine, leaving his mark and presence upon them, seeking to transform and transfigure them into his presence as hope and forgiveness in the world. And they worship, understanding more and more who Jesus is, and they obey, returning to the city, awaiting the coming of the promise. Now the community of the Risen Lord is characterized by joy and the blessing of God. The story is starting to come true.

Raymond Brown writes of why Luke ends his story in Jerusalem (while Mark and Matthew have Jesus appearing to his disciples and leaving them in Galilee). Place for gospel writers is not just location, but it reveals relationships and speaks a language of truth that is more revelatory than just a description of place.

Luke spotlights Jerusalem as the setting for Jesus' appearances and ascension. Matthew has the appearance of the risen Jesus to the Eleven take place in Galilee. This region was a fitting selection from the tradition of Matthew's purpose since for him Galilee is the land of the Gentiles (4:15) and Jesus after his resurrection is instructing his disciples to go and make disciples of the Gentiles (28:19). Luke has the appearance to the Eleven take place in Jerusalem. This was a fitting selection from the tradition for his purpose. For him the Gospel began with the appearance of Gabriel to Zechariah in the Jerusalem Temple; now it ends with Jesus' disciples in the Temple blessing God. (pp. 14–15)

Luke's Gospel ends waiting on a promise, creating a bridge to what comes after that he will later describe in the Acts of the Apostles—the birth of the church and its story in the world and how the Spirit came and did clothe them from on high with power and that power is loose in the world in those who tell the story of Jesus's forgiveness, calling for repentance. This is the story of hungry people, always needing the bread of the stories of God, Jesus, and the Spirit, and the bread of forgiveness, and the bread of hope, and the bread of the Eucharist. It is all the same bread. God in his goodness stays among us in so many presences, tangible, burning our hearts and seeding our imaginations and releasing our souls to bring hope and bread to those who are the most hungry and in need of bread and mercy.

AND NOW TODAY THE STORY CONTINUES

There is the story told of G. K. Chesterton when he became a Catholic. Many berated him for his conversion, insulted him and accused him of deserting his religion for a shallow way of life that was based on mindless acceptance of faith. On one occasion when he was giving a lecture, he was repeatedly interrupted by a reporter, who kept harrying him. Finally, he turned his attention to the man and asked him if he wanted to ask him a question. If so, please do. The man had been waiting for his chance. He scornfully said, "So you are now a Catholic?" "Yes," Chesterton answered him. And the reporter continued, "You now believe in the Resurrection, that Jesus was raised from the dead and is alive." "Yes," Chesterton said. "That is precisely what I believe." "Well then," the reporter asked, "in light of your belief, what would you do if this Jesus was standing behind you right this moment." Chesterton looked the man right in the eye and answered solemnly, "He is, sir. He is!"

Luke's Emmaus account reminds us of the continual presence of God, everywhere in the world, but most especially in the guise of a stranger, someone we meet along the way, who falls in with us and accompanies us for part of our journey, especially at points in our life when we are in pain and suffering. Then especially, the Crucified and Risen Son of Man is with us.

The world is still a place of violence and terror for many people. There is starvation that kills people. Approximately twenty-five thousand people a day die of preventable starvation. In fact the Bureau of Statistics released these figures for 2001. Approximately twenty-five thousand people died from terrorist attacks in the previous six years. During that same period of time, about fifty-two million people died of starvation, about twenty-five thousand a day. There are hungers first for food, for life, and life without violence, and hunger for justice, for peace, and a life that is more than surviving, a life with hope, freedom, dignity, and grace. There is still much we want to run away from and blot out of our lives, erase from our spirituality and ignore. But we can't. We are not allowed to as those who believe that our God walks with us.

I read this piece years ago in Roberto Goizueta's *Caminemos con Jesus: Toward a Hispanic/Latino Theology of Accompaniment* (Maryknoll, N.Y.: Orbis Books, 1995), and it has haunted me ever since. He quotes an experience narrated by a Dominican missionary, Brian Pierce, in Lima.

> I remember standing for hours as a young Dominican theology student in Lima, Peru . . . holding a large crucifix, as hundreds and hundreds of mourners approached to adore and kiss the feet of the crucified Christ. The women wept as if their only son had just been gunned down by a death squad . . . Three days later, there was just a scattering of folks to celebrate the Resurrection. "They are obsessed with suffering," I screamed in my heart, trying to understand it all. "Where is the hope? Where is the promise of new life?" . . . Little by little, the scales have fallen from my eyes, thanks to the patient accompaniment of the people. It is now that I can see the failure of Jesus as a source of hope. . . . There is no contradiction between the bloodied statue of Jesus in the Church and faith in the Resurrection. . . . God is, like us, on a pilgrim journey. The Resurrection is experienced, not as final victory, but in recognition of the close presence of the living God who chooses to walk with and suffer with his people. (p. 211)

This is the mystery of Emmaus. Our God accompanies us, but our God especially chooses to walk with the poor, the victims of violence and injustice, the widows and the orphans, and our God expects to find us on that same road, accompanying them, if we wish to see him by our side. In the third century, these words are found in the Didascalia Apostolorum: "Widows and orphans are to be revered like the altar." The presence of God lingers most strongly among those whose hearts are beaten down by the callousness of human beings and who find themselves pushed to the edges of life, on the borders, running from bombs, landless, homeless, hungry, and without health care because of preemptive strikes and sanctions enforced for decades out of vindictiveness and greed.

Jesus asks his disciples for something to eat, and they feed him broiled fish. He eats it while they watch. Jesus is always asking us for something to eat in the nearly 85 percent of the world that goes to bed hungry every night. He breaks bread, and we recognize him in that breaking and sharing of bread in communion, but for that ritual to be whole and true, we must break and share our food with strangers and all among us who are struggling just to survive day to day. Part of our hunger for the presence of God can only be satisfied when we are found among his own, obeying his imperative of the gospel: giving to the poor, walking with the poor, standing in solidarity and communion with the poor of the earth.

There is a great Jewish story told to children often at bedtime, after they have had a full meal and given thanks and are ready to fall asleep. It's called "Fresh, Hot Breakfast Rolls."

Once upon a time, not so long ago that your grandmother and grandfather would not remember, in the 1930s in a place called Scranton, Pennsylvania, there was a good rabbi whose name was Chaim Guterman. He was a friend to the whole neighborhood and everyone in his congregation respected him. People were always trying to give him gifts and take care of him and his family. The baker down the street made fresh hot rolls for his breakfast every morning, wrapped them still hot from the oven in a basket, and ran them down to the rabbi's house and left them on the front door. It was a good way to start his morning, and he knew the rabbi was often so busy that he didn't think about eating. But the rolls smelled so good that they lured the rabbi out of his house. The rabbi and his family always had a grand breakfast gift. And the rabbi was always careful to thank the baker for his kindness and remembrance of him and his family.

This had been going on for years and had become a way of life. But then one morning, unexpectedly, there were no rolls. The rabbi came out— nothing. Looked down the street and wondered if the baker were sick, or if something had happened in his family. It went on for a few days, and every morning when the rolls weren't there, he reminded himself that he must go and check on the baker to see if he and his family were all right. But he was busy and kept forgetting to do it. After nearly a week, he stopped into the bakery on his way home from a very long day seeing people, and he greeted the baker and asked if he and his family were well, adding a blessing for them all. The baker assured him he was fine. In fact, everyone was just fine. And in response, the baker inquired after the rabbi's family, and added on, almost as an afterthought so as not to embarrass the rabbi, "and the rolls, you are still enjoying my rolls for breakfast each morning, yes? I haven't heard from you lately."

The rabbi looked rather confused and stuttered a bit, finally telling the truth. "There haven't been any rolls for over a week. I stopped by to see if you were all right, or if something had come up where you were too busy or needing to take care of your family. There haven't been any rolls lately to thank you for!" "What?" the baker responded loudly. "I've made the rolls and left them on your front porch every morning, as I always do." "Hmmm," said the rabbi, "then someone must be taking them before I get up and go out to get them." The baker was furious. "We will watch and wait for them, and catch them and punish them, immediately. Stealing from the rabbi and his family! I've never heard of such a terrible thing." "No, no," said the rabbi. "We certainly must find the person, but not to punish them or embarrass them. If someone is reduced to taking the rolls off someone's porch for food in the morning, they must be always hungry, poor and in terrible need. We have to find them and get rolls for them every morning. That is the least we can do, a place to start to help them. Come, early tomorrow you will bake as you always do and leave the rolls and I will get up early and come meet you here and then we will go together to see if we can find our hungry friend."

We must search out anyone who is poor and share our good hot breakfast rolls with them. And the children know that this is the way they are to live—watching and seeing if they can help anyone who is hungry to eat and get what they need without being embarrassed. Some learn it as children. As Christians we are always being reminded that our God stays with us as food to be shared and passed around.

A friend of mine, Herman Hendrickx, has lived for decades in Manila, and for the last decade he has been writing a commentary on Luke's Gospel, currently being published by Liturgical Press in Collegeville, Minnesota. It is eight volumes in all, called *The Third Gospel for the Third World.* But he had struggled with illness for many years and was trying to finish it before he died. He died in May 2002. The last entry in his computer is the lines from this last chapter on resurrection. They read, "But they urged him strongly, saying, "Stay with us, because it is almost evening and the day is now nearly over" (Luke 24:29). That is as far as he got in his commentary. And he died. Some friends of his are finishing his work, continuing his way of looking at the Scriptures and interpreting them from the point of view of the poor, the marginalized, the hungry, and those victimized by pollution, globalization, land and resources drained out of local economies, and those despairing of ever seeing their children well fed, healthy, and living with dreams. "The Lord is risen indeed!" That short pithy statement that welcomed the two on the road from Emmaus is still being spoken, cried out, written, and proclaimed by those who accompany the poor who live on the way of the cross, walking all the way to its end in the tomb and glory. And it is still being written for those who don't want to look, who want to rewrite the story their way, by prophetic voices, theologians, and ordinary believers who walk with dignity, confessing the truth and witnessing to the God who can be hidden from our eyes, but visible in his friends. We must learn again in every age, in every land and nation, to bring hope and joy to those whose lives have been violated and rejected by society, religion, and governments.

Sometimes the way is revealed in startling ways that can make us laugh and cry at the same time, marveling at the tenderness that is shared among those who are hurt and rejected. A newspaper account told of an experience at the Seattle Special Olympics about six years ago. There were nine contestants for the one-hundred-yard dash, all lined up at the starting line. All were physically or mentally disabled. The gun sounded, and they were off and running. It didn't look much like a dash. It was helter-skelter, start and go, but they were all intent on finishing the race. But then one of the them fell head long, rolled over and over, and started to cry, hurt and frustrated and disappointed.

All of the others, all eight of them, heard him crying. They all slowed down, turned around, and eventually just stopped where they were. And everyone of them turned around and went back to him. A young girl with Down's syndrome got to him first, bent over him tenderly and kissed him, saying, "This will make it better." Up they pulled him, wobbly but okay, and then they all linked arms and the nine of them went on with the race, getting to the finish line together.

Of course, by this time everyone in the stadium was stunned, but they were getting on their feet and screaming and cheering them on, all the way home together. People are still telling this story, and people are still sending me this in clippings to tell. How you make your way and whom you travel with makes the way. Are we walking the way of the cross, all the way to the tomb and glory? Are we walking it together and making sure everyone gets there at the same time and has a good time, a life, along the way? Do we remember that anyone we meet along the way, especially a stranger who just falls in with us, asking us questions, is the Lord of Life, the Son of Man who walks with us always?

And I must end with this blessing for the way, just sent to me by friends who understand the Scriptures and have been traveling with me for a long time, though by long distance, as companions on the way. It was penned by Edward Abbey. It reads:

> May your trails be crooked, winding, lonesome, dangerous, leading to the most amazing view. May your mountains rise into and above the clouds.

Luke's Resurrection account reminds us that Jesus's stories and all our stories are merged into one story and that all ways not only lead to life and resurrection, but that our God walks with us, always. And our God loves eating out, or dining in, as long as we are remembering to eat and live in communion with all those who are hungering for God to stay with them and crying out, "Don't go!" We were meant to be found always blessing God and living in great joy.

6

John 20

I have no refuge in this world other than thy threshold.
My head has no resting place other than this doorway.

—Hafiz

*W*e are back at the empty tomb again, early on the first day of the week, while it is still dark. John's Gospel is finely crafted, playing on strong words and symbols that are repeated again and again, but rearranged with other words and symbols, so that he constructs an intricate pattern that becomes a grid for understanding life, the universe, and Jesus. One of the words that are foundational to that grid is, of course, "light." Over a decade ago on my first trip to Ireland, one of the first places I chanced upon as I was driving around was the newly opened site of Newgrange on the River Boyne, in the hills north of Dublin, inland from the sea. Dated from the Stone Age, around 3000 B.C.E., it is an ancient burial chamber, massive in its dimensions, built of 250,000 tons of stone with ninety-seven huge outer boulders carved with circles, snaking lines, and knots that stand in a great circle, as though guarding the mound and the entrance to the main chamber. Those who study the site and its construction are at a loss to explain where the boulders and stones, many weighing two tons or more, came from and how they were transported to the place.

It was not a well-known site yet, and I almost had the place to myself. It was spring, the day bright with sunlight, lushness, and wildflowers. The guide gave me detailed information on how it was built at a perfect angle for the sun to penetrate the opening to the tomb on the solstice. Then we entered the tomb and were immediately enclosed in pitch blackness in a narrow passageway that

113

angled upward. Soon we entered into a round room carved out of the earth with a number of smaller chambers, like niches, on the outside of the circle. We stood silently in the tomb, smelling the ancient ground, and I ran my hands over the great stones where the bodies had lain. Then the guide told me to wait there in the dark, and he went outside. It was chilling and enormous in the silent dark earth. After only minutes the light came creeping slowly up the passageway. He held his hand over it until it reached the room where I was standing, and then opened his fingers letting the light pour in. I tried to imagine what it was like for the light to enter on the solstice, just that one day, cutting through the long night and filling the burial room with the warm light of the sun. It would last no more than seventeen minutes, and then it would recede and the tomb would be filled with utter and total darkness again for the year. Utterly amazing! These people, whoever they were, hungered for light and connected it with not only darkness, but death and some glimmer of hope. That burst of illumination brought such rejoicing in the midst of momentary terror. He let me stay alone in the tomb awhile, and I wondered what it was like in the tomb of Jesus that night, that holy night before the Resurrection. What filled my soul was the sense of emptiness and mystery. Now whenever I read the accounts of the Resurrection, the reality of the empty tomb is itself a silent-sounding, deafening proclamation. I sense in a small way how it must have engendered a deep-seated fear, confusion, hurt and anger, even terror. If there was hope initially, it would have been but a pinpoint in the dark.

This story begins in darkness too.

> Early on the first day of the week, while it was still dark, Mary Magdalene came to the tomb and saw that the stone had been removed from the tomb. So she ran and went to Simon Peter and the other disciple, the one whom Jesus loved, and said to them, "They have taken the Lord out of the tomb, and we do not know where they have laid him." (John 20:1–2)

What should strike us immediately upon hearing this reading is the use of pronouns. We are told that it is Mary Magdalene who has gone to the tomb and sees the stone rolled away, but when she frantically tells Simon Peter and the other disciple, she says *they* have taken his body and *we* do not know where he is. Obviously, she is the one who has run to tell them the disturbing news, but there were others with her at the tomb. She doesn't enter, only sees and panics and runs. Grave robbing was common at the time, and she seems to think that the grave of Jesus has been desecrated and his body taken away by thieves. She is shocked, distressed, and distraught, anxious to get the others involved in looking for the body. She sees from the outside, runs, and tells only of loss, the body gone. The reaction she gets from Simon Peter and the other disciple is instinctual—they bolt and run to see for themselves if what she has said is true.

If so, what could this mean? Hard as it was to just live through the past few days, without a body their grief would have no focus and they could be accused of a plot, in trouble with both the Romans and the Sanhedrin. They run to the tomb.

> Then Peter and the other disciple set out and went toward the tomb. The two were running together, but the other disciple outran Peter and reached the tomb first. He bent down to look in and saw the linen wrappings lying there, but he did not go in. Then Simon Peter came, following him, and went into the tomb. He saw the linen wrappings lying there, and the cloth that had been on Jesus' head, not lying with the linen wrappings but rolled up in a place by itself. Then the other disciple, who reached the tomb first, also went in, and he saw and believed; for as yet they did not understand the scripture, that he must rise from the dead. Then the disciples returned to their homes. (John 20:3–10)

The text is careful never to name the "other disciple, the one whom Jesus loved." We traditionally assign that title to John, who is the writer of this gospel, but the community of the Beloved Disciple, John's community, deliberately leaves this disciple nameless, for each person baptized into that community became the "disciple, the one whom Jesus loved," and each member of the community was to have the same relationship with Jesus that the beloved disciples knew and experienced. Always these are essential belief statements of the community, as well as baptismal catechetical texts. Entering the tomb is the ritual of baptism, initiation into the life, death, and resurrection life of the Risen Lord. Mary did not enter the tomb, just saw and ran to tell the other two disciples what she surmised, the worst possible scenario in her grief and fear.

They run together, but then the other outruns Simon Peter. In John's Gospel, Peter's name keeps changing. His name before he ever encountered Jesus was Simon, and it is Jesus who changes his name, calling him Cephas or Peter. There is a subtle shifting of the names that tells us where Peter is in his relationship with Jesus in every story. When he acts like he did before he met Jesus, he is called Simon. When he is acting as a true disciple, he is Peter, and when he is waffling or hesitant and reluctant, he is called Simon Peter, what he is named here. He has betrayed Jesus publicly and with the others absented himself from the site of the crucifixion and has heard secondhand how Jesus died. Others, Joseph of Arimathea and even Nicodemus, who had once come to Jesus at night, prepared the body hastily for burial—these "secret" disciples are the ones who attend to the body of Jesus in death.

The other disciple pulls ahead; he is younger, faster, more intent on getting to the tomb, perhaps more hopeful, more devoted to Jesus. He arrives at the tomb, but pulls up short of entering. He waits on Simon Peter, the older man who was the leader of the disciples whenever Jesus was absent. He bends down and sees the linen cloths that had wrapped the body in spices, as was the custom, lying there. The tomb was probably a cave, the entrance low, so that you had to bend to get in and could straighten up once inside. He bends, reverently, and sees and takes it all in. And Simon Peter comes and barges straight into the tomb. He sees the same wrappings, but also the head cloth that covered the face or was put into the mouth and that is rolled up and off to the side. Bewilderment, dismay, wonderment—the positions of the burial cloths say that this was not a robbery. Robbers don't fold up things they leave behind. Something has happened here—but what? And then the other disciple enters and sees and believes. That line is pivotal. Mary saw, assumed the worst, and ran to tell her perceptions. Simon Peter hears, runs, goes into the tomb, sees and nothing registers. But the Beloved Disciple hears, runs, waits on Simon Peter, enters the tomb, sees, and believes. None of them understand the Scripture saying that he must rise from the dead, but the Beloved Disciple sees with eyes of faith and love and believes. And the disciples return to their homes. An odd ending—where are their homes? Is that the upper room or places where they were staying in Jerusalem, in the houses of other disciples?

There are three disciples in this story, very well-known and famous ones in our history: Mary Magdalene, Simon Peter, and the Beloved Disciple. John is interested in believers and stages or development of belief and practice within his community. There is ample evidence that these three people are used to reveal three types of disciples and how each comes to believe, and what keeps them from seeing and believing. Mary of Magdala figures in all the gospel accounts. It is as though she has a story, or a life, separate from the other women who followed Jesus, precisely because of these accounts and her presence at the tomb with others on the morning of the Resurrection. And as the understanding of the meaning of resurrection occurs in the gospels, her position changes accordingly, but she is always there. Here she is nearly frantic with fear and grief when she thinks that the body has been stolen, and she finds that she has no body to weep over (in this story, the body has already been prepared prior to burial with the linens and spices). She is not expecting anything but a tomb with a body in it, the body of the one she has followed and loved in her own singular way. Whatever her relationship to Jesus was among his other disciples and friends, it was intense and she is shattered by his death and her loss of him. Her message to the disciples has nothing of the announcement of hope; it is angry, frustrated, and pained. The body has been taken away from her and she (along with the others) has found that her grieving has been short-circuited violently. She is primarily relating to her past, her memory of Jesus and what her relationship was with him. All she wants is his body. It is all that she thinks there is left to her. We will look at her more when the story continues.

Simon Peter enters the tomb. He has been a follower of Jesus, publicly known as one of his company, in that sense, but he has severed that relationship by denial, angry shouts and words, even curses, and though driven to bitter tears, he has also kept his distance from Jesus's way of the cross, crucifixion, and burial. He is steeped in his sin of betrayal, fear that made him lash out in anger at those around him and Jesus, and he has failed to be a leader, acting with cowardice, paralyzing and disheartening the other disciples. He is blinded by his present state of distancing himself from Jesus. His state of being, his state of grace or sinfulness clouds any hope, any glimmer of light even as he stands in the tomb and sees evidence that Jesus is not buried here anymore.

But the other disciple, the one who stood near the cross, witness to the sufferings and death of Jesus, the one who stays close, who loves more, who is faithful, enters and sees and believes. Even as he runs, his heart sings, and he reaches beyond what his eyes told him when he watched Jesus die on the cross, and his love cries out, "Yes!" He even stands and waits at the entrance to the tomb. This is the image of the Beloved Disciple, the community of John, who loved and stood faithful, and waited until Simon Peter, who became the leader of the church, caught up, and then stood aside to let Simon Peter enter the tomb first. Love, its power and authority, always gets there first, comes to belief first, and always waits for the others, especially the leaders, to catch up! This is the reality of what happened among the disciples and the community of the Beloved Disciple, John, and those closest to Jesus, called his friends. They mature and develop differently from the other disciples, and the community of the church has to struggle with the fact that the last one anyone thought would be the leader was the one who betrayed him and contributed to the dissolution of the disciples when Jesus was arrested and crucified. In the community today, love and faithfulness, the friends of Jesus always get to the point of understanding, of believing and seeing first, but their authority is of a different sort, and it waits on all the others, so that the whole community can move together in unity and communion. This is the "other disciple," the model for John's community, the model for all of us today.

And while the other two go back, pondering and wondering, half hoping and truly believing that something glorious is happening, Mary stays at the tomb. Obviously, she too has run back with the others, but she doesn't go in and she doesn't go back with them. She stays, weeping, frantic with grief.

> But Mary stood weeping outside the tomb. As she wept, she bent over to look into the tomb; and she saw two angels in white, sitting where the body of Jesus had been lying, one at the head and the other at the feet. They said

> to her, "Woman, why are you weeping?" She said to them, "They have taken away my Lord, and I do not know where they have laid him." When she had said this, she turned around and saw Jesus standing there, but she did not know that it was Jesus. Jesus said to her, "Woman, why are you weeping? Whom are you looking for?" Supposing him to be the gardener, she said to him, "Sir, if you have carried him away, tell me where you have laid him, and I will take him away." (John 20:11–15)

Poor Mary! She is so caught up in her grieving, her need to have Jesus's body, his dead corpse, that she cannot see anything else but what she thinks will bring her some comfort. She cannot imagine any other option, cannot let in any shred of light or hope. She does not remember anything from before, just what he was to her and what she had and loved, the way he treated and loved her. If she can't have that anymore, she will settle for his body and mourn over it, keening and hanging onto the body itself. She bends down to see and is given a vision of angels! But she sticks to her one line: "they have taken the body away and I don't know where it is." Even when she senses there is someone else there near her, she assumes again it is a gardener and anyone, everyone is part of the plot. When Jesus asks her the same question, adding in "Whom are you looking for?" She accuses him of taking the body and implores him to tell her where he has put it. The story is pitiable, undeniably sad, but she cannot see anything other than what is. That line is crucial to the text—the one in which Jesus asks of her, "Whom are you looking for?" In the very first chapter of John, the two disciples sent by John the Baptist follow Jesus, and he turns and asks them, "What are you looking for?" She should have picked up on that question. It is Jesus's invitation to intimacy, to discipleship, and she misses it altogether. Her past relationship with Jesus has her stuck, and she, like so many of the others, made him what she needed and wanted him to be, without much sense that he was so much more, so other than that limited relationship each had with him. But Jesus is both careful of her loss and her love that grieves his human relationship with her and intent on having her let go of what holds her back from him now, so he reveals himself to her.

> Jesus said to her, "Mary!" She turned and said to him in Hebrew, "Rabbouni!" [which means Teacher]. Jesus said to her, "Do not hold onto me, because I have not yet ascended to the Father. But go to my brothers and say to them, 'I am ascending to my Father and your Father, to my God and your God.'" Mary Magdalene went and announced to the disciples, "I have seen the Lord"; and she told them that he had said these things to her. (John 20:16–18)

"Mary!" It is said as a command, a wakeup call, demanding her attention, wresting her out of the emotional grieving that is blocking anything from getting through to her other than what she thinks she wants so desperately—his dead body. Her name in his mouth—finally she can hear that word, what was, although she could not hear any of the others he spoke to her. And when she replies and calls him Rabbouni, it reveals that she has no understanding of who he really is—it was what he was—teacher. The next line is strong. In this translation, it says, "Do not hold onto me." In others it reads, "Do not touch me," or even more strongly, "Do not cling to me." It follows that she went to grab hold of him, putting her arms around him (the other women in Matthew approached, embraced his feet, and worshipped him). And he is trying to wean her from what was between them, with them, to shock her into a new awareness of him and of what she is before him and God. His message reveals that when he says, "go tell my brothers I am ascending to my Father and your Father, to my God and your God." She does not have a prior claim on him. She must learn to relate to him in community (along with his brothers), and she must come to know him as he is in relation to God his Father. This is the relationship to which he has been inviting all of his disciples and friends—to share and live with him as he dwells with his Father. It is intimacy with God in him, not just whatever she wanted or thought she had with him. It is an encounter and a meeting that is full of power, truthfulness, and compassion, but always he is trying to draw her and all his disciples beyond what they had wanted him to be for them, into the awesome deeper reality of who he is with God. She is locked in her past and tries to cling to what was, her old ideas, her old ways of relating, what she would settle for, rather than the unlimited Word that is being offered to her. He is trying to draw her into the Risen Body of Christ, larger than her personal connection to him. She goes to the disciples and tells them that she has seen "the Lord" and repeats what she has been told, but there is not the sense that she knows what is happening at all. In this gospel the Beloved Disciple is the first to believe and Mary is the first sent to proclaim the reality of the Resurrection, but there is little understanding as of yet.

Each of us has known the experience of Mary, clinging to what was and what we wanted in spite of the crying need to change. Tina Beattie, in an article titled "Christ and the Women" (*The Tablet* April 14, 2001), states:

> Mary clinging to Christ in the garden could also be a symbol of the Catholic Church in our own time. With the Second Vatican Council, Catholics were asked to relinquish the past and their possessive hold on Christ in order to share the resurrection with the modern world. But for many people, the old familiar practices and liturgies made Christ tangibly, vividly present. It has been a wrenching experience for them to let go of that certainty and to leave the place where Christ seems real and alive, and to go out into a disbelieving world. Can we really be sure that God's spirit goes with us, that we are not alone, that in dying and rising again the body

of Christ has become the body and breath of the universe? Perhaps—if we only knew how to look—we would recognize in the shards and fragments of our post-modern world a cosmic mosaic which bears the face of the risen Christ. And if that is the case, then the Church, like Mary Magdalene, can go out joyfully, fearlessly, passionate in her love of Christ and her message for the world. (p. 525)

It seems this coming to believe in the Resurrection is a process that takes time, and only some immediately take that leap of faith into the presence of believing that he is risen from the dead. So much can hold us back—what was, what we had, what we grew up with, needed and wanted, experienced in the past and want to stay the same, concentration on our particular individual relationship with Jesus. The past can become a prison if we do not let go of it and learn to live in freedom. Conversion, constant conversion, is the message of the gospel, the Resurrection accounts even more so than many of the other stories Jesus told his disciples. What we have done or failed to do, our sin that affects our own ways of seeing and perceiving reality, our effect on the belief and faith of others who look to us for direction and example, our words and our public allegiances or our defensiveness and protection of ourselves first: these can keep us from believing. Our pasts and our presents can keep us from seeing and believing. It is love, faithfulness, staying with Jesus, near to the cross and becoming the beloved disciples, the ones whom Jesus loves, that allows us to be truly members of his community and know his God and our God and his Father and our Father. The Resurrection is an invitation, an unbelievable invitation into the community of Jesus, his Father and his Spirit. Believing and understanding is a never-ending process that requires letting go, risk taking, virtue, and practice, that becomes a lifestyle for all personally and in the community of believers. It is being torn from death's gripping hold on us and thrown into hope and life. This witness to the Risen Lord, this seeing and believing, is lived out in the world, and it is a process of radical reintegration of all that we are and know, and it is the Risen Lord who keeps coming to us. The Dominican mystic Meister Eckhart wrote:

> For however devoted to God you are, you may be sure that God is immeasurably more devoted to you. Whoever possesses God in their being has him in a divine manner, and he shines out to them in all things; for them all things taste of God and in all things it is God's image they see.

The Risen Lord comes to us primarily in community. If we are given a meeting with the Risen Lord, it is to pull us into the community and send us back to them with words of hope from the mouth of God.

But, for many of us, we meet one person who draws us beyond our limited awareness into something far larger than our eyes permit us to see. That person introduces us to the light in him- or herself, and we follow that person to the Christ, as Simon Peter is described following after the Beloved Disciple as they run to the tomb. Or, equally marvelous, someone sees that light in us and trails behind us, until we ask of him or her those words Jesus asked of Mary: "Who are you looking for?" Bill Kreidler, speaking at the Friends (Quaker) General Conference in 1994, wrote about why people become Quakers:

> One reason that many of us become Quakers is that we met someone whose life spoke. Whose life was an embodiment of listening, acting, being. Someone who showed us a light so lovely. The theologian Philip Brooks was once asked by one of his students why he was a Christian. Brooks answered that he was a Christian because of his aunt in Teaneck, New Jersey. She showed him a light so lovely that he wanted with all of his heart to know the source of it.
>
> Aren't we all called to be aunts from Teaneck, New Jersey? Here I am Lord, send me. Victor Hugo wrote in *Les Miserables,* describing an old Catholic woman:
>
> "Her life, which had been a series of pious works, had cloaked her in a kind of transparent whiteness. And in growing old she had acquired a kind of beauty of goodness. What had been thinness in her youth was in her maturity, a transparency, and this ethereal quality permitted glimmers of the angel dancing within." [quoted in *Heron Dance* (Autumn 2002)]

These are the morning stories, when light came back into the world and now light is a person. It begins with the overwhelming sense of absence, but a lingering absence that is a foretaste of an altogether new presence, the presence of the One who shattered the hold of death and, in living now, gives us all abundantly new life. This section of the story is about the power of death to hang onto us in spite of the dawning awareness that Jesus has been raised from the dead. Sometimes it can seem to take forever for us to come to understanding what it meant for Jesus, what it means for each of us in our dyings, and for all of us facing death inevitably as believing followers of Christ. Years ago, around 1988, I read a story by Ida Mae Kempel called *What Was in Jeremy's Egg* the subtitle being, *The Lesson of Easter from an Unlikely Child.* It was said to be a true story, but with the names changed. I tell it around Easter time, and on rare occasions at funeral liturgies and wakes, but it is a hard, hard story to tell. Something in it loosens tears, which is very comforting for those listening and struggling with death, but not so for the teller, who can get choked up and then can't finish the story. Here is the way I tell it.

> Once upon a time there was a young boy, named Jeremy Forrester. It was hard to be around Jeremy. By the time he was twelve, he was still in the

second grade. He had been born slow, halting, often unable to control his body that was so bent physically. He was in a regular school living far from any special education classes. He'd drool, laugh out loud, cry, and fidget. His teacher often wondered if he learned anything. Her name was Doris, and Jeremy was a constant drain on her attention and teaching. Yet, every once in a while Jeremy would say something profound, his eyes shining and his voice very clear, articulating his words with care. But mostly, he was an irritation and a problem in the classroom. Finally, his teacher made her decision and called in Jeremy's parents to tell them that he had to be removed from her class. She just didn't have the skills and time to attend to his needs and had to honor her commitment to teach the other students in the room. His parents were distraught, and pleaded with her to keep him. A special school was so far, he'd have to board and it would be a terrible shock to him, setting him back, maybe causing him to lose all that he had managed to learn in the past years at school with people who knew him, and cared about him, and even put up with him. She was trying to be fair to her other eighteen students, and she knew that Jeremy had a terminal illness, who knew how long he'd live, but he couldn't read or write and she doubted if he was learning anything. They prevailed; she'd keep him until the end of the year at least.

She practiced patience and tried not to let his noises get to her. He'd bring her an apple and embarrass her with his loud, "I love you, teacher." And the class would laugh. The months dragged by, winter lasted so long, but finally it was spring, and towards the end of Lent, she asked the children if they knew what they were celebrating at Easter. She told them the story of Jesus, some of his stories, and how he died on the cross and was buried, but on the third day his Father loved him so and raised him from the dead, brought him back to life. She gave each of the students a plastic egg and told them to go home and bring back something they put in the egg that for them said there was new life. They all were excited and took their eggs. Jeremy sat quietly, staring at her, listening, drooling, but she wondered if he understood what he was supposed to do. She decided she'd call his parents and tell them so that he wouldn't make a mistake and disrupt class the next day. But that night everything seemed to pile up and she totally forgot to call them. She only remembered the next day when everyone came with their eggs and put them in the basket on her desk.

Towards the end of the day, it was time to open the eggs. She picked the first one and opened it. Inside was a tiny flower with bright colors. Yes, that's a sign of new life, something that grows from a seed in the ground. Good! And a girl from the back waved her hand and said, "That's my egg." The next one held a gorgeous real butterfly. "Yes, that's good—we all know that butterflies come from caterpillars, changing so much it's hard to believe that it came from that cocoon." One of the boys said, "I need that back. I borrowed it from my big sister's collection." Again, she picked up an egg. This time there was a rock with moss on it. A boy said, "My dad helped me. I found the rock, but didn't know until he told me that moss grows on the rock!" The next egg she picked up and opened was empty. Oh dear, she thought, it must be Jeremy's egg. He didn't understand and I forgot to call his parents. She just closed the egg up and went to put it back in the basket.

But Jeremy was waving his hand and squirming about yelling, "That's my egg. Talk about my egg." What could she say? There was nothing in it. Everyone starting laughing again. She tried to calm them down and said, "Jeremy you're egg is empty." "I know! I know! Just like Jesus's tomb. It was empty too! They killed him, but his Father took him out of the tomb, like you said. He raised him back to life." She was stunned. He had listened and had understood, more than any of the others, more than she herself had understood. The bell rang and school was out. When they were gone, she cried.

Three months later Jeremy died. His whole class came to the wake in church and everyone who came to pray and comfort one another were surprised to see nineteen eggs sitting on top of his casket—all empty.

There is no body! Now the Body of Christ, crucified and risen from the dead, lives in the world. Resurrection is hard to believe in, let alone explain. We need a community to help us with words, with remembering, and with holding onto hope in the face of death. And sometimes belief expressed by those being persecuted and threatened if they so much as speak about their hope and religion can startle us into a shock of wonder at and awareness of what we claim to believe, and ask us if we really do, and if so, how do we show it to others. Faith is nascent, but growing, and when expressed, it can sustain hope in those who speak out. A friend of mine wrote this story for his parish bulletin one Easter.

In 1930, a Bolshevik named Bukharin was sent from Moscow to Kiev to peddle the party politic among the people. For more than an hour he addressed a huge assembly on the subject of atheism. In the course of a long harangue, he presented argument after argument in an attempt to ridicule Christianity. When he concluded, he felt sure that he had diminished his hearers' faith and hope to a mere whimper.

"Are there any questions?" Bukharin challenged the silent crowd. Suddenly, one man snapped to his feet and requested permission to speak. Given the nod, he climbed the platform and stood near the Communist. Not a sound could be heard as he looked out over the people, first to the left, then to the right. At last he shouted the ancient Orthodox greeting, "Khristos voskryes!" ["Christ is risen!"]. Immediately the entire assembly stood up together and with one voice thundered their response: "On dyestivityelno voskayes!" ["He is risen indeed!"].

Nothing, not even the mind-bending and will-wrenching force of the party's propaganda, could threaten the faith of the Russian believers in Jesus.

Seventy years or more after the death of Jesus, John's community is seeking ways to speak of resurrection, of their belief in the Risen Lord and how believers must be converted to life, wondrous, unexplainable, new, vibrant, unheard of life! But now there are the evening stories of John to look at and experience. And it is this story of Jesus that completes and fully interprets the presence of the Risen Lord for John's community. For John, the mysteries of the Resurrection, Ascension, and Pentecost all take place in a single moment, on Easter night when the disciples are huddled in fear, hiding in the dark.

PART 2: THE LOCKED ROOM, JOHN 20:19–30

> Above the shouts and the shots,
> The roaring flames and the siren's blare,
> Listen for the stilled voice of the man who is no longer there.
> Above the tramping of the endless line of marchers along the street,
> Listen for the silent step of the dead man's invisible feet.
> Lock doors, put troops at the gate, guard the legislative halls,
> But tremble when the dead man comes
> Whose spirit walks through walls.
>
> —Anonymous

John has told the story of Mary Magdalene, of Simon Peter and the other disciple, the Beloved Disciple, and their summons to belief, each brought to a crisis point by the empty tomb, the linen cloths, and even his presence calling out a name. Now, in his closing story (the original ending of John's Gospel), he looks at the group of disciples and one who is absent from Jesus's appearance to the community, Thomas. And lastly, all those who come after the gospel writer—all of us are described and summoned to resurrection life. This is the story of Jesus's breaking into the locked room where his disciples are hiding. It is his first meeting with all of them since his rising from the dead. It says "the disciples" and includes among them ten of the twelve who followed him from the beginning. Since this is the original ending of John, this segment pulls together many of the major themes of the gospel and what it means to believe in Jesus, the Risen Lord. He tells us in the last line why he has written about this experience specifically.

> Now Jesus did many other signs in the presence of his disciples, which are not written in this book. But these are written so that you may come to believe that Jesus is the Messiah, the Son of God, and that through believing you may have life in his name. (John 20:30–31)

This is John's summation, the reason why he wrote the gospel—so that we could come to believe. Gustavo Gutierrez writes, "Believing is having life. Having faith is believing in life." And to the point, the life of Jesus, Son of God, risen from the dead, live in his name. We are now made in the image of God, whose purest, clearest image is Jesus, and we live as the beloved children of God, with Jesus, in God. This whole story describes the essential elements of this life. It has three major sections, each summed up in the proclamation of resurrection in the words of Jesus, "Peace be with you." There will be much to say about his "peace," but here is a place to begin thinking about the first peace. It is from the words of Black Elk, an Ogalala Sioux medicine man who was a Christian and a catechist on the reservation.

> The first peace which is the most important is that which comes within the souls of people when they realize their relationship, their oneness, with the universe and all its powers, and when they realize that at the center of this universe dwells Wakan-Tanka, and that this center is really everywhere, and it is within each of us.

Here we begin to delve as deeply as we can into the mystery of the Resurrection and the depth of understanding that the early church, after believing it and struggling to live it in the face of terrible persecution, has come to know and profess as the basic core and heart of its belief. And it begins with the universal experience of fear, and immediately begins to root out that fear by breaking it open and bringing freedom into the places where fear stunts and imprisons us.

> When it was evening on that day, the first day of the week, and the doors of the house where the disciples had met were locked for fear of the Jews, Jesus came and stood among them and said, "Peace be with you." After he said this, he showed them his hands and his side. Then the disciples rejoiced when they saw the Lord. (John 20:19–20)

They are locked in a room, seeking security, protection, consciously living in fear. The description is of a "safe house." But Jesus is not so easily locked out. Jesus has died. He was gone. But he comes back to reclaim his own, to bring them together and keep them together with his Peace. He shows himself to them, and he shows them the marks of the cruelty, pain, hate, and torture that he has endured. Look! He demands of them. The Risen Christ is the Wounded One, the Suffering Servant, the Crucified One. His woundedness attests to the core of who he is—it cannot be ignored, turned away from, run from, rejected. His words of peace are bound intimately to his wounds, which have revealed him as human, vulnerable, suffering, and subject to all of life, even violence and death known in his own flesh and blood. He is here among them. He is alive! He has passed through the ferocious killing of his body and emerged from the tomb bearing the marks of his passion and death, but bringing peace in his words, his presence, and his very body. This is the peace of the Father who raised him from the dead, newborn from the grave, the Father of life, the maker, creator, keeper of all life surging, breathing, speaking in the body of Jesus risen from the tomb. This is the peace of the Father that makes whole what is torn to shreds and broken beyond repair. This is the peace that makes holy, makes luminous, makes wholly pure and true, as it was in the beginning, as it was meant to be—as all of us were meant to be as those made in the image of God. A friend once said, just in passing, "The touch of glory always stings!" and this is the risen and crucified Christ. His very presence is a reminder of what they and we are not and how we have failed, and yet it is the sheer unbounded presence of wild joy that bursts forth from human beings as Jesus burst forth from the tomb.

This greeting, "Peace be with you," is forceful, a command, summoning them back to life, to hope, to be present to him and to the world again. It is a shout of confidence, of freedom, and suddenly we can see Jesus's life and death and our own lives and deaths as all of a piece, revealing a design writ large on God's horizon. He comes through locked doors for now; because of the resurrection, the veil, the boundary between this life and that other life of resurrection is more permeable than we could know. This is the announcement in flesh and blood of the earlier testament's statement, "Thou shall not die, but live!" Now, before this Jesus we once again have solid ground to stand on. This greeting is welcome grace. As John Shea has said, "This presence of God is that of tender regard present in accidental signs, nocturnal communiqués, the ordinary stuff of pedestrian lives." We are not on our own—not ever! With Jesus's entrance again into their lives, presence, not absence, will linger like perfume or the echo of a bell rung, sounding deep in the soul.

But he is a sight to behold, and they must look at what they would not stand to see before: he is nail scarred. That is the hand he raises in glory and greeting. There are holes in his hands, his side, his feet, his heart. He has been through a ferocious life-and-death struggle and come through the other side. Now we must begin to face that same struggle with death, violence, sin, evil, injustice, limits, community, failure, the cross, fear, and despair. This is peace breaking in, exploding, threatening, and exhilarating. His presence says, "Don't run, don't hide, don't blend into the world, don't disappear." Or as Etty Hillesum wrote in her journal as the net of the holocaust tightened around her, "we must safeguard this little piece of God in ourselves." Jesus's presence now radically alters forever the direction, scope, and horizon of history and our lives. And it is almost too much to take at one sighting. The disciples react in joy at the sight of him, as they had been caught up in sorrow at his death and their failure to stand with him.

There are two kinds of sorrow: the honest grief of knowing what you lack and what you have lost versus the incessant brooding over misfortunes that makes one cower in a corner, that despairs of life and spreads gloom among everyone like a virulent infection. And there are two kinds of joy: that of trying to fill up the emptiness with pleasure to avoid the reality of not being whole versus the joy that builds in the deepest places of our soul, pouring up and out in gratitude, for which adequate thanks can never be given and that can only be shared. The reaction of the disciples runs the gamut of rejoicing, hysterical fear, hope, confusion, disbelief, shock—after all how does one deal with the shock of resurrection from the dead? And so he speaks to them again.

> Jesus said to them again: "Peace be with you. As the Father has sent me, so I send you." When he had said this, he breathed on them and said to them, "Receive the Holy Spirit. If you forgive the sins of any, they are forgiven them; if you retain the sins of any, they are retained." (John 20:21–23)

It is as though he is trying to get their attention, to pull them back together so that they can actually see him present in their midst, lock onto him, and let it sink deeply into their minds and souls. It would have been a loud, demanding shout of "Peace be with you!" No soft, gentle, barely audible sound. The first peace would have washed over them like a wave: shalom with its sound and blessing coming in from out in the universe, from the heart of God, Jesus's Father. This peace is the Peace of Christ, not like any other in the world. It is the peace of forgiveness. They are all forgiven, no strings attached, no need to say anything. It is the gift of peace immeasurable, freely given, spread around. And it comes with the gift of the Spirit, his own breath breathed out upon them, sighed into them, bringing them back to life, instilling in them the power of the Spirit of God, his own risen Spirit. His words ring loud and clear: "As the Father has sent me, now I send you!" Those words in themselves are terrifying. This is the power of resurrection poured into each by the mouth of Jesus, as creative and evocative as the Spirit of God that brooded over the emptiness before creation and then, as God, breathed, and all that is came forth at his Word. Now this Word made flesh among us bids us go forth, return to the world, and remake it in the image of God, the community of the Trinity and the kingdom of enduring peace with justice for the poor. John Paul II speaks of this peace when he says, "It is up to you to make God's love which welcomes and reconciles, which forgives and renews the hearts of believers, drawing into a consoling embrace every man and every woman."

Jesus in one sentence after breathing on them draws them and us into his mission, his way in the world, the depth and power of the Incarnation and

Resurrection. What he has begun, we are to take up and complete. And there are so many realities hidden in this peace. This is the breath of peace, the last dying breath of Jesus on the cross sent out into the world in his death, and this is his breath of resurrection given first to those who will follow him and are his friends and disciples, his presence, especially when they are together in the world as his witness to life. Dorothee Soelle speaks of one such reality: "In the face of suffering you are either with the victim or the executioner—there is no other option." Jesus was the victim, the Crucified One, and his wounds attest to that, but his hands extended in blessing and commissioning ordains them to stand and live in communion with the victims, opposing the executioner, the one who does violence to other human beings, to creation, and seeks to mar the face of God. Rene Girard speaks of Jesus in this way: "Jesus is the only one who achieves the divine goal for all of humanity, the only person who has nothing to do with violence." This is our command now, our vow of obedience among one another and in the world. This is both resurrection and Pentecost, the giving of the Spirit.

But the giving of the power of the Spirit is twofold, two pronged. It demands that we forgive those who seek forgiveness and that releasing from bondage and setting free will be honored by God. And in the same breath, we are told that whoever's sins are retained by the disciples are retained by God as well. In other translations, that verb is much stronger: the phrase used is "held bound." If you hold bound the sins of anyone, they are held bound. It is the word of someone chained, imprisoned, and it has another specific meaning found only in John, in chapter 12. When Lazarus is summoned forth from the tomb by the sound of the Word of God crying out, "Lazarus come forth!" Lazarus does come forth to the shocked and horrific joy of those standing witness. He was probably buried in an upright standing tomb, so that he fell out. He would have been wrapped in his linen shrouds, bound round and around with cloth tightly like a mummy, with a cloth over his face. Then Jesus cries out to the bystanders, his friends and disciples, "Unbind him and set him free." Or it reads, "Unbind him, loose him and set him free." The sisters would have run to him and painstakingly untied, unbound, the wrappings that they had so sorrowfully bound him in just four days before. Now they would be unbinding him, setting him free from what held him in death. Then they would have helped him to his feet and turned him toward Jesus. This is the word, bound or unbind, that is used.

Just as the power of the Spirit is given for freedom, for forgiveness, the power of the Spirit is also for binding, for holding bound, those who do evil, convicting them of sin, evil, and injustice, and refusing to let them loose further on the world. Evil, death, violence, sin, injustice must all be held in check, bound. We must live with the power of the Spirit refusing to let evil run loose in the world. We must resist nonviolently and stand against death. The Spirit is given for the large issues, the signs of goodness, love unto death and beyond death, the burden of the cross, justice that is stronger than hate and mean-spiritedness, forgiveness and restitution, repairing what was destroyed, redeeming every situation. We are sent into the world, as Jesus was sent, but with the Spirit of Jesus to sustain us, enlighten us, give us courage, and speak and work through us.

Hold bound! Who and what needs to be held bound for evil and violence and the death that they let loose in the world, the havoc they wreak on earth and the despair they sow in the souls of people? Governments and leaders, corporations, those who manufacture weapons and research and design ever more deadly nuclear weapons, stockpiling them and shuffling them around, rather than dismantling them; those who lie, steal from the poor, with their greed, insensitivity, and mockery of human dignity, and deny people the basic necessities of life, food, water, clothing, shelter, and medicine; those who must make a profit on these things, or refuse them to those in misery and great human need; those who decide who lives and who dies, legally and horrifyingly inhumanly playing god with the death penalty, euthanasia, monetary choices, refusals to remit loans or remitting them with exorbitant interest rates, abortion, preemptive strikes and wars, who use sanctions to punish whole nations of people indiscriminately, but affecting the children, the elderly, women, and the weak most; those who use religion to destroy people, condemn them to living hells of exclusion, refuse to leave doors open for rehabilitation, change, repentance—three strikes and you're out—or now—one strike and you're out; those with power, authority over others, and who use it selfishly, lying and bending circumstances to their own ends, using vengeance and fear, insecurity and hatred against others, claiming that they act in the name of God; those who are to be held bound are found everywhere, in politics, economic institutions, every profession, churches and religions, and, of course, among each and all of us.

What does it look like? In words, it can be as simple as a document. The Vatican issued a document on the Holocaust (Shoah) called "We Remember" (March 16, 1998). John Donahue, SJ, writes in his column "The Word" in the April 9, 2001, issue of *America* what we are called to do and not to let go by without response:

> *We Remember* calls on Christians to keep alive the scandal of its memory and to admit that in the past they "departed from the spirit of Christ and his Gospel." It concludes that the victims "from their graves, and the survivors through the vivid testimony of what they have suffered, have become a loud voice calling the attention of all humanity." Voices continue to be raised

from the graves of victims of worldwide acts of genocide and other forms
of lethal violence. (p. 47)

And these worldwide acts of genocide and other forms of lethal violence include terrorist attacks by individuals and fundamentalist religious groups engaging in hate and murder, as well as the equally devastating and often more
pervasive acts of governments attacking countries where individuals and
groups live, punishing whole peoples in retaliation and making war a way of
responding to any group or nation that disagrees with them. Anyone who uses
violence and death, torture, the death penalty, legal killing, institutional greed,
and fear to control people and hold power needs to be held bound, held responsible and stopped, if necessary by laying down one's life, as Jesus did to
make a statement that life is God's, and we serve the God of Life, Jesus's Father,
in the power of his Spirit. The truth must be told, the words must be spoken,
and all manner of resistance must be part of our lives. Our baptismal vows
promise that we will both live in the freedom of the children of God (given to
us in the peace of resurrection) and that we promise to resist evil and refuse to
be mastered by any sin. This is the peace of Christ.

This would be a good place for the gospel to end. But it doesn't. One of
the eleven wasn't there: Thomas. And what isn't written is the bridge between
these lines of power and hope and the fact that one week later they are still
locked in the room, and they haven't moved. They have seen the Risen Lord,
been blessed and breathed upon, commissioned and sent forth with the gift of
the Spirit to forgive and hold bound, the very life of Jesus within them, among
them, and they haven't moved an inch. They are still caught in the grip of fear.
The Word of God is going nowhere fast. Why? The rest of the story tells us
why. We read this whole gospel on Low Sunday, the Sunday following Easter,
but we read just the portion we have already read on Pentecost. Hopefully, each
Easter season fifty days of rejoicing in the presence of the Risen Lord teach us
how to go out into the world, as Jesus did in obedience to his Word.

> But Thomas (who was called the Twin), one of the twelve, was not with
> them when Jesus came. So the other disciples told him, "We have seen the
> Lord." But he said to them, "Unless I see the mark of the nails in his hands,
> and put my finger in the mark of the nails, and put my hand in his side, I
> will not believe." (John 20:24–25)

Two lines and the truth is told. Someone was missing. The community
was not whole, or together. Thomas absented himself. Why? Perhaps the reason is hidden in his name: the Twin, the word for an identical twin. When people are living in fear and insecurity, many want to be with others and some,
who have other options, an alibi, prefer to go out on their own. Thomas had

an out. If he was recognized as one of Jesus's disciples, he could always feign ignorance and say, oh, you must mean my twin brother. Has he gone back to his old way of life, before he met Jesus and went off as part of his company? Has he parted company with them now that there is persecution and the possibility that he will be arrested? It would seem so. The other ten disciples who have traveled with him and Jesus, prayed, eaten, learned, and been his followers, all try to tell him the same story: we have seen the Lord! And he steadfastly refuses to believe any of them. He flat out rejects the community's word, hope, and passing on of Jesus's command. He won't listen, obey, believe them. He might, but he has his own criteria for belief—very callous, insensitive, and violent criteria, impossible in his mind to fulfill. He wants to see for himself, and then he wants to open up the wounds of Jesus again, sticking his finger in the nail holes and thrusting his hand into his side, to see if he bleeds and is really Jesus? It is insulting, degrading, and horrible to think about. So a week later, none of them has moved. His refusal, his selfish response to their hope and newborn belief is to kill it dead, abort it. Thomas, one of their own, is the reason why fear prevails and none of them obey Jesus's Word. A week goes by, seven days, signifying a lifetime, an entire cycle of life, and this time he's with them.

> A week later his disciples were again in the house, and Thomas was with them. Although the doors were shut, Jesus came and stood among them and said, "Peace be with you." Then he said to Thomas, "Put your finger here and see my hands. Reach out your hand and put it in my side. Do not doubt but believe." Thomas answered him, "My Lord and my God!" Jesus said to him, "Have you believed because you have seen me? Blessed are those who have not seen and yet have come to believe." (John 20:26–29)

This is the third peace, the peace of the Spirit, breathed upon them, the Spirit that forgives and holds bound those who need to be held bound. It is given to all, this peace that is forgiveness, but now Jesus shows the disciples how to hold one another bound. Thomas has paralyzed the community with his disbelief and refused to obey the Word that they brought to him, seeking to obey Jesus's command to them. He has insisted on impossible personal attention because he wasn't with the community, a decision he made by his own choice. Now Jesus turns toward Thomas and singles him out, calling his bluff, repeating his own words back at him, holding him bound to actually try and do what he has claimed for his criteria. He tells him, in this translation, "Do not doubt but believe," but so many other translations read, "Do not persist in your unbelief, but believe." This is not doubt: this is stubbornness and hardness of heart that has hurt the whole community. This often happens in community and is not to be tolerated and allowed to go unchecked. This is what the power of the Spirit is about: binding and holding the community together in forgiveness, truthfulness, the command to obey and be faithful to Jesus's Word, summoning us out into the world; as the Father sent Jesus in the Incarnation, we are now sent in the Spirit. We are to believe one another in community, especially any story of hope, or freedom, of resurrection and life.

There is the sense, the tone, that Jesus is not easy on Thomas, but hard, strong, and fierce, jolting him out of his selfishness and sin. When Thomas blurts out his one line that he now decides to speak, "My Lord and my God!" it's a bit late and not based on faith, but sight—he got part of what he asked for—personal attention from God. It is hardly an act of faith. It's just a state-ment of fact, now. The proof is there. This may be Thomas's faith, but it is not the faith of the community, not the way to belief. We must look outside our-selves for the source of our belief, in Word, community, sacrament, and the presence of the Crucified Lord in those who suffer still. And so the very last line of Jesus in John's Gospel is a response to this kind of person who holds back the believing community from God's mission entrusted to them and in-sists on individual experience for his or her own coming to belief. He pro-claims a blessing for all time and people, "Blessed are those who have not seen and yet have believed!" This is a blessing, a heart call to all of us who come to belief, relying on the belief of the community that has gone before us in faith, staking our lives daily and enduringly on others' belief and the stories of res-urrection that others have known in their flesh and their lives. The peace of the Spirit, the peace of unity, of mission and obedience to the Word of God, the peace of communion and encouragement that we owe to one another, the peace of the Spirit that is strongest together is proclaimed.

This is the peace of the Trinity, the Father, the Son, and the Spirit, the God revealed in the mysteries of the Incarnation, the Resurrection, and the church borne on the breath of the Spirit of God. Now they will once again be blown out of the locked room, blown on the winds of the Spirit out into the whole world, breathing in the Word and Sacrament of Jesus, sent as the Father sent him, with the Good News of resurrection. And this is the community of peacemakers, the presence of the peace of God in the world. It is our mission, our work, our gift, and our power, our authority, to make and keep peace among all.

It works on large-scale ventures and in small interpersonal ways.

There is a story told in the recent history of South America. There had never been a war between Chile and Argentina, although they shared a long border. But in 1899 there was a frontier border dispute that spread all up and down the hundreds of miles that they shared with only a traditional line be-tween them. It had terrible possibilities and by Easter of 1890 there were two armies, thousands, poised and ready to strike at a moment's provocation or or-der. A disastrous and long war seemed inevitable. But for one man. Monsignor

Bonaventa in Buenos Aires during Holy Week preached a mission with a passionate appeal for peace between the two nations that had been neighbors for so long. And news of the sermons spread throughout the country, and a bishop in Chile picked it up and began preaching on his side. And the message and plea for peace put pressure upon both governments.

The will of the people forced the leaders to submit to arbitration presided over by King Edward VII of Britain. A treaty was signed, war was averted, and all the guns that had been assembled and gathered along the border were declared useless now. They were brought overland to an arsenal in Buenos Aires and melted down. They were used to cast a towering bronze figure of Jesus, now known as "The Christ of the Andes," with his arms flung wide in the sign of the cross, outstretched in blessing, and in his left hand he held aloft a cross as his standard.

Then, it was decided that the statue would be taken up to thirteen thousand feet in the mountains to the border. A train took it to the end of the railway and then gun carriages drawn by mules picked it up, continuing its journey. On the final, steep ascent to the top of the mountain it was dragged up with ropes pulled by soldiers and sailors. On March 13, 1904, it was firmly established and unveiled, and it still stands there today.

On one side of its base are written the words, "These mountains themselves shall fall and crumble to dust before the people of Chile and Argentina forget their solemn covenant sworn at the feet of Christ." On the other side is the text from Eph. 2:14, "He is our peace who has made both one."

A little anecdote concerns the grumbling on the Chilean side when they found that the statue faced Argentina and gave its back to Chile. Some peacemaker in Chile said, "That's alright. They need watching over on that side" (from Christopher notes and friends in Chile who sent me pictures and told me the story). After reading the words, I wondered, do we need watching? We certainly need to melt down the guns, the tanks and missiles, the nuclear weapons, and make covenant with each other in this new century and stand together in peace at the feet of Christ. If two countries can do it, then all countries can do it—make peace and be peace. A good place to begin would be with all the Christian nations making peace among ourselves and then reaching out in peace to all. This is the peace we are blessed with, challenged to bring to the world and be, as presence to all in hope.

On a more individual and personal note, one of the first times I went to Japan I worked on this gospel with a number of communities, teaching them to study and delve deep into the Scriptures, and together we sought ways to make them come true in our own lives, taking them to heart. After a week of working with John's Gospel, it was time for me to leave, and as was the custom, I was given a gift. But as part of the formal presentation, I was called before the community and the person holding the gift spoke to me and to all gathered. He held in his arms a huge bouquet of flowers, huge peonies, chrysanthemums, green sprays, absolutely gorgeous, bearing a strong scent that I could smell more than three feet away. And I was first told this story, which is very famous in Japan.

Once upon a time there was a monk-poet, Basho, who spent his time traveling in the mountains and villages when the weather was fair and then burrowing in for the winter months in a tiny hut, living simply. He played with children, wrote poetry, told stories with old men, and shared his meager food with anyone and everyone. It was his custom to save money all winter so that in spring he could make a trip, a pilgrimage to a place where he could sightsee, watch the world, rest and write poetry, specifically haiku, a short terse three-line form that had a strong syllable pattern. The best time to write haiku and the content were traditionally found between seasons: winter into spring, spring into summer, and so on. This year he had heard about the gardens in Kyoto and decided that would be the place of pilgrimage for his haiku (which he will see, give away, and live on for the following year). He knew he would need a good deal of money because the *royokan* ("guesthouses") and gardens were expensive, and he needed funds for ink, brushes, good rice paper, sake—and, of course, food. It was a long, long winter, and he had time to save up much, but he couldn't wait for the first signs of spring to come. It was April before he got on the road, and even then there was mud and patches of snow, bits of fierce wind, and miserable days of blustery weather.

But finally he arrived in Kyoto, and already the trees were budding, against snow mountains and remnants in corners of the temple. He got himself quickly settled in his royokan and went out to explore and see. And he discovered something magical and unbelievable that first day. It was a person who gave away gifts. But it just wasn't any usual way of giving (the Japanese have a ritual of giving, what, when, to whom, and so forth, that is complicated and based on many sets of relationships). This was an altogether different way, and it intrigued him. She would give what she had to someone in need: food, a warm jacket, a cup of sake in a small teahouse. And then she would beg for anything that others would give away. And she kept lists. Lists of what she got and lists of what she needed, for she would also walk around asking people what they needed and then, even more startling, asking them what they didn't need, and would they give that to her. Basho decided this would be a marvelous way to spend his spring, following her around and watching what she did and how people responded to her, in need, or begged from, or given gifts, whether they asked for them or not.

Spring flew by like birds darting about in the morning. After watching for awhile, he started giving her some of the money he had saved and took to sleeping in fields and ditches, under the awnings of temples and in doorways, begging for food and sake himself. He sold his papers, brushes, and ink, and even gave away his outer garments. It was an incredible trip. He ran out of money and spring turned into summer, and before he knew it, it was late summer, and it was time to head for home in his mountain pass and settle back into his hut. It would be a hard fall and winter though; he had no haiku to sell or share or give as gifts. He'd been too busy watching and following her around to write.

When he arrived back in his valley, his friends and neighbors harried him for his poems, wanting to hear his new haiku, but there was nothing. All he would say was that it was a most magnificent spring, that he couldn't remember such a marvelous season in all his many decades. Just marvelous. He kept saying: I found something better than spring! Better than poetry! Better than haiku! Even better than sake! Someone who begged, and gave, and took, and questioned, filling up what was lacking in others, relieving people of burdens they didn't have to bear, pulling people together, making strangers into friends, and spreading joy around. Marvelous, absolutely.

It was months and months later, in the heart of winter, when he wrote his first haiku about that spring and summer spent in Kyoto. It has become one of the most famous in Japan, and it is often used when giving a gift to someone, in their honor. The story was told and then my gift presenter stood formally before me and bowed low. Then, he recited solemnly the haiku.

The scent of the flowers remains on the hands of the one who gives them away.

And then he repeated it again, and still a third time. Then, he formally presented me with the great armload of blossoms. Then he continued. "We love his haiku, but we have made our own that we wish to share with you as some of the first Japanese Catholics you have visited and come to know," he said. And he bowed again and solemnly declared this blessing.

May the blessing of the Father who raised Jesus from the dead
Be peace in your heart.
May the blessing of the Son who sends us forth and walks with us
Be peace in your heart.
May the blessing of the Spirit who forgives and tells the truth
Be peace in your heart.
May the blessing of the Trinity that makes us one mind, one heart, and one spirit
Be peace in your heart.

And may the peace that you give away be peace abiding with you.
May the scent of the flowers remain on the hands of the one who gives
them away.
Peace be with you!
Amen. Amen. Amen.

And very uncharacteristically among the Japanese, I cried. And they were thoroughly delighted! This is a fitting prayer for all of us who fall into the category of believers who have not seen and yet believe these two thousand years after the Resurrection of Jesus, relying on one another in community for the strength and power of our belief, given to be shared with a world so fearful and in need of peace. Peace be with you. Peace be with us. Peace be with all. Amen.

7

John 21: Jesus and Peter on the Beach

God is present at the point where the eyes of those who give and
those who receive meet.

—Simone Weil

*T*his chapter is an add-on to John's Gospel, and it is about practical, hard, and
down-to-earth forgiveness, the really difficult kind that comes with the destruction of relationships, the killing of human beings and hope, the violence
of the world and our fear of it, which cause us to betray our best intentions
and cast us headlong into despair. This is about Peter's betrayal of Jesus, but it
is about all of us human beings who do terrible things and must live with one
another ever after. And it is about the church and the pragmatic necessity to
be honest about sin and evil in its members, its leadership, and as a community
and how we live in collusion with evil that eats at the heart of many who seek
to live faithfully, but are discouraged by those who claim to be faithful followers of the Crucified and Risen Lord, and yet do such terrible things to one another or do nothing to stop the pain and the evil all around us.

But it is good news! And it is a story of hope, reminding us that absolutely
everything in the world is redeemable because of the Father's raising Jesus from
the dead in the power of the Spirit. There is a Hassidic tale that will set the
stage for this last account of Jesus's appearance after his resurrection for us. I
call it "Someone Waits," and it is one of the Baal Shem Tov's ("The Master of
the Good Name") stories, so it is more than two hundred years old.

> Once upon a time there was a man who came to visit the Baal Shem Tov,
> intending to become one of his disciples. But the Besht (as he was called)
> told him that his path lay in another direction—that he was a storyteller, but
> that he was welcome to stay with him for a year and he would keep him

close to him, including him among his closest disciples. He was to listen and watch and collect stories that he was to spend the rest of his life telling. It was a year unparalleled in wisdom, in wonder, in marvelous things to behold, in songs, stories and visions, encounters with strangers and so many believers who came to hear the Besht, to ask his counsel, and prayers, to tell of history's events and to see how the Besht responded.

One day the Besht called him over and told him to be silent and to collect another story for his memory. Soon after, a very distraught young man came in and poured out his soul, saying that he was a Jew, but had become a Christian, lured by greed and material wealth and power in the city. Now he was very rich, but he had lost his soul and his community. What was he to do? There was a long silence, and then the Besht told him, "You must remain a Christian outwardly in your practice, but in your heart you must do penance and be a Jew, honoring the God of your ancestors and the covenant. Give away your money to the poor year after year and someday you will know that you are not only forgiven, you are freed from your bondage to your sin. Now go and do as I commanded you." He leaned over the man, put his hand on his head, blessed him, and whispered a final bit of comfort into his ear. The man wept and turned and went back to his life.

There were so many stories, the man wondered if he would remember them all, but the Besht told him that the Holy One, blessed be His name, would remind him of the stories as needed. And the time came for him to go. He was reluctant, and yet he knew that the Besht saw into peoples' hearts and he was a storyteller and it was his way. He left with a blessing and the memories of that year. And he traveled the roads of cities and countries, among the rich and the poor, illiterate and well educated, and he told stories. There were times of famine and drought, persecution and exile, and still he made his way telling stories of truth, of hope, of laughter and joy, marvelous, unbelievable, fanciful tales, whatever was needed. He was paid in food and drink, shelter and clothing, friendships and places to stay spread out across half of eastern Europe. And he grew old and wondered if his old master, the Besht, was still alive. Times had grown very hard. It was winter, and there was no money, nothing extra, and so there were many places he went that were not interested in stories. They were too busy just surviving.

One night he was so hungry and tired, exhausted from traveling and fighting the wind and snow and inhospitality. He tried telling stories in a tavern, and the barman suggested that he'd do better elsewhere. But where, he asked. The man told him that just outside of town there was a huge mansion and inside lived an old man who would pay for any story he'd never heard before, and probably he'd get fed while he told his collection. Off he went and found a house well lit, a huge winding driveway, and servants at the door. He announced that he was here to tell stories and was ushered into a long dining room with one long table, heavy dark curtains, and food and drink and candles laid out. It was a banquet! There were only two chairs, one at each end.

He was fed and the table cleared, and then the owner came and sat at the end of the table with a stack of kopeks, and he stayed seated at the other end. "Tell," he was commanded. And he did—story after story after story. And the coins were slid down the table, the stack slowly being transferred from one end of the table to his end. He'd have enough to live on for months, a year at this rate! But the man who listened, and he did listen intently, never showed any emotion, never responded. He only sent a coin down the table if he had not heard the story before. Nothing moved him. And the teller began pulling out all his best stories and telling them with all the power he had, trying to get the man to respond. Nothing. And the night wore on, and dawn came. And he was spent, out of stories, but richer in money than he'd been in years. It was time to go.

He rose from the table and for the first time the man reacted. He rose and said, somewhat panicked, "Is that all? Are there no more stories? You don't know any others?" "No," the teller answered, "I can't remember another one." "Please," the man begged, "think, any one at all." "I'm sorry," the teller replied and started to leave. The man was right next to him now, begging, pulling on his arm. And then he remembered that young man who was a Jew, but betrayed his belief and the covenant for wealth and power and lost his soul.

"Ah, yes, there is one more, but I doubt if you'd be interested." The man's glare told him to get on with the telling. He did, exactly as he remembered it, describing the Baal Shem Tov, his time with him, the man who came to visit, and as he spoke, the man actually started to respond. He breathed deeply, swallowed, his eyes brightened. He become agitated, then attentive, and then he began to weep, tears running down his face. The teller could not think of why; he ended the story with the Besht blessing the man and bending down to whisper in his ear. And at that point the man spoke, finishing the teller's tale. "Yes," he said, "that man is me. And the Besht whispered that on the night that someone came and told me this story, I was forgiven, I was free and that all restitution and amends had been made. I was a Jew again, at one with my people and with God. Your story has liberated me from these long, long years of hidden pain and bondage. Blessings on you!"

They say when this story is told (very, very rarely) that it is stories that save us and that somewhere someone waits for yours, for the one you will tell that will set another human being free, and there will come the moment when your eyes and your words bring another back to life. That person is out there now waiting for your story, and when you meet, all history will shift and hope will reign again in that part of the earth.

This is what we must bear in mind as we read these last stories in John, and we must remember that always they are about us too and our need to practice this resurrection life begun in our baptisms, imitating among ourselves what Jesus does with his disciples and Peter, so that we retain the integrity of the gospel and the commitment to our baptismal promises that is essential if we are to preach the gospel to the world. Evil is not just out there. It is in us, and among us, and we accommodate our belief to its power, betraying our relationships to the Crucified and Risen Lord. The following are a few statistics recently published in the *Casa Maria Catholic Worker* newsletter.

> More children have died in Iraq than the combined death toll of the two atomic bombs in Japan and the ethnic cleansing of the former Yugoslavia.
>
> The U.S. has used sanctions of food and trade/investments against Vietnam, Cuba, Iran, Iraq, Nicaragua, and other states that have not complied with our wishes.
>
> The U.S. has used more chemical weapons against other countries than has any other nation, including Iraq. It used them in Vietnam and Cuba and tested them on its own soldiers without their knowledge.
>
> Israel has an estimated 60–80 nuclear warheads. They are pointed at every Arab capital and at nuclear facilities in Pakistan and some states of the former U.S.S.R. (from *Z Magazine*)

Sin and evil are realities worldwide. We are responsible for ours individually and collectively, within our nation, our institutions, and our church, in our collusion with others and the effects that they have on others by force and example as Christians and Catholics who profess publicly belief in forgiveness, nonviolent resistance to evil, love unto death, and justice with mercy. We are called to lay down our lives for one another and for what we believe in, but we are not called to kill anyone in God's name, for any reason. And we are not to kill hope in others, or kill the presence of God and the call to discipleship in others by our cowardice and sin. This is the hard edge of resurrection, the practice with all our hearts and souls, minds, strength of forgiveness and reconciliation, restitution, and atonement—in a word, the gospel.

Peter vehemently denied Jesus publicly in words, and all the disciples, men and women, abandoned him and betrayed their relationships with him. We all do. We have all been forgiven so many times that we cannot begin to count them. We are commanded to forgive so many times that we do not try to count: everybody, for everything, all the time, no exceptions to the rule. And some things are infinitely harder to forgive than others. By now, many people know the story of Bud Welch and his daughter, but it is a good place to start; it is about as hard a thing to forgive as most of us will ever have to face. It is a story that is about death and about life after it, and about resurrection life in the face of death that has torn a hole in us (like the wounds of Jesus) that will not ever be fully healed. The scars are always there, and they must be looked at and faced with the Spirit of God.

Bud Welch lost his twenty-three-year-old daughter, Julie. Before that, life was simple. In his words, "I had a little girl, and I loved her a lot." He ran a gas station for thirty-four years in Oklahoma City. Then on April 19, 1995, his Julie and 167 others were killed in a bomb explosion that destroyed the Alfred P. Murrah Building. The day she was killed, he found out that she was about to announce her engagement. He is clear: all his life he opposed the death penalty, but that changed on April 19. He describes what he was like inside afterward.

> The first four or five weeks after the bombing I had so much anger, pain, hatred, and revenge, that I realized why, when someone is charged with a violent crime, they transport him in a bullet-proof vest. It's because people like me would try to kill him.

For months his life fell apart—he smoked and drank—and then he went to the bomb site and stood there, thinking about Timothy McVeigh. He wanted him dead, but he also started thinking whether he'd feel any better once he (and any others involved) were executed. He writes:

> Every time I asked myself that question, I got the same answer: No. Nothing positive would come from it. It wouldn't bring Julie back. After all, it was hatred and revenge that made me want to see them dead, and those two things were the very reason that Julie and 167 others were dead.

This was the first step, and he once again began to come out publicly against the death penalty, for Timothy McVeigh or anyone, for anything. It wasn't the answer. And in the process of constantly standing up for what he believed, he also had to come to grips with forgiveness. It began with a television program that he watched that tried to interview Timothy McVeigh's father. The man wouldn't talk to the interviewer, but just looked up for a moment with eyes filled with pain, and Bud Welch recognized that look. He knew it intimately. He had been living with that kind of loss, sorrow, pain, and hurt for months. That day he decided to visit McVeigh's father.

They met in the man's garden and talked, picking weeds, and then went inside to meet his daughter, Jennifer, who was twenty-four. There were pictures on the wall of all of them and Tim's high school graduation picture. His father had trouble talking and had told him earlier that he couldn't cry, but when Bud commented on the photograph, he cried a little. They talked together the three of them, all in awful pain for over an hour and a half, and then Bud got up to leave. He shook hands with Timothy's father and extended his hand to Jennifer. But she did not take it, instead she grabbed him and held on and hugged him, weeping. He describes it:

I don't know who started crying first as we embraced, but we were both in tears. Finally, I said, "Honey, we're in this together for the rest of our lives. And we can make the most of it, if we choose. I don't want your brother to die, and I'll do everything in my power to prevent it." Never in my life have I felt closer to God than I did at that time. I felt like a thousand pounds had been lifted off my shoulders.

He did not want to meet Julie's killer and wasn't sure that he'd forgiven him. It was a daily struggle that exhausted him. He would find that he had fits of rage and anger and terrible feelings about Timothy McVeigh, but he was sure he did not want him executed. He wants to forgive him and has said that if he were to die, that it will be too late to choose to forgive him.

It's a struggle, but it's one I need to wage. In any case, forgiving is not something you just wake up one morning and decide to do. You have to work through your anger and your hatred as long as it's there. You try to live each day a little better than the one before. [Story and notes taken from NPR interview and Johann Christoph Arnold. *Plough Reader* (Spring 2001): 21–23, quoting from sections of his book, *Why Forgive*]

Timothy McVeigh is dead, executed, and hundreds of people must deal with their pain and emotions and whether or not they will forgive. We all have to live with what has happened to us and what we ourselves have done to others. On some things, there is no closure, only as Bud Welch called it, "a hole in your heart that doesn't close." This kind of forgiveness is hard, hard as nails, and yet it is a power given with grace by the Spirit and a practice of a lifetime. It is a process. It deals with feelings, but it is not based on feelings, but actions and responses. And because of that, Bud Welch did forgive, even if the words never actually were spoken silently or aloud.

The practice of gospel forgiveness involves four steps:

1. Forego. This means to forego retaliation, revenge, the expression of anger, hate, resentment, attacking, doing violence, vengeance, and letting your emotions control your actions. This takes discipline and is hard to do alone. We need a community that helps us, holds onto us, and sometimes restrains us, and allows us to vent our feelings and reactions with them, calming us and acting as a buffer zone.
2. Forebear. This is long term, bearing our pain with grace, bearing our share of the burden of the gospel's command to forgive. Forbearing is bearing the cross and filling up with what is lacking in the sufferings of Christ. Forbearing is sharing in others' pain in solidarity and communion with others. When members of families who lost loved ones in the bombing of the World Trade Center towers went to

Afghanistan to meet with families who had lost loved ones in the U.S. bombing against their country, many came back realizing that they were not alone in their pain, and while they had lost a child, a husband or wife, a relative, most of their Afghani counterparts had lost so many, whole families, three, four, and five children, aunts and uncles, cousins. It did not stop the pain, but put it in perspective and gave them others to bear the burden with.

3. Forget. This is choosing deliberately not to dwell on what was done to you, what the other person is like, and what you'd like to do to him or her. Stop it in your mind. Begin to pray for that person, even just saying the Our Father over and over again, or Lord, Jesus Christ, Son of the Living God, have mercy on us all. And pragmatically making new memories so that the sight of that person does not immediately bring to mind what he or she did, or what we think he or she did to us (these are general suggestions to follow in all cases where we must forgive; in some instances it is only prayer that we can do at this stage, either because of circumstances or what was done to us or those we love).

4. Forgiveness. This is a gift, returning the favor of the gift of God to us and passing it along to others. We need to forgive for our own integrity and humanness. And it frees us, as God has freed us. It is given on behalf of another. We are called to live under no sign of power, but the sign of the cross, and that sign and power is forgiveness. It stretches our minds and hearts, our souls, to include more and more people. It is the practice of mercy giving, of being a merciful person, of living in the mercy of God, leaning on the mercy of God, and as it is given, giving it again.

This is a long introduction, but a necessary one to this last gospel account and appearance that was born of the experience of the early church that struggled with forgiveness, learning with time that it is the core of the gospel, baptism, and resurrection life. After two thousand years it is still hard to practice and live with all our hearts, but this is the Word of God showing us how to do it, and it is graceful and freeing always.

Religion consists of God's question and our answer.

—Abraham Joshua Heschel

This is a Resurrection appearance along the shore of the Sea of Galilee, unique to John's tradition. The first part appears to be a fishing story, much like the one where Peter goes fishing and cannot find anything, and Jesus tells him where to find the fish. Peter's response is to see himself in the eyes of Jesus, as a sinner. Listen to Peter's being called to be a disciple and a missionary in Luke.

> When they had done this, they caught so many fish that their nets were beginning to break. So they signaled their partners in the other boat to come and help them. And they came and filled both boats, so that they began to sink. But when Simon Peter saw it, he fell down at Jesus' knees, saying, "Go away from me, Lord, for I am a sinful man!" For he and all who were with him in the boat were amazed at the catch of fish that they had taken; and so also were James and John, sons of Zebedee, who were partners with Simon. Then Jesus said to Simon, "Do not be afraid; from now on you will be catching people." When they had brought their boats to shore, they left everything and followed him. (Luke 5:6–11)

This story is familiar to us, but strange. Simon Peter is a fisherman but it seems all too often that he isn't all that good at his profession. They'd been out all night and caught nothing. They are tired and frustrated, and here comes a traveling preacher who gets into their boat and then tells them to cast out into the deep for a catch. They obey, even though they do not think much of his suggestion, and are overwhelmed by all the fish. Peter's response is to fall on his knees and declare that he is a sinner and that Jesus should depart from him. He hasn't done anything wrong. He has committed no sin, and yet what he says is all too true, not only for himself, but for all of us. Defining oneself as a sinner is acknowledging a state of being, of being less than what we claim to be or not living as a human being must, in right relationship to God, to others and to the earth, living holy, wholly devoted to obedience to God, especially for Peter, who is an Israelite, a member of God's chosen people, bound to Yahweh, his God, in covenant and law. Jesus's words, and the effect they have had on him, their power over the seas and what dwells in them, his very presence, have touched Peter in his depths (like the sea's own depths that he was commanded to launch out and cast his net into). Thomas Merton writes succinctly, "People are in every way prevented from getting inside themselves. Our greatest problem is fear of depth." And in this circumstance, Peter is in over his head. He senses something in Jesus, something more fully human, something holy. And in relation to Jesus, in Jesus's presence, he stands and kneels, knowing his own lack of humanness and grace.

Yet, Jesus assures him, by name, that he has a new vocation, a mission, not with fish, but with people, in Jesus's company and that he has no need to be afraid. And Peter, James, and John leave their boats and follow him into another life. Jesus has earlier, before the catch, taught the crowds from Simon's boat, because the people were pressing to hear the word of God. Peter has heard and has been drawn into the net of God, and he has no idea what lies ahead of him.

This story, in many ways, foreshadows Simon Peter's life. As a fisherman, he is Simon. An encounter with Jesus changes everything, alters his direction, plumbs his depths and reveals him to himself in the gaze of God in Jesus. But he has a long way to travel before he understands any of this. In the first chapter of John, it is his brother, Andrew, who brings Simon to Jesus. There are only two sentences, and they are life changing and both threatening and transformative: "He brought Simon to Jesus, who looked at him and said, 'You are Simon son of John. You are to be called Cephas' [which is translated "Peter"]" (John 1:42–42).

One look and Peter is seen, known, and his name and identity are changed forever. He is taken from his father's lineage and becomes a part of a foundation of Jesus's making. Oftentimes *cephas* is translated as "rock," perhaps because of Matthew's story of Peter being the rock of the church (Matt. 16:18), and the image in Mark's Gospel where Jesus turns on Peter who has become a stumbling block on his way to Jerusalem and the cross, and calls him Satan, the hinderer who does not think like God, but who is trapped in human designs (Mark 8:33). In this story, Jesus again looks at Peter, who is in the process of remonstrating with, or rebuking, him and turns on him ferociously, along with the other disciples. Again and again, Peter gets that look from Jesus: warning, searching, disappointed, demanding, asking, and more often than not, Peter misses its intent or refuses and turns away. Peter's walk with Jesus is not always that of a follower. He has his own ideas of where they are going, how to get there, and who Jesus is and his own place in the group that follows Jesus.

And there is that story in Luke's account of the last supper where Jesus tries to warn Peter of his coming downfall and failure and tells him that he is praying for him, but Peter is quick to place himself in a better light, proclaiming his stalwart loyalty to Jesus. He doesn't listen well to Jesus's words.

> "Simon, Simon, listen! Satan has demanded to sift all of you like wheat, but I have prayed for you that your own faith may not fail; and you, when once you have turned back, strengthen your brothers." And he said to him, "Lord, I am ready to go with you to prison and to death!" Jesus said, "I tell you, Peter, the cock will not crow this day, until you have denied three times that you know me." (Luke 22:31–34)

It is all to no avail. Jesus even calls him Simon, his name before he met him and that doesn't register with him either. And that night when Jesus is being interrogated at the high priest's house, Peter follows him, "but at a distance." The story is devastating. Peter's failure, his cowardice, his fear, and his denials mark him forever. His moment of testing, his a chance to witness to belonging to

Jesus's disciples, to call him friend and to defend him even for a moment to some anonymous strangers, becomes his downfall.

> When they had kindled a fire in the middle of the courtyard and sat down together, Peter sat among them. Then a servant-girl seeing him in the fire-light, stared at him and said, "This man also was with him," but he denied it, saying, "Woman, I do not know him." A little later someone else, on seeing him, said, "You also are one of them." But Peter said, "Man, I am not!" Then about an hour later still another kept insisting, "Surely this man also was with him; for he is a Galilean." But Peter said, "Man, I do not know what you are talking about!" At that moment, while he was still speaking, the cock crowed. The Lord turned and looked at Peter. Then Peter remembered the word of the Lord, how he had said to him, "Before the cock crows today, you will deny me three times." And he went out and wept bitterly. (Luke 22:55–62)

Not a flattering portrait of Peter, named as a public disciple, in the company of Jesus and publicly disavowing any connection. It starts with his keeping his distance. And then he tries to be anonymous, blend into the crowd, waiting around to see what happens to Jesus. Then, when first questioned, he replies bluntly with the first level of denial: I do not know him. Disassociation. The second denial is in anger: I am not! I am not a disciple. I am not with anyone connected to him. He puts more distance between himself and Jesus. And the third denial, which is translated here as "I do not know what you are talking about!" is more often translated as curses, separating himself, severing any thin tie at all, even that of fellow countryman. And then this small scene is zeroed in on when Jesus is led out and he overhears that last vehement denial and curse and Peter looks up to see Jesus looking at him. No words needed. The deed is done, the course shifts; Jesus is taken away and Peter goes out and weeps bitterly.

That is the last we hear of Peter. He disappears from the rest of the passion, crucifixion, and death of Jesus—all accounts. What did that look say to Peter? What did Peter's words and angry heart do to Jesus's heart? Sebastian Moore, in his book *The Crucified Is No Stranger,* writes, "You prefer not to face the full situation, which is that you have hurt another person by shrinking yourself. When you hurt another person, your true self, the lover in you, goes into hiding, and uses every possible ruse to stay in hiding." Peter will live with his guilt, his remorse, regret, his self-pity and -loathing, and the other disciples will scatter, knowing not even Peter would stand up for Jesus. Perhaps others who heard about Jesus's death would have relayed some of Jesus's cries in agony on the cross, one of the most startling being, "Father, forgive them; for they do not know what they are doing" (Luke 23:34). Peter is publicly no longer a disciple.

And that is the reason for all this background and for this story in John. Peter in actuality went on to become the leader of the community, of the church until he died in 60 A.D., and the church struggled with this leader who had so forcibly denied any association with their Crucified Lord and Master. In Mark's Gospel (written in the 60s) Peter is mentioned in the Resurrection account, when the young man in the tomb tells the women, "go tell his disciples and Peter" (Mark 16:7). There is nothing in Matthew, except there is another Simon, of Cyrene, the disciple who carries Jesus's cross and follows him to Calvary (Matt. 27:32). And in Luke, when the two disciples return from Emmaus, they are greeted by the eleven and their companions, gathered together, who cry out, "The Lord has risen indeed, and he has appeared to Simon!" (Luke 24:34), but there is no account of that appearance.

How did someone so without honor, cowardly and a public sinner, become the shepherd who led the church for the thirty years after the death of Jesus? And it seems that the church struggled with that fact from the day of the Resurrection right up until this account was added to John's Gospel, probably as late as 110 A.D. It was most likely written after even the death of John, because the text intimates as much, after it describes Peter's own execution as a martyr and witness to Jesus.

These stories begin again on the Sea of Galilee and almost rewrite Simon Peter's story in light of the Resurrection and what that meant for him, for the other disciples and the church and, consequently what it means for us today. These texts are the fruit of seventy or more years of experiencing the power of the Spirit to forgive and hold bound and the practical and difficult reality of putting that into practice personally and publicly.

This is the scene depicted on the cover of this book. The title of the painting is *Easter Breakfast*, and Jesus is sitting on the beach looking straight out at us, his face and eyes filled with unbearable sadness and inexpressible peace. You can see farther off, on the sea of Galilee, the boat and the disciples fishing. It is the moment when Jesus is looking both at them, their pasts, presents, and futures, and beyond and through history right up to the present moment, when he is looking straight at us. It is a look that questions us ultimately, truth-telling us to our depths, and knowing us completely. In a sense these two lines from Sebastian Moore, in his work *God Is A New Language*, sums up Peter's story and all our stories gathered in this moment of being seen, of God looking at us: "Human living as it is normally pursued is an escape from reality. The gospel message is a recall to reality, revealed as the mystery of forgiveness." This is the story of bringing Peter back as a disciple, connecting him again to the disciples, and back home to dwelling with Jesus. Listen to the homecoming.

> After these things Jesus showed himself again to the disciples by the Sea of Tiberias; and he showed himself in this way. Gathered there together were

> Simon Peter, Thomas called the Twin, Nathanael of Cana in Galilee, the
> sons of Zebedee, and two others of his disciples. Simon Peter said to them,
> "I am going fishing." They said to him, "We will go with you." They went
> out and got into the boat, but that night they caught nothing. (John 21:1–3)

Some things don't change. All night fishing and nothing to show for it.
Peter has gone back to his former profession and hasn't improved much with
the hiatus. And the others follow him backward. This section lists seven of the
disciples, naming them as they are described in earlier chapters, namely the first
and the last chapters of John. The scene has the feel of discouragement,
lethargy, filling up time, reverting to old ways—almost as though they haven't
integrated much of the appearances of the Resurrection. Now the story shifts
to the beach.

> Just after daybreak, Jesus stood on the beach; but the disciples did not know
> that it was Jesus. Jesus said to them, "Children, you have no fish, have you?"
> They answered him, "No." He said to them, "Cast the net to the right side
> of the boat, and you will find some." So they cast it, and now they were not
> able to haul it in because there were so many fish. That disciple whom Jesus
> loved said to Peter, "It is the Lord!" When Simon Peter heard that it was the
> Lord, he put on some clothes, for he was naked, and jumped into the sea. But
> the other disciples came in the boat, dragging the net full of fish, for they
> were not far from the land, only about a hundred yards off. (John 21:4–8)

Only a hundred yards offshore and they're still not good at seeing. As in
the account on the road to Emmaus, they can't recognize the Risen Jesus. It
eludes them, perhaps as the earlier story in John asserts, because their past and
present way of relating to Jesus and one another are clouding their vision. And
the figure on the beach questions them, calling them children. And with
echoes of the other stories and all the other times that he directed them where
to go, what to do, how to catch fish, and showed them how to catch people,
he commands them again.

Now it is the beloved disciple who sees and cries out to Peter, "It is the
Lord!"—the announcement, the Easter proclamation—and Peter listens to and
hears the other disciple's words, trusting his eyes and heart, though he can't see
for himself. And Peter reacts strangely. He dressed for fishing—that is, with
nothing on. And then he goes into the water, but not until he puts his clothes
on! This is baptism! And Peter now wears a baptismal garment as he draws near
to Jesus on the beach. He has heard Jesus's words, and he and the others have
obeyed, and he has come to see and believe through the sight and belief of the
beloved disciple, and he plunges into the waters of life and sight. He has forgotten all about the fish and is intent once again on getting to Jesus. The oth-

ers haul in the net, fishermen still, and not wanting to waste the catch that Jesus gave them so graciously.

> When they had gone ashore, they saw a charcoal fire there, with fish on it, and bread. Jesus said to them, "Bring some of the fish that you have just caught." So Simon Peter went aboard and hauled the net ashore, full of large fish, a hundred and fifty-three of them; and though there were so many, the net was not torn. Jesus said to them, "Come and have breakfast." Now none of them dared to ask him, "Who are you?" because they knew it was the Lord. Jesus came and took the bread and gave it to them, and did the same with the fish. This was now the third time that Jesus appeared to the disciples after he was raised from the dead. (John 21:9–14)

Jesus is waiting for them and has breakfast on the beach all prepared, good fish, bread, and his company, and now he waits on them, feeding them. This is Eucharist and forgiveness. It's a done deal; it's a given. His very presence is forgiveness, acceptance, a welcoming back, and peace and communion shared among them all. Jesus feeds them the bread and the fish, food of friendship. But it must have been an awkward meal, quiet, with none of them asking any questions or saying much of anything. Jesus is doing the cooking, and Jesus is doing the talking, moving among them as a servant, just as he once washed their feet. He calls them children, his Father's children, not his brothers. They are all the beloved children of God again, in baptism, Eucharist, and forgiveness.

Jesus tells them to bring some fish, and it is Peter who now moves, going back to the boat to grab hold of the net and pull it closer and get the fish to eat. This is Peter the fisherman obeying his master, and we are told two things: no matter how many fish there are, the net is not torn and that there are 153 fish—big ones. Some fishing story! People who research such biblical trivia say that this was the known number of species of fish at the time of Jesus—this is a universal catch of all the nations and folk in the world! And this is the bark of Peter, and the nets hold secure.

But this story isn't about fishing; it's about facing reality and shepherding. The story isn't about mission or the great catch; it's about breakfast on the beach and the great catch of Jesus, who has just caught some big ones himself, seven of his wandering sheep. This story isn't about these seven, even about Peter and John; it's about us. And this story isn't about fishing; it's about forgiveness. This is the Good News. This is the essence of who Jesus is—the forgiveness of God extended to us, always, everywhere, for everything, again and again, no matter what we do or don't do. This is the first step, forgiveness, and for almost a century, Eucharist was the way sins were forgiven after baptism. The community would fast, do penance, give alms to the poor, and go to Eucharist to be fed the bread of peace and communion, making them whole and one again.

But now it's time for the second step: reconciliation. The word in Greek literally means "to walk together again." It's time for Jesus and Peter to go for a walk on the beach together and draw Peter back into intimacy with Jesus. It is part of the public ritual that must be attended to and witnessed by the other members that knew him as designated leader and despaired when he failed publicly. This is the second gift of the gospel—to pull the community back together again so that it can walk the way of the cross all the way to Easter's glory as one body in Christ. It's a harder gift and a richer and truer, more complete one than forgiveness even!

> When they had finished breakfast, Jesus said to Simon Peter, "Simon son of John, do you love me more than these?" He said to him, "Yes, Lord; you know that I love you." Jesus said to him, "Feed my lambs." A second time Jesus said to him, "Simon son of John, do you love me?" He said to him, "Yes, Lord: you know that I love you." Jesus said to him, "Tend my sheep." He said to him a third time, "Simon son of John, do you love me?" Peter felt hurt because he said to him the third time, "Do you love me?" And he said to him, "Lord, you know everything; you know that I love you." Jesus said to him, "Feed my sheep. Very truly, I tell you, when you were younger, you used to fasten your own belt and to go wherever you wished. But when you grow old, you will stretch out your hands, and someone else will fasten a belt around you and take you where you do not wish to go." [He said this to indicate the kind of death by which he would glorify God.] After this he said to him, "Follow me." (John 21:15–19)

Oh, the love and the pain, and how hard it is to look at who we are, what we have done, and its effect on others. How do we undo things? How do we live with what we have done to others? How do we live with failure that reveals us as so much less than we make ourselves out to be before others? How do we reconcile ourselves with Truth? This is how it's done. This is reconciliation, the second stage and gift of forgiveness that makes forgiveness mutual, with acceptance and confession, and it's a process, a walk back, a coming together, a coming home to ourselves.

The first step is acknowledgment: basically, we are flawed. And Jesus does this by calling Peter by his given name before he met him, when he had another primary relationship, Simon son of John, and he will stay with that form of address until Peter turns again and again back to facing Jesus and acknowledging what he is and what he has done and the effects his actions have had on others—those who are witnesses to this ritual confrontation in the essential meaning of that word, "face to face with one another."

Then comes confession: three times Jesus asks the question, do you love me? to offset the three times that Peter denied any relationship or friendship with, any love for him. It has to be worded so. It is direct, honest, and explicit, although even on the third asking, Peter does not seem to be getting it. The text says that Peter was hurt and that it could be that he still doesn't know how much he tore the heart of his master and friend or that he is now beginning to see and sense what he has done, and it hurts—he shares Jesus's pain at the rending of friendship and how hard it is to mend that relationship. Jesus is so kind to Peter; instead of reminding him over and over again of his fear, cowardice, curses, and distancing from him, he asks him to tell him that he loves him. Amazing courtesy, kindness, careful regard for the one who sinned by the one who was sinned against; this is the grace and art of forgiveness that are to mark and characterize all the followers of Jesus.

The third step is restitution, righting the wrong, apologizing directly, reconstituting reality with the Spirit and grace. The traditional word for this is "penance." And Peter is given three penances, one for each of his denials. The penances come in the forms of exhortations, calls to change patterns in Peter's life. They are worded in theological language: feed my lambs, tend my sheep, and feed my sheep. We shift now from fishing to shepherding, because that is what Peter became, the shepherd of the church. And he will spend the remainder of his life doing penance, not only for his personal failure, but for the demoralizing consequences it had on the community, scattering them, sheep without a shepherd. That is never to happen again. And this is the way it is remedied.

Feed my lambs. We start with the young ones, those most damaged by what Peter did, and so the first penance is to tell the story, in every generation, to confess the sins of those who are leaders and keep telling as well of the incredible mercy of our forgiving God. This is the Good News made personal and communal to each church. Tend my sheep is next. Peter was the lost sheep, and Jesus went out after him, and now that is Peter's penance, to seek out the lost, to find and carry them home, to keep them all together and to make sure that they have fresh water, pastures, peace, and strong presence. He is to spend his time, searching out the ditches, leaving the ninety-nine if necessary to go after the one that needs finding the most. This is to be Peter's new way of life, his vocation. And lastly, feed my sheep. Peter is to lead the community and keep them together, emphasizing the expression of forgiveness, mercy, and love of God for us and in return our forgiveness and mercy and love for one another. Is there anything worse that what Peter did? All must be forgiven and all must be held bound, responsible for what we do or do not do, and we must be publicly held accountable for our effect on the community around us. That is what leadership is for—the accounting of those with power over others and influence and the extension of mercy to all, especially those most in need of it, as an example to the community of believers and to the world. This is the preaching and the living out of the gospel. This is not a one-time response to sin, but an active commitment not to sin, to resist the evil and injustices we have committed before, and not to return to our old ways, alone or with others. Like the asking of the question, do you love me? over and over again, and the command to feed and tend and feed the sheep, over and over again, we are to be known as those who forgive and forgive and forgive, over and over and over again. It is the refrain, the music of our lives.

But there is a third gift that accompanies forgiveness and reconciliation—it is atonement. The word can be broken up to read "at-one-ment." It is the way we bring all the community back together again, with one heart, one mind, one body in Christ. It is the hard work of undoing, redeeming what was done, sharing in the pain of what tore things and people apart. For Peter it is Jesus' words about his dying, his finally giving glory to God, and staying true in the face of persecution and suffering, facing the cross he once turned and ran away from. But Peter's atoning reveals again how unworthy he still is to die the way his beloved Lord died—he'll be led to crucifixion, but he will be crucified upside down, paradoxically righting the wrong and righting his piece of the world that he bent out of shape with his sin and unfaithfulness.

In the early church, this forgiveness, reconciliation, and atonement that became the sacrament of reconciliation were aptly named second baptism. It was a starting over, a new beginning, and when it was first practiced, it was only for three major sins that ate at the foundation of the whole church, where the communities were small, intimate, and what anyone did had tremendous influence for good or evil on all the members. It was enacted, as a long process, sometimes years in the making, for the sins of murder, giving up one's faith in public, and breaking one's marriage vows, when married as a Christian. And it was only done once in a lifetime, publicly celebrated in the liturgical seasons of the church, when the sinner, the penitent, was enrolled in the Order of Penitents. These sinners were welcomed back into the church when the community decided that they had changed, done restitution, penance, and atoned for the evil they had subjected the church to by their behaviors, or words, or failures. On Holy Thursday, they were drawn back into the net, for Eucharist before the Paschal mystery of the Body of Christ was lived through once again, and the catechumens became new Christians, born in the tomb and waters of the death and resurrection of Jesus.

This add-on ending of John's gospel is at its heart a story of mercy unbounded, of God's teaching us how to follow Jesus in his life, death, and resurrection after betrayal, after sin, and after missing once again the depth we are called to as the servants, the followers, and the friends of God in Jesus. We have known such mercy ourselves that we are schooled in it and are sent forth to bring the Good News to the torn heart of the world, practicing it publicly as witnesses and resisting evil with all our hearts and souls and minds and strength. We are to make the world and its inhabitants whole again, holy, redeeming every situation and bringing mercy's presence among those who are most in need of it. This is what we are initiated into at our baptisms, this is the practice of resurrection life, and we are fed the Body of the Risen Lord in community for the strength and courage to practice this and resist falling back into the dominant powers of the world. We preach mercy in forgiveness, reconciliation, restitution-penance, atonement, and always the peace of Christ. This is our calling, vocation, mission, and honor. And Jesus's last words to Peter are the first ones: follow me, follow me all the way to the cross and resurrection.

But this is John's gospel, and though it was crucial to draw Peter back into the net of Jesus, establishing him as the shepherd of the church and providing a model for daily practice of forgiveness and the Good News, the last word, the final story is about the Beloved Disciple, who has no actual authority in the church, but whose love is stronger than anything institutional, ordained, traditional, or learned. It ends with a moment of intimacy between Jesus and the Beloved Disciple.

> Peter turned and saw the disciple whom Jesus loved following them; he was the one who had reclined next to Jesus at the supper and had said, "Lord, who is it that is going to betray you?" When Peter saw him, he said to Jesus, "Lord, what about him?" Jesus said to him, "If it is my will that he remain until I come, what is that to you? Follow me!" So the rumor spread in the community that this disciple would not die. Yet Jesus did not say to him that he would not die, but, "If it is my will that he remain until I come, what is that to you?" (John 21:20–23)

Always this disciple follows after Jesus, never letting him out of his sight, and Peter is curious about him, about this other disciple's relationship in life and death to Jesus. But he is not given entrance into that relationship; he is exhorted instead to look to himself and begin once again with passion and intensity to "follow only Jesus." The language is steeped in Johannine theology. Jesus's words at the core of the gospel are, "I am the Resurrection and the Life. Those who believe in me, even though they die, will live, and everyone who lives and believes in me will never die. Do you believe this?" (John 11:25–26). What if the Beloved Disciple remains until Jesus comes—remains faithful, remains truthful, remains loving, remains near to the cross, remains believing and seeing? This is the image of the Community of the Beloved Disciples, who all remain true to life, resurrection life, and their baptism vows—this is the essence of what it means to be a beloved disciple. We are called to love, love unto death, willing to die daily so that others' faith might be strengthened. This is the focus and intent of John's gospel—to make beloved disciples. This is mirrored in the understanding of the early church. Listen to this, in the writings of Clement of Alexandria.

> If martyrdom consists in confessing God, then every person who conducts himself in purity in the knowledge of God and who obeys his commandments is a martyr in his life and in his words: for in whatever way his soul is separated from his body, he will pour out his faith like blood, both during his life and at the moment of his death. This is what the Lord says in the Gospel: "Whoever leaves his father, his mother, his brothers, his wife, or his lands, because of the Gospel and my name," such a man is blessed because he has realized in himself not only an ordinary martyrdom, but the true knowledge of martyrdom, in living and acting according to the rule of the Gospel, out of love of the Lord. For the true knowledge is to know the Name and to understand the Gospel. (*Prayers of the Martyrs,* p. 11)

For John there is no dying, only living in the death and resurrection of Jesus, remaining close to the heart of the Beloved Disciple and following as closely as you can in the Crucified and Risen Lord's shadow. The journey, the walk with Jesus is always deeper and deeper in, being seen more and more truly and responding in love. This other disciple now ends this last story and draws the gospel to a close.

> This is the disciple who is testifying to these things and has written them, and we know that his testimony is true. But there are also many other things that Jesus did; if every one of them were written down, I suppose that the world itself could not contain the books that would be written. (John 21:24–25)

The other disciple is wise, leaving the gospel open-ended. There are so many stories to tell that the world couldn't contain the books, because Jesus is alive, in the world, and the story is still being told, and all believers are called to give testimony that is true, with their own lives and words. The world cannot contain the Risen Lord, just as the tomb could not hold his body in death, and the world cannot contain that presence and power loose among his beloved disciples either. Persecution, exile, death, martyrdom, sin, evil, injustice, torture, betrayal, dissension in the community, failure to practice resurrection here will not stand against the Crucified and Risen One walking the world, going after his wandering disciples and friends, asking them over and over again, "Do you love me? Do you?" and reminding us again and again that God is peace, and we are to become God's living, breathing, merciful, and forgiving peace in the world and let loose the power of the Resurrection now. "Follow me! Through life, into death and the tomb, and out again, standing in resurrection light, more alive than you have ever been." And we all do that by feeding the lambs, tending and feeding the sheep, loving them as we would love the Risen Lord—it is the only way we love the Risen Lord. And the world needs to see us walking together again with the Risen Lord.

There is a short, marvelous Japanese poem to help us remember how we are to live.

> I fall down
> I get up
> I fall down
> All the while I keep dancing.

This is the dance of resurrection, of forgiveness, of reconciliation, of restitution, of atonement, of love. "Come, children, eat your meal. Come follow me." This is the Gospel of the Lord. Amen.

8

The Acts of the Apostles

Don't run. Don't hide. Don't blend back into the world!
We must give an account of our hope!

The Acts of the Apostles describe the birth and the coming of age of the believers in Jesus who became known as the Followers of the Way, then as Christians, and then as the church, the church at Rome, the church in Jerusalem, the church in Ephesus, and so on. It is the gospel of the Spirit of Jesus given as gift, their clothing and power from on high, sent from the Father upon the disciples of Jesus, as it was sent upon Jesus at his baptism. The Spirit is what birthed the church in fire and word and founded it in community that shared all in common, caring for the Body of Christ among them and in the world. It is the Spirit that held them together as they were persecuted, as they became distanced from the Jewish community and as they disagreed among themselves on how to do things and who was to do what in house, church, and in regards to outsiders, Gentiles and those who refused to believe what they were proclaiming with their public life in community, their worship, and their proclamation of the gospel.

It was the guiding Spirit that taught the leaders to appreciate the universality of God's goodness and salvation, even though these leaders often required remedial education in order to accept the fact that Romans and Greeks, as well as Jews, were following the lead of the Spirit into the church—ahead of the church's leadership to recognize what the Spirit was doing in the world. But above all, it was the Spirit that revealed the Risen Lord in their midst and called them to conversion, to courage, and to strengthen the churches in peace, holding them together, as though the Spirit is the glue that binds us together in love. With this in mind, there is an old story from Ladakh in the Himalayas that will lay the foundations for what the Spirit is doing in the churches, as we are

157

called to imitate in the Book of Acts. It is called in some versions "Happiness," but I call it "Communion."

Once upon a time, there was a kingdom that was hidden away among mountains in a lush valley. Crops were plentiful, its waters clear, and they say that the words "thief" and "beggar" did not exist. They lived in peace, in harmony, and without war, together. Now it may be hard to believe that such a place existed, but it did. And when a neighboring king heard about this place, he immediately sent one of his advisors to them to learn their secret of peace and prosperity. His own kingdom could use a good dose of whatever it was that held this kingdom so together.

So the ambassador arrived, was brought to the king, and stated his question, because, of course, it was the leader who would be able to answer it satisfactorily. What was the source of his kingdom's peace and plenty? The king was flattered and answered, "Why, of course, my kingdom's happiness springs from my leadership, my wisdom, and my vision as surely as a valley's harvest springs from the waters that irrigate the fields!" The ambassador was not pleased with this answer. It would not bode well to return to his king with this response.

But the king's councilors weren't all that pleased with the answer either. They were quick to point out what was missing in the king's reply. "Well if it weren't for our management and careful planning, where would we all be," sputtered the treasurer and his advisors. "As commander in chief of the armies, I bet the kingdom would be a lot less peaceful without my strategy for the protection of the borders and my courage against any invader," muttered a general. And the astrologers, magicians, and priests whispered back and forth among themselves, "If it weren't for our interpretations of signs in the heavens, events, and the rituals, the king wouldn't have a whit of wisdom, and the kingdom would be in chaos." Soon everyone was disgruntled, and when they went home it was all they talked about at the dinner table and at the gates and in the places where they met.

Soon the whole town was talking about the ambassador's questions, and the people did not agree with their leaders at all. "What about us? Do we count for anything? We're the ones who keep everything going, the building, the food, the shops, commerce and business and living." And the people, every man, woman, and child, agreed that it wasn't their leaders who made for peace and prosperity, not at all; it was all of them who were responsible for their kingdom's well-being. And they were right, but they kept up the complaining, grumbling against the leaders, whom they thought did not do much of anything that was useful, and arguing with each other, and soon there was little or no work being done in the kingdom. The fields were not tilled; the teachers ignored the students and off they went; wives refused to clean and cook, while their husbands spent more time talking than working. Everyone soon was on edge, fights broke out, and soon the happiness and peace, even the prosperity, of the kingdom were nowhere to be found.

A week later the king and his council met, looking bad, hungry, and annoyed. "Bad times." "Awful." "Terrible" "Where is that pesky ambassador? Look what he started with his fool question. If I could get my hands on him, I'd wring his neck before sending him back to his kingdom," said the general. The king was trying to restore order among his advisors. "Please, remember the head, or the neck, of an ambassador is sacred, as though it were that of the other king! Besides, he seems to have vanished," said the king. "Well that makes his question moot," said the astrologer and the priests. There was only silence after that remark. And they sat there, unhappy and agitated, thinking and disturbed.

Finally it was time for tea, and the serving girl arrived, served her tea, and looked at them oddly. And instead of following custom, tiptoeing in and out, she stood on the threshold and spoke, rather boldly. "When the mighty ones lose their way, sometimes a shepherd can find it. And right now we humble folks believe you should go see the Old Man of the Forest and ask for his advice! You need it." They were troubled, and for once there was no sense that she spoke out of place. The king decided immediately: tomorrow at daybreak, be here and we will go see this shepherd.

Now no one remembered the shepherd's name, or how old he was, or where he had come from, but he'd been around for so long that everyone, young and old, knew him and trusted him. He had a radiant face and shining eyes. He was frail of figure, but strong, listened to anyone and exuded insight and protection, like the stars above did on clear nights. The next morning he was standing outside his hut and waiting to receive the king and his royal visitors. He heard them out and then instructed them that they were to follow him on foot, leaving their horses and servants behind. Off they went into the forest. Within minutes the path nearly disappeared, and they were stumbling over vines, falling over downed tree trunks, and getting caught in creepers and spider webs. The sun disappeared, and there was an odd twilight among the trees. Strange noises were all around them. And it grew hot and they grew sweaty. They fell over boulders, fell into streams, slid down embankments and tried to keep up with the old shepherd. If they could have turned back they would have, but they were lost, and the shepherd ignored groans, complaints, sighs, and just followed some invisible path he seemed to know by heart.

Finally, they arrived in a clearing, all of them sopping wet, covered in mud and stickers and not happy. But oh! What was right in front of them was a giant tree, towering above them, casting a great shadow. The sun shone through it, and there were all sorts of leaves, fruits, blossoms, on it. They'd never seen anything like it before. And even more strange to behold was this pyramid of creatures that seemed to live in its long shadow. At the bottom was a magnificent elephant, and on top of it was a monkey, and on top of that was a rabbit and still on top of that was a tiny little bird, and they were all picking fruit and blossoms off the tree and sharing what they could reach and take with the others.

The shepherd greeted them and sat down on the grass near the pyramid and gestured to his visitors to follow suit. And berries and fruit were passed down to them to slake their thirst, which were delicious, unlike anything they'd ever tasted before. "Now," he said, "listen and I will tell you a story. Years ago, these four who look so friendly and get along so well came to me, and they were all furious and about to go to war with each other. It was when this tree was first discovered and just beginning to bear fruit. Every one of them was angry and yelling at the others, 'It's my tree. I found it. They're all thieves. There will not be enough. Besides, it's mine. And the tree isn't giving as much as it used to.'

I asked each of them why they thought it was their tree and got these answers.

'Because I watered it, whenever the rains were late,' bellowed the elephant.

'I kept watch over it so no other animal would knock it down when it was still a sapling and needed to be protected,' screeched the monkey.

'I pulled out the weeds and brush growing around it that was making it hard to grow when it was little,' piped up the rabbit.

'No, it's mine because I was the one who planted the seed in the first place. I brought it from far away on an island,' chirped the bird. 'And I only want to have a little bit of its fruit.'

When the others heard the bird, they were a bit ashamed of themselves. Nobody remembers who had the idea for the pyramid, but they climbed on each other, with the bird at the very top and apologized to the tree, telling it that they all loved it, and needed it, and would be careful of it. They became one heart. And the tree, surprised to see the four united, began to blossom, give fruit, and shed a perfume that was enchanting. Its leaves murmured and the wind carried the scent to every corner of the kingdom."

"Oh," said the king, "and the peace and prosperity, the friendship and the happiness spreads from here out into my kingdom." The astrologer spoke up and said, "I guess that harmony will return when everyone gets a chance to see this and know really where their peace comes from." The treasurer spoke up, "We'll have to build a road and set up places along the way for people to rest and get something to eat, or a place to stay for those who come from far." "And," chimed in the general, "I'll position my men as guards to protect the tree and the travelers and make sure that no one steals anything and that no one decides to come from outside the kingdom and take it for themselves."

The shepherd looked at them in disbelief. "No! Crowds would come, and the forest would be destroyed, and the grass made into mud and then, what, you'd put a fence, made out of gold with your crest on it to protect the tree and its friends?" They all fell into an awkwardly long silence then. The king finally spoke up. "If I hadn't seen this for myself, I wouldn't have believed it, so how can I expect my people to believe it without seeing it?" "There are other things you could do," said the old shepherd. "You could paint pictures of it. Better yet, you could tell its story and have people take the story to the far ends of the kingdom and even past your borders. And you could invite people to act the story out, celebrate the tree on certain days, and vie with one another on how it would look in their villages." And so it was passed on, told and sung of, and taken into the whole world.

But that was a long, long time ago and there aren't a lot of storytellers anymore, and sadly there aren't any kingdoms that live like that anymore. Almost nobody even remembers this story, but now you do. And you know that stories and memories have power, stronger than any king, any astrologer, any general, any treasurer. And the tree is still there; in fact, the storytellers used to end the tale with these words: "The tree lies hidden in your kingdom and the tree's friends still share its fruits, its blossoms, and its company, and the scent is found wherever all is shared in common."

This story from a Himalayan kingdom, a children's story, has much in common with the Acts of the Apostles, its major difference being the tree is the cross and life, and its friends are known as the friends of God, and our story is a reality still in the kingdoms of the world today. However, in every age, the church and its believers must be born again in the power of the Spirit and learn to make their own way in history, uniquely developing new fruit, blossoms, and structures so that the scent and reality of peace with justice is known by all, even if they do not realize its source. So during the entire fifty days of the Easter season, practically every first reading in the lectionary is from the Book of the Acts of the Apostles. This is the time of the early Church, and we are shown vignettes from its life, its prayer and work, its liturgy and quarrels, its failures, its astounding outreach as the Spirit adds to its numbers, its members' imprisonment and beatings and their words as they stand up for what they believe. This is the story of the Body of Christ, crucified and risen and living in the world with them still. There is no body in the tomb—this is the silent sounding proclamation of the Resurrection Gospels. And the reason there is no body is that the Risen Lord has ascended into heaven, but his body remains here with us in his Spirit that gave birth to his community, in the Word, the breaking of the bread—the Eucharist—in the poor, in those persecuted for the sake of the gospel and in marvelous things to behold, the first being the spread of the gospel out into the world.

It is Luke who is the author of Acts, and the beginning stitches together his gospel with this account of the early church that is the Good News to those around them, disconcertingly so, yet full of passion and grace. The genius of Luke as he puts these pieces together to form a single garment to be read in tandem is simple, deliberate, and ingenious. He writes in the opening of Acts:

> In the first book, Theophilius, I wrote about all that Jesus did and taught from the beginning until the day when he was taken up to heaven, after giving instructions through the Holy Spirit to the apostles whom he had chosen. After his suffering he presented himself alive to them by many convincing proofs, appearing to them during forty days and speaking about the kingdom of God. While staying with them, he ordered them not to leave Jerusalem, but to wait there for the promise of the Father. "This," he said, "is what you have heard from me; for John baptized with water, but you will be baptized with the Holy Spirit not many days from now." (Acts 1:1–5)

So Luke begins Acts with a wide-sweeping summary of his own gospel, sliding immediately into what happened after Jesus's ascension, when the disciples stayed in Jerusalem to await the coming of the Spirit of God upon them—their baptism with the Holy Spirit. This, called Pentecost ("fifty days"), is the birthday of the church and the baptism and confirmation of the disciples, followers and friends of Jesus. The coming of the Spirit in wind, fire, tongues, and gifts of the Spirit, the first being courage to boldly proclaim the gospel, is presented as the catalyst, the seed sown that became the church. So Acts both describes this newly born and often wiggling and squirming community in its ways of living and worshipping and provides sermons that collected the growing understanding of Jesus Christ risen from the dead, his gospel and relationship with God his Father, and the experience of how this Spirit of Jesus worked among them, pushing them out into the world. There is no body in the tomb—the body is alive and breathing, proclaiming, praying, working, and suffering in the world. This body is the extension of the Kingdom of God, the believing community that will become the church, the Body of the Risen Lord.

Raymond Brown describes Luke's genius in putting these two books together, so that one builds on the other and their ideas and meaning go back and forth, both giving us a glimpse of Luke's community and a history of the beginnings of the church. This is how book one describes the gospel, what Jesus did in the world, and how in book two, Luke describes what the Spirit of Jesus was doing in the world, as model and example of what we, followers today, are to be doing in the world, baptized into this same Spirit, making the gospel come true in our lives.

> Most of us are familiar with the imagery at the beginning of Acts (1:3, 9–12) where Jesus ascends into heaven from the Mount of Olives 40 days

after the Resurrection. Yet at the very end of the Gospel (24:50–51) Luke has him ascend into heaven from the same region on Easter Sunday night.

In this "double exposure," we see Luke's theological perceptivity. In one sense (dramatically portrayed in the Gospel) *Jesus' return to God was the end of his earthly career*, a career beginning and ending in Jerusalem and thus symbolically lived within the confines of Judaism. In another sense (dramatically portrayed in Acts) *Jesus' return to God begins the life of the Church* that starts in Jerusalem (Judaism) and extends to Rome (the Gentile world). (p. 15)

From the fourth century, the Easter season readings from Acts reintroduce the believing community to its roots and what should define us as community and church: the proclamation of the life, passion, cross, death, and resurrection of Jesus, the giving of the Spirit and our mission to bring the kingdom of peace with justice, the imperative of compassion and care of the poor, and the welcome of the stranger and the outcast into the world first in our own living of the gospel as witnesses and then as mission to draw others into this community of the Risen Lord. Basically, Acts takes us in the first fifteen chapters with Peter and the council in Jerusalem, and the community's movement out in mission through the last fifteen chapters with Paul's missionary journeys that lead him to Rome, where he dies (around 60 A.D.). It is not so much a history book as a primer in how to be Church, how to live as a believing community that is attentive to the workings of the Spirit in its members, in the world, in new believers, and in experiences and situations that are new, troubling, painful, and demanding. And core to this growth and expansion is how to remain together in the Spirit, one in heart, with care for the poor, one in mind and strength, with shared resources, one in body through the Scriptures and building up of the communities, and one in spirit, with true worship, in prayer and the Eucharist. This is the story of how the followers of Jesus and the kingdom of his Father grew in the gift of the Spirit and became church that learned, in fits and starts, dissension and bending to the will of God, to stand up for what they proclaimed, to stand behind the Word of God, the cross and resurrection and to stand with the Crucified One in his poor and suffering body in the world. And so it is our story, to be read among us as checklist, as examination of conscience, as investigation of actual priorities in our communities and as exhortation to remind us of the core of our lives as church. There are a number of descriptions of what we are to look like early in the text. These are the blueprints, the foundational bases essential to being church in the Spirit of Jesus. They are usually found in the text after a major sermon or preaching where we are told that the Spirit added to their number so that we know how to live the gospel, as well as preach it. The first comes immediately after Peter's sermon on the day of Pentecost. The reaction begins mixed as Peter begins to speak: "All were amazed and perplexed, saying to one another, 'What does this mean?' But others sneered and said, 'They are filled with new wine'" (Acts 2:12–13). But the reaction shifts dramatically after they have heard the Word of the Lord in the power of the Spirit, in Peter's impassioned and inspired preaching.

> So those who welcomed his message were baptized, and that day about three thousand persons were added. They devoted themselves to the apostles' teaching and fellowship, to the breaking of the bread and the prayers.
>
> Awe came upon everyone because many wonders and signs were being done by the apostles. All who believed were together and had all things in common; they would sell their possessions and goods and distribute the proceeds to all, as any had need. Day by day, as they spent much time together in the temple, they broke bread at home and ate their food with glad and generous hearts, praising God and having the good will of all the people. And day by day the Lord added to their number those who were being saved. (Acts 2:41–47)

It sounds like a honeymoon, and in some ways it is, because it is the first flush of enthusiasm with the Spirit moving them and stirring inside them the risen life of the Lord, animating them as his body in the world. But this is what the passion settled down into on a pragmatic basis, day to day, as well. And the Spirit was given to both preach the gospel and to make the community of believers into that good news themselves. There are, it seems, four elements that are essential to this community, which constituted the foundation of the new way of life for those baptized into its belief:

1. Devoting themselves to the apostles' teaching, which is the Lord's teaching. This is in effect our Gospels.
2. Fellowship, further described as "they had all things in common; selling their possessions and goods; distributing the proceeds to all, as any had need." This is the care of the Body of Christ. Just as all the gospel accounts of the Resurrection begin in some way with the need to tend to the broken and crucified dead body of the Lord with the corporal work of mercy of preparing the body for an honorable burial, so now this need to express the love believers have for the Crucified and Risen One is practiced with those crucified, in pain, suffering from lack and need—the poor. Whatever one wishes to do for God in Jesus the Crucified and Risen One, now one does for the poor. They are seen as one and the same.
3. Breaking the bread, both the ritual celebration of Eucharist, with bread and wine and the actual sharing of the meal of thanksgiving and transformation, sacrifice. This is described as eating their food together

with glad and generous hearts. It seems no one in this community ever went hungry, not for food as sustenance for life or for the bread of life in Eucharist and the Word of the Lord.

4. Devoting themselves to the prayers, still in the temple initially, the tradition of the Jewish covenant, psalms, prophets, readings, and daily liturgy.

In effect, the Spirit was making a new family, a new kinship group, not bound by blood and marriage ties, but bound by belief in the Risen Lord and desire to share the Good News, and bound by commitment to those they broke bread with and shared wine with, the Body and Blood of the Risen Christ. At the time of Jesus and still today in many cultures, to share bread, to eat meals with others is to share equality and commit to their welfare, as surely as your own. And as the Acts of the Apostles develops, this binding will be ritually celebrated in baptism and the coming of the Spirit that will proclaim the New Covenant of the Spirit of God with this people and their binding together as one family. In following Jesus, one's horizontal relationships revealed the purity of one's vertical relationship with God. The community made a virtue of universal poverty! But this is a poverty that the majority of believers had known before, but without the joy of shared resources according to need, and without the security of support and the devotion to one another that was, in belief, their devotion to the Crucified and Risen One in their midst.

This way of life continued in the face of arrest and persecution, along with the preaching of the Good News of the life, cross and death, and resurrection of Jesus. In chapter 4 the description of the community of the Risen Lord becomes more precise, astounding, and, for us today, a far, far cry from what most of us experience as church. And since the writings are for believers having difficulty living the gospel, calling us to conversion of heart and life, and questioning us on our faithfulness, these readings are essential to any notion of our spirituality, liturgy, or daily lives today.

> When they had prayed, the place in which they were gathered together was shaken; and they were all filled with the Holy Spirit and spoke the word of God with boldness.
>
> Now the whole group of those who believed were of one heart and soul, and no one claimed private ownership of any possessions, but everything they owned was held in common. With great power the apostles gave their testimony to the resurrection of the Lord Jesus, and great grace was upon them all. There was not a needy person among them, for as many as owned lands or houses sold them and brought the proceeds of what was sold. They laid it at the apostles' feet, and it was distributed to each as any had need. (Acts 4:31–35)

This description follows the release from jail of both Peter and John, after they have been threatened and warned strongly "not to speak or teach at all in the name of Jesus" (Acts 4:18). Persecution begins almost immediately in response to the preaching of the gospel. And it seems that what hastens the spread of the gospel is twofold, bound to this preaching: the experience of suffering, being persecuted for sharing the gospel with others, and the experience of sharing one's goods, lands, and resources with the poor. These soon become the characteristic marks of the newly empowered and impassioned believers.

This experience of persecution escalates with more arrests, floggings, and warnings, all to no avail. The response of those punished for preaching about Jesus is joy—an undeniable mark of the presence of the Spirit of God. As Peter and John are described, "as they left the council, they rejoiced that they were considered worthy to suffer dishonor for the sake of the name" (Acts 5:41). And along with the escalation of arrests and punishment, the community of the poor grows apace, and the need arises within the community for order and distribution to ensure that those most in need are taken care of first, and no one is excluded. Chapter 6 tells the story of how the Spirit imaginatively inspires the community to new ideas, ministries, works, and ways of dealing with any situation that might develop, especially as regards in-house demands. The description is simple, clear-cut, and pragmatic.

> Now during those days, when the disciples were increasing in number, the Hellenists complained against the Hebrews because their widows were being neglected in the daily distribution of food. And the twelve called together the whole community of the disciples, and said, "It is not right that we should neglect the word of God in order to wait on tables. Therefore, friends, select from among yourselves seven men of good standing, full of the Spirit and of wisdom, whom we may appoint to this task, while, we for our part, will devote ourselves to prayer and to serving the word. What they said pleased the whole community, and they chose Stephen, a man full of faith and the Holy Spirit, together with Philip, Prochorus, Nicanor, Timon, Parmenas, and Nicolaus, a proselyte of Antioch. They had these men stand before the apostles, who prayed and laid their hands on them. (Acts 6:1–6)

And thus the first deacons, those who wait on tables and serve the food to the poor, are born of need and of a community that now has two groups: Hebrews, or Jews, and Hellenists, Greeks who could have been Jews, but who lived apart from the city and temple. It seems those with power from the old tradition, the locals, are taking care of their own first, rather than looking at all as equals. The whole community chooses the seven, and all seven who become deacons happen to be Greeks who will balance the ministries within the growing community.

The two primary ministries and works of the church are preaching the Word, and so becoming vulnerable to persecution and caring for the poor, especially with food and basic necessities of clothing and shelter, becoming vulnerable to the sufferings of the world. This is the Body of Christ, crucified and risen among them: those persecuted for justice and truth's sake and the poor among them. And from this group will come the first newcomer who is deacon, preacher of the Good News and martyr, Stephen. Stephen will be set up for trial with false witnesses and killed, following in the pattern of Jesus. He is described almost like Jesus in Luke's Gospel: "Stephen, full of grace and power, did great wonders and signs among the people" (Acts 6:8). The response to his presence is that people argue with him, but "they could not withstand the wisdom and the Spirit with which he spoke." And in their frustration and anger, they instigate false witnesses against him and stir up the people, the elders, and scribes, and "they suddenly confronted him, seized him, and brought him before the council." He is falsely accused, and "all who sat in the council looked intently at him, and they saw that his face was like the face of an angel" (again echoing all in the synagogue looking intently at Jesus as he declares that the Spirit of the Lord is upon him to preach the Good News to the poor and care for the blind, the imprisoned, and the oppressed). The whole of chapter 7 is Stephen's witness and proclamation of who Jesus is, interpreting the writings beginning with Abraham, Isaac, Jacob, Moses, David, the temple and the prophets who always found the people resistant to the word of God. His long sermon culminates in including his hearers and accusers in the same long history of rejection and blindness. And this is what provokes the killing of Stephen.

"You stiff-necked people, uncircumcised in heart and ears, you are forever opposing the Holy Spirit, just as your ancestors used to do. Which of the prophets did your ancestors not persecute? They killed those who foretold the coming of the Righteous One, and now you have become his betrayers and murderers. You are the ones that received the law as ordained by angels, and yet you have not kept it."

When they heard these things, they became enraged and ground their teeth at Stephen. But filled with the Holy Spirit, he gazed into heaven and saw the glory of God and Jesus standing at the right hand of God. "Look," he said, "I see the heavens opened and the Son of Man standing at the right hand of God!" But they covered their ears, and with a loud shout all rushed together against him. Then they dragged him out of the city and began to stone him; and the witnesses laid their coats at the feet of a young man named Saul. While they were stoning Stephen, he prayed, "Lord Jesus, receive my spirit." Then he knelt down and cried out in a loud voice, "Lord, do not hold this sin against them." When he had said this, he died. And Saul approved of their killing him. (Acts 7:51–8:1)

Stephen intimates his master in life and in death. He proclaims the belief of the early community that is written in the last chapter of the gospel and the first of the Book of Acts, calling Jesus, the Son of Man, the Righteous One (meaning the Suffering Servant, the judge of the nations from Isaiah and Daniel), and he uses Jesus's own words from the gospel to hand over his spirit, and his last words are the proclamation of the Good News: forgive them. His death is the last word, and the young community has its first martyr, who was a deacon, one who cared for the poor in the name of the larger community and so preached the gospel with his work, his presence among the poor, and who attracted the attention of others, who found his compassion and inclusion of the poor with dignity and love offensive. His words follow upon his relationships and his company with the poor. Jesus, the Righteous One, is preached first in life, followed by words that can bring you to imitation of the Crucified One in death. And in the tradition of the Gospels, these accounts are written looking back; we find Saul, the Jewish rabbi who will become Paul the missionary to the Gentiles, present at his martyrdom. The church has from its foundation had the saying that "the blood of martyrs is the seed of Christians." Paul's conversion and baptism is seeded in Stephen's dying.

The church is obeying Jesus's words in the gospel: to be witnesses to his presence, his words, and his compassion in the world, and the world is responding in the same way, by rejecting the Word, threatened by this group of people who break with Jewish custom and laws, care for the poor, and never cease speaking of this Crucified and Risen Jesus, in spite of threats, arrests, floggings, humiliations, and persecution from their own neighbors. After the death of Stephen, the young church experiences its first great persecution in Jerusalem, scattering the apostles throughout the countryside. From here on in the text, the church will be pushed to stretch its vision of who it is out into the Gentile world, breaking with the Jewish religious bodies and people, becoming "the followers of the Way." In chapter 10, Peter, after baptizing Cornelius, a Roman centurion, and his household, realizes that the horizon of what it means to be the church has just crossed its first border, and now the gospel and the community are to go into the whole world. He preaches a sermon that becomes both a testimony and a summary of what the community now believes about Jesus the Risen Lord.

> Then Peter began to speak to them: "I truly understand that God shows no partiality, but in every nation anyone who fears him and does what is right is acceptable to him. You know the message he sent to the people of Israel, preaching peace by Jesus Christ—he is Lord of all. That message spread throughout Judea, beginning in Galilee after the baptism that John announced: how God anointed Jesus of Nazareth with the Holy Spirit and with power; how he went about doing good and healing all who were op-

pressed by the devil, for God was with him. We are witnesses to all that he did both in Judea and in Jerusalem. They put him to death by hanging him on a tree; but God raised him up on the third day and allowed him to appear, not to all the people but to us who were chosen by God as witnesses, and who ate and drank with him after he rose from the dead. He commanded us to preach to the people and to testify that he is the one ordained by God as the judge of the living and the dead. All the prophets testify about him that everyone who believes in him receives forgiveness of sins through his name." (Acts 10:34–43)

This is, in reality, Peter's last will and testament, the last great sermon he preaches in Acts. In the tradition of the Easter accounts, we are told that "While Peter was still speaking, the Holy Spirit fell upon all who heard the word." The Jewish circumcised believers are stunned to find out that Spirit doesn't discriminate according to old Jewish law, but comes as gift to the Gentiles as well. This is a shift of cataclysmic proportions in the community that will become an entity born of the Spirit no longer tied or connected to the Jewish religious institutions or practice. Peter cries out, "Can anyone withhold the water for baptizing these people who have received the Holy Spirit just as we have?" (Acts 10:44–47). So he ordered them to be baptized in the name of Jesus Christ. It seems in the early church that the sacraments of initiation weren't as ritualized as they are now—the gift of the Spirit, confirmation, could be experienced before baptism. But all of the sacraments, in fact, only make public in rite and word what is already a reality in persons and communities. The Spirit takes the lead and the church follows. Peter will report what has happened exuberantly to the church in Jerusalem, and then James the brother of John is killed by Herod, and Peter is imprisoned. When Peter is released, led out by an angel, he goes to the home of Mary, the mother of John Mark (one of the witnesses to the empty tomb in Mark's account) (Acts 11:12). The first chapter of the church has been told, and from here on the story shifts to Paul (converted in chapter 9), his rise as preacher, prophet, and missionary to the Gentiles, and how the base of power shifts from the poor church in Jerusalem to the church in Rome, which will become the model for the community as it grows throughout the Greek and Roman cultures, languages, lands, and people.

Paul will be converted, and as a Jewish rabbi begin almost immediately to preach, but the disciples in Jerusalem are wary of him and their all-too-close memories of his stint as the one who hunted them down, had them arrested in the synagogues, reported them to authorities, who then flogged and tortured believers wherever he could find them. Many of the disciples do not believe in his conversion, and Barnabas stands up for him so that they can hear his story and preaching, but his presence causes dissension and violence. He retreats to

Tarsus, and it will be perhaps as many as seven years before Paul once again begins to preach and is sent on his missionary journeys. In the meantime, we are told that "the church throughout Judea, Galilee, and Samaria had peace and was built up. Living in the fear of the Lord and in the comfort of the Holy Spirit, it increased in number. And after the council in Jerusalem welcoming Gentiles into the believing community, Barnabas goes and gets Paul in Tarsus and brings him to Antioch, where they work for a year, and it is here that the community acquires its new name, Christians (Acts 11:26).

In chapter 13 Barnabas and Paul are commissioned by the church in Antioch, in obedience to the Spirit that has inspired those praying to know that they have a work to which God has called them. They learned this while worshipping and fasting together. And when they are finished, they lay hands on them and send them off. The rest of the Book of the Acts is primarily the travels of Paul and Barnabas, who separates from him over whether or not John Mark should accompany them, and then Paul and Silas, who travel through Syria and Cilicia strengthening the churches (Acts 15:36–41). This split or bridge in the missionaries reveals how human they were and how personal their struggles were while they were also learning to reach beyond their own communities. Soon after, Timothy, whose mother is Jewish and father is Greek, joins Paul and Silas and the litany of their journeys, jailing, shipwrecks, persecutions, being run out of towns, and their conversions, like Lydia, whose home was in Philippi.

Chapters 16 through 28, the end of Acts, read like a travelogue: Paul in prison, Paul in Thessalonica, Paul in Beroea, Paul in Athens, Paul in Corinth, back to Antioch, Paul in Ephesus, riot in Ephesus, Paul in Macedonia and Greece, Paul saying goodbye to Troas, and Paul's journey to Jerusalem, where he is arrested (Acts 21). In the course of Paul's defense, it becomes known that he is a Roman citizen (Acts 24), and he is sent to the governor Felix and is held in custody for two years in Caesarea. Paul appeals to the emperor through King Agrippa and is sent to Rome. After a shipwreck on Malta, he arrives in Rome and lives by himself with a guard. He gathers the local leaders of the Jewish community together, telling them of his background as a Jew and his preaching to the Gentiles and preaches to them over a period of two years. Some believe; many others do not, refusing to listen to him. The last words of Paul in Acts describe what has happened in those ensuing years between 35 and 60 A.D.: the church, the believers of Jesus, the Christians broke from the Jewish community, and the parting, the severing, is not peace filled or promising. Paul's last words are harsh and accusatory.

> So they disagreed with each other; and as they were leaving, Paul made one further statement: "The Holy Spirit was right in saying to your ancestors through the prophet Isaiah,

'Go to this people and say,
You will indeed listen, but never understand,
And you will indeed look, but never perceive.
For this people's heart has grown dull,
And their ears are hard of hearing,
And they have shut their eyes;
So that they might not look with their eyes,
And listen with their ears,
And understand with their heart and turn—
And I would heal them.'
Let it be known to you then that this salvation of God has been sent to
the Gentiles; they will listen." (Acts 28:25–28)

Paul separates himself from the Jewish community, as a Christian, yet relies on his Roman citizenship to protect him from being killed by them. When he is martyred, it is by beheading, which was reserved as a right for Roman citizenship. And the parting words we have in Acts reveal stubbornness on the part of those who refused to believe his preaching (thus reminding us that preaching and proselytizing alone are not enough to convince anyone of belief in Jesus the Crucified and Risen Lord) and stubbornness on the part of Paul himself, who was both an apostle and missionary to the Gentiles, and yet, did not often (as reported in the Acts) discern with his communities how to live with others who were not becoming believers. This is the story of the spread of the early church throughout the Roman Empire and through Greek culture, but what is not written also reveals that the seeds of hostility and separation that have marked Christianity's rise in the West and caused scandal, misery, and the persecution of the Jewish people are still with us in regard to the Jewish religion.

Paul and Peter both are martyred in Rome around 60 A.D., and the church begins a new age of growth and persecution. These two individuals, Peter and Paul, have become legendary figures that affected the image of what church is in the two thousand years that have transpired since their lives and deaths. Each had massive gifts and equally massive weaknesses. Each sought to obey the word and the will of the Spirit in his time, among his people, as history engaged him and reacted to his belief and his living out of the gospel. Each had a remarkable and lasting effect on his community and the church that has evolved into the Roman Catholic Church today. But each must be seen in retrospect and in relation to the gospel and the person of Jesus Christ, crucified and risen from the dead. It is not individuals that should characterize what church is today, but communities, as it was in the beginning of the Spirit's work in the disciples of Jesus. The descriptions of the early church are what is core to being church, not what individuals do. The early church, like Jesus's own followers, was known by the company its members kept and how they treated one another and how they lived in their history, culture. and world. Pheme Perkins, in notes for *The Catholic Study Bible* (New York: Oxford University Press), writes about how these disciples acted and what marked them as believers in Jesus.

> The disciples do not simply preach about Jesus and the Kingdom of God, they also participate in the reversal of roles, status, and concerns that the coming of salvation brings. Some disciples renounce everything that ties them to the social structures of the world. Others use their material resources in ways quiet different than those around them. They do not seek exchanges between friends which would create obligations to reciprocate. They do not try to pile up wealth or to indulge themselves or their friends in consuming luxurious goods. Their lives are not dominated by concern for acquiring and preserving material things. They give away wealth to meet the needs of other people. Their only "anxiety" is acquiring heavenly treasure. All disciples are willing to follow Jesus' example of suffering service rather than demanding that others honor and serve them.

They remember the story of the rich man who is instructed to "sell all that you own and distribute the money to the poor, and you will have treasure in heaven; then come, follow me" (Luke 18:22). Or they have learned what in more contemporary writing was stated by Simone Weil: "The feeding of those that are hungry is a form of contemplation." Bread, money, resources, and wealth were all one with bread broken and shared, the company you kept and your intimacy with Jesus's Father in the Spirit's strength and compassion.

Early in the second century, the church is described in a small book called *The Didache.* Here is what it says about the church and how the Spirit lives in the church more than a hundred years after the Acts of the Apostles is written:

> The Spirit of boundless voluntary giving alive in the early church caused Christians to take on anything out of love to their brothers [and sisters] and all people. Everybody was expected to seek out street by street, the poorest dwellings of strangers, with the result that the Christians spent more money in the streets than the followers of other religions spent in the temples. Let the gift from your heart sweat in your hands until you find someone to give it to.

One of the lines in *The Didache* that sums up how to spot the Christian communities is startling and sobering when we read it today: "See how those Christians love one another, there are no poor among them." The Spirit led the believers in Jesus to care for the poor, which was more than 85 percent of the population at that time. (The statistics really haven't changed that much; the gap between the rich and the poor has just become a gulf. Americans are less than 5 percent of the world's population, using more than 85 percent of the world's resources, and contributing more than 75 percent of the world's pollution and refuse. American Catholics are now the richest religious group in the country, while they are last in what they give to the poor. This has been the state of affairs for over a decade, which leads us to the Spirit's question, is the American church Christian or following Jesus in the understanding of the gospel and the Acts, and how does this contradiction of life with the Scriptures and tradition affect what the church is preaching as the Word of God made flesh?

And we must remember that this same Spirit that founded and enlivened and shook the world of the first century after Christ is the same Spirit that is given to us in our baptisms and calls us to holiness and obedience to the Word and will of God in our history, calling the churches to reform, conversion, and new ways of practicing and proclaiming belief in the Resurrection. What we have become in two centuries is always to be seen, critiqued, converted, and transformed in that Spirit that is strongest in the Scriptures, among the poor and those who are victims of injustice, among prophets and peacemakers, and in the churches that are known by their love for the poor, the hungry, the oppressed and marginalized, the speaking of truth to power, and work for the Kingdom of God in justice, nonviolent resistance to evil, and the strengthening of peace, as the early Church proclaimed with its living witness. It was the practice and the life lived that drew people into the believing community as much, if not more than, the preaching with words. These early chapters in Acts (1–9) reveal how to make church, how to do church, and how to attend to the Spirit's will in the churches, allowing for diversity, new gifts, and ministries, according to needs, and how to deal with dissension and disagreements theologically and culturally. The presence of fasting, praying, and waiting on the Spirit precedes any new ministry, and reconciliation is a constant among the apostles, disciples, and churches.

But most important in Acts is the reality of the Body of Christ as the community and the necessity to preach the gospel in word at the same time it is preached in the believers who are publicly known by their care for the poor and the outcast, the widow, the orphan, the slave and stranger. Without these essentials, looked upon and used as we use our two eyes, two hands, two ears, two feet, our hearts and our mouths, the church disintegrates and becomes an organization, an institution without soul, a business corporation, an organized religious body, like any other among the three thousand or more denominations of Christians registered in the United States as churches. Christianity without community is at best an aberration. Community is the corrective to almost everything that causes the church to lose its priorities and its power for the transformation and its vocation to make the world holy.

What does community do for us as believers? An African sister in her traditional dress, which was tied in the back, with her hair piled up and wrapped gave me this image that has stayed with me, especially because I often wear my hair piled up and have worn a sari and other indigenous clothing that must be held together in the back. She said, "My community is a mirror [there were no actual mirrors among those she lived with often]. They tell me if I have done it right and when it is coming down or I am coming apart. Without them I would unravel and become disheveled and embarrassed. They are a necessity for my daily living and being clothed correctly." The images and connections to baptism, of course, are staggering. Communities within church are essential to our actually being Christians and knowing if we are living as witnesses to the Crucified and Risen Lord in our daily lives in the world. It is essential that we each belong to a small community and devote ourselves to the Scriptures and the tradition of the Kingdom of God among the poor, making peace with justice a visible beacon of hope for those in need around us, so that when we gather in our churches for the breaking of the bread we are seeking to be what we claim to be: the Body of Christ, making holy the world. The members of our community are our mirror, telling us whether or not we have done it right, providing challenge and calling us to conversion, and we return that favor to them in the wisdom and demand of the Spirit. This must be a weekly binding together of the Sunday Scriptures, prior to our going to Eucharist, that makes sure we are more than "church-going Sunday Catholics," but actually believers who witness boldly to the presence of the Crucified and Risen Lord among us.

A hundred years ago a man named Josiah Royce said, "My life means nothing, either theoretically or practically, unless I am a member of a community." This is absolutely true in regard to the church. And the work of the church is impossible to do without a community. John XXIII wrote:

> Peace will be an empty sounding word . . . unless it is founded on truth, built according to justice, vivified and integrated by charity, and put into practice in freedom.

This sentence could, in fact, be describing what church must be today if it is to be true to the Gospels and our beginnings in the Acts of the Apostles. These small communities bound in the Word of Scripture and the Eucharist must be tied equally strongly with other communities in sharing resources with those in need. This communal witness is what makes us church and what gives us clout when we stand up before society and government and the world to speak the truth of Jesus's words in the gospel and speak out morally and ethically in solidarity and communion with the crucified Christ, hungry, poor, living in misery, and shunted to the edges of life today, let alone the specific moral issues of life and death, from abortion, capital punishment, torture, and euthanasia on a personal level to the horrific global levels of terrorism, nuclear proliferation, the gulf between obscene wealth and grinding poverty for the majority of the world, nationalistic aggression, preemptive strikes, and war. All these issues are about death and life and impact human beings, whole nations, and the state of the Earth itself. These are the issues and realities that demand witness from believers in the Resurrection of Jesus and impassioned preaching of the God of Life, "ever-more abundant life for all" (John 10), not death-dealing power and greed that continues to crucify millions today as surely as the Romans lined their roads into Jerusalem with crosses to announce their sovereign authority, their claim to be God, and their power over life and death of all in their domain. This is witnessed to and resisted, and presented clearly in the words of Jack Nelson-Pallmeyer in a short quote from *Sojourners Magazine* (March/April 1996):

> Silence about moral behavior is feeding a mean politics which helps cover up an essential truth: In our society, poverty is ugly, dysfunctional, and crippling, and it is rooted in class divisions and a corporate-dominated system which distorts political and economic life. The huge and widening gap in income, wealth, political power, opportunity, and privilege which separates a prosperous minority from the vast majority of U.S. citizens is at the heart of the family and social crises gripping our nation.

And this is a society and nation that claims to be Christian! These words were published in 1996, almost seven years ago, a lifetime gone. Since then the same words could be used to describe the widening gulf between the United States most especially and a few other first-world nations and the vast majority of the rest of the world. This despairing and distorting and demeaning distance between the wealth of the few, often in Christian countries, and the glaring poverty of the many, without hope for even survival or a future, is at the root of the rise of violence, terrorism, suicide attacks, bombings, and the lashing out in destruction of many against those who have and do not share. John Paul II has reiterated that "security is impossible while there is such disparity among the nations of the world" (Vatican document to the United Nations, delivered by Cardinal Renato Martini, September 2001).

This is really not a new phenomenon, and there have been those who have exhorted us to attend to the suffering around us in every generation. We heard it from someone in our own country as recently as Jane Addams in this past century who wrote, "The good we secure for ourselves is precarious and uncertain . . . until it is secured for all of us and incorporated into our common life" (on a wall in a community center in Chicago).

As Christians who were originally steeped in the Jewish tradition and Torah, we must live the Word of God with integrity and use it for what it was intended when it was given to us. Rabbi Greenberg, preaching on this issue, said, "We're here to uphold the fundamentals of Torah . . . it is *hillul haShem* [a desecration of the holy name] when Torah is not used to relieve injustice, protect dignity, and redress grievances." And in today's society, as in the first century, to use the Scriptures in this way, they must be used together, first on ourselves in constant conversion and then together on behalf of the world that waits for our witness. In this same light, there is a simple Muslim story of a holy man who stood before God crying out incessantly, his heart breaking as he witnessed the pain, the suffering around him, and the callousness of those who passed by and did nothing. The world was just too unbearable and he prayed, "Lord God, look at what is going on everywhere! There is so much killing, so much pain, so much starvation, so much anguish and distress everywhere! Why don't you do something? Why don't you interfere to stop it, relieve it? Why don't you at least send someone like you did of old?" And they say, God answered him rather curtly, "I did! I sent you! I did! I've sent so many who claim to be mine! I did! I do!"

We believe that God sent his only beloved son, Jesus, who showed us how to do it, how to begin to stop the pain, and to begin by embracing the poor, by feeding them, and by living with one heart and body. This Jesus, the Suffering Servant, lived and died proclaiming love, justice, forgiveness, and communion and was raised from the dead. We who are baptized into him are to continue his work on earth, bringing his kingdom and creating places of refuge, of sanctuary, where the poor are honored as the Body of Christ and those who are persecuted by nations for standing up for the Good News of justice and peace, nonviolence, forgiveness of enemies, and compassion, for a way of the Spirit in the world, are to be his shining presence in the world. We do this primarily in communities that attract the attention of others, for both good that will draw believers into our midst and the negativity that will result in persecution for the sake of the Word. And we will be characterized by joy, considering it an honor to suffer with Jesus for the sake of the glory of God, who is the God of life for all. The Spirit is given to each community in every age for new, imaginative, life-giving and death-defying ways to resist evil nonviolently and to create new ways of being the presence of the Risen Lord in the world.

But we must remember who we are and how we live here, practicing resurrection now, not losing our way or being diverted from the command to be hope, forgiveness, and life for others. How we live is our first and most powerful preaching. Here's a story called "Night Flying" that someone told me just recently before I left on a long plane ride from Singapore to San Francisco.

> Once upon a time, in fact not very long ago, a plane was on a long stretch of a night flight across the Pacific Ocean. The plane had long ago settled down: dinner had been served, the movies were over, the cabin was dark, and there were only the sounds of sleep, snoring, breathing, occasional coughs, and the squirming of people too long in seats. Unbeknownst to everyone except a few in the cockpit, the plane's communication and nav-

igation systems failed and the instrument panel went dark. They were hours out from landfall. Even the automatic pilot was gone. Frantically, the flight engineer worked on basic systems. Nothing seemed to work. The pilots were trying not to panic, yet they were not sure even what direction they were hurtling in or what country they were flying toward at over 600 mph.

There were no landmarks, and finally they decided to tell the stewardesses and stewards if they could discreetly find anyone among the passengers who might have electronics skills. It seemed a long, long wait. Finally a passenger was brought to the cockpit by a stewardess. "What do you know?" the woman was asked. "What field of electronics are you an expert in?" She answered that she wasn't knowledgeable in any electronics field, but she was sure that she could be of help. They were irritated. "Then why are you here? If you do not know anything about electronics or computers get out of here!" one of them said. "Sir," she tried calming him, "tell me what your problem is and I'm sure I can help you." Her voice was quiet and sure. One of the others in the cockpit snapped back, "Can't you tell? Our instrumentation has stopped working. We do not even know where we are and here we are at least five hours out from land, stranded over an ocean in the middle of the night!"

She smiled and said, "Ah, I can help you. I have some knowledge that is failsafe. It never has failed in the past, and it won't fail us now." They looked at her in disbelief and mistrust. "What are you talking about?" "The heavens, my friends, are what I am talking about! The stars will be our guide. Show me your maps over the ocean and the ones for your destination. This I know like the back of my hand."

The woman, in her late fifties, was an astronomer. She sat beside the pilot for the rest of the trip and guided him into land. She sat with the map on her lap and her eyes glued to the skies. She kept them steady and calmed them with her skill at reading the heavens, her obvious love and familiarity with the night sky and the stars, and just at dawn, the plane landed on schedule at its destination, with the majority of passengers utterly unaware of the drama of the night.

As Christians, we have a knowledge that never fails in the Scriptures, a star to steer home by, a constellation of communities, light in the darkness and the peace of the Risen Lord's Spirit, no matter what is going on around us or in the universe. We must remember, and then practice resurrection and make sure that our Acts, our book of the great things that the Spirit is doing in us, who are the followers of Jesus in this century and place, is being written truthfully, with hope, with clarity, and with compassion for those most in need. It is our time now to boldly proclaim and steadfastly, to joyfully share the presence of the Risen Lord in our surprising ways. Our lives and our souls depend on it; in fact our world and all the children of God depend on it.

9

Baptism: The Sacrament of Resurrection—Hymns, Prayers, and Rites

> No language about God will ever be fully adequate to the burning mystery which it signifies.
>
> —Elizabeth Johnston

*T*hroughout this book, while looking at the Resurrections accounts, the sacrament of baptism has been seen as integral to our understanding of the mystery of Jesus's and our own resurrections. Our resurrection begins in baptism, and Christian life is the practice of resurrection in the community of believers. We live resurrection now because we have died with Christ and risen to his own mysterious life in God. And this life "hidden with Christ in God" will know fulfillment at our deaths when we as individuals, all human beings, and history and earth are judged. And in the fullness of time all creation will know the presence of the Risen Lord and the completeness of the power of the Resurrection. This sacrament of baptism, and more specifically the Rite of Christian Initiation for Adults (RCIA), is the jumping-off place for our life as those called and chosen to live as believers and followers of the Risen Lord.

Our faith is predicated on this experience of resurrection at our baptisms, and all our lives are spent remembering and incorporating this event more completely and more deeply into our person, in our community and in church in the world. Peter writes to his community of this need, and calls his young believers to attention.

> Simeon Peter, a servant and apostle of Jesus Christ.
> To those who have received a faith as precious as ours through the righteousness of our God and Savior Jesus Christ.
> . . .
> Brothers and sisters, be all the more eager to confirm your call and election, for if you do this, you will never stumble. For in this way, entry into

the eternal kingdom of our Lord and Savior Jesus Christ will be richly provided for you.

Therefore I intend to keep on reminding you of these things, though you
know them already and are established in the truth that has come to you. I
think it right, as long as I am in this body, to refresh your memory, since I
know that my death will come soon, as indeed our Lord Jesus Christ has
made clear to me. And I will make every effort so that after my departure
you may be able at any time to recall these things. (2 Peter 1:1–2; 10–15)

Remembering, being reminded, recalling, revisiting our baptism, and knowing
again its power and mystery are essential to our living as those who have died
and risen with Christ. And since the majority of Catholics in the past hundred
years were baptized as children, and most often have no memory of the rites
of baptism and few childhood memories of confirmation and Eucharist separated from baptism, it is crucial for adult believers to experience this sacrament
of baptism within the larger community as it welcomes new believers during
the Easter vigil. This is when the church knows an intensity and concentration
on the mysteries that make new Christians. Vicarious experience, through solidarity and communion with newly baptized adults, is literally a lifeline to our
own baptisms and lifeblood for the survival of the Christian community and
church.

There is a Zen story that succinctly and forcefully shocks us into a realization of what baptism actually means for us.

A great Zen master commanded an initiate to sit by a stream until he heard
all that the water had to teach. He was to sit in the tradition of the Buddha
himself, faithful and enduring until enlightenment came to him. He sat
there for days and days, seeing, thinking, breathing in the water, the edges
where land and water and air met, watching, attentive, hearing it with his
eyes closed, trying to absorb everything that he could. Then after days of
this exercise, a small monkey dropped from the tree above him, chattering
away. Then, seeing the clear stream of water glinting in the sunlight, the
monkey dropped even his bananas and chattering and jumped wildly into
the water! He splashed about, playing, throwing the water up in the air,
floating and diving under, flying out sputtering and wet to rest nearby on
the bank. The initiate sat stunned and then wept. Then, he returned to his
teacher to tell him what had happened. The master scolded him gently saying, "The monkey listened. You just saw and heard." Then, he looked at him
sadly and told him to return to the water and this time to imitate the monkey and plunge into the waters and let the waters actually teach him what
he needed to know.

In many languages, including Latin, to "listen" means to obey. The waters of baptism summon us to a way of life, but literally and figuratively

plunge us into the current of God inspiriting us with grace and the very life of God. With every newly baptized person, with every celebration of the Paschal mystery of Holy Week and Easter, with every renewal of our baptismal promises and being sprinkled again with the shower of Easter water, we are urged to plunge once again into the waters of life and to enter the stream of life and power that sources us and carries us along throughout our lives. Everything in our spiritual, liturgical, and ethical lives is sourced in this sacrament that initiates us into resurrection life and stands us with Jesus before the Father in the grace of the Spirit. Peter continues in his letter reminding his community and us.

> For we did not follow cleverly devised myths when we made known to you the power and coming of our Lord Jesus Christ, but we had been eyewitnesses of his majesty. For he received honor and glory from God the Father when that voice was conveyed to him by the Majestic Glory, saying, "This is my Son, my Beloved, with whom I am well pleased." We ourselves heard this voice come from heaven, while we were with him on the holy mountain.
>
> So we have the prophetic message more fully confirmed. You will do well to be attentive to this as to a lamp shining in a dark place, until the day dawns and the morning star rises in your hearts. (2 Peter 1:16–19)

What has been begun in us must continue to thrive, and we must learn to express ever more clearly and truthfully what it is we have been called to live out as witnesses to others. And basically what we have been called to is a life that witnesses with others to the gospel and passing on that belief to others, often in a world that resists, or ignores the Word of God that has been born in us. Paul writes to Timothy, who received his impetus to believe and live as a missionary, accompanying Paul, from his grandmother Lois and his mother Eunice, encouraging him to hold fast and endure with gracefulness what they have passed on to him as their best gift.

> You then, my child, be strong in the grace that is in Christ Jesus; and what you have heard from me through many witnesses entrust to faithful people who will be able to teach others as well.
>
> . . .
>
> Remember Jesus Christ, raised from the dead, a descendant of David—that is my gospel, for which I suffer hardship, even to the point of being chained like a criminal. But the word of God is not chained. Therefore I endure everything for the sake of the elect, so that they may also obtain the salvation that is in Christ Jesus, with eternal glory. The saying is sure:
>   If we have died with him, we will also live with him;
>   if we endure, we will also reign with him;

if we deny him, he will also deny us;
if we are faithless, he remains faithful—for he cannot deny himself.
(2 Timothy 2:1–2; 8–13)

We, the church, are God's "elect," chosen to witness to the presence of God in the world, witnesses to the Father's raising of his first-born beloved Son from the dead in the power of the Spirit. We stand firmly rooted in this hope, shared and experienced, and in the future faith of how God works in history through us. The liturgical cycle of the Paschal mystery, the lectionary readings, ethical choices, and the lived spirituality of care for the poor, holding all in common, while seeking to manifest the kingdom of justice with peace for all, is our calling, our honor, and our responsibility. We, as Church, are a visible and tangible sacrament of the presence of the Risen Lord summoning the world to a radical redefinition of what it means to be human and to live together "in the freedom of the children of God," as our first baptismal promise proudly and steadfastly proclaims with joy. Our baptisms begin our immersion into Christ's mystery and our "putting on Christ" becoming words of truthfulness and clarity for all to hear and read. It is a long apprenticeship, a lifelong conversion, that transfigures us in gracefulness. Peter tells his small community again and again what sources them and how they are to present themselves before others.

> So we have the prophetic message more fully confirmed. You will do well to be attentive to this as to a lamp shining in a dark place, until the day dawns and the morning star rises in your hearts. (2 Peter 1:19)

The ritual of baptism brings us to a point, a place of convergence with the Holy Spirit that will reorient all of our lives forever. Even as the ritual itself begins, the opening prayer reminds the whole community that it is God "who has called them and brought them to his hour. May he grant them the riches of his light and strength to follow Christ with courageous hearts and to profess the faith of the church. May he give them the new life of the Holy Spirit, the Spirit whom we are about to ask to come down upon this water" (#213. "Christian Initiation of Adults." *The Rites.* New York: Pueblo Publishers. Co., 1975, p. 95).

These waters are a wellspring of life, and they are the tomb of the buried and risen Christ. This prayer over the waters (#215) tells the history of water from creation, through the flood and the waters of the Red Sea to the Jordan River, ending with the blood and water that flowed from Christ's own side at his death on the cross. The last line of the blessing brings it to completion:

> We ask you, Father, with your Son to send the Holy Spirit upon the water of this font. May all who are buried with Christ in the death of baptism rise also with him to newness of life. We ask this through Christ our Lord. Amen.

The celebrant touches the water as it is blessed, and the font is meant to be deep enough to stand in, to be immersed in, to actually go down into the waters, as one would enter a tomb, but this is a rarity in actuality, rather than the norm. Perhaps some words that describe the power of this symbol, water and its meaning, can take us deeply into what is happening to our bodies and souls in a way that we can also sense and touch again. This is from Nikos Kazantzakis.

> I undressed, dove into the sea, and swam. I felt the sacrament of baptism in all its deathless simplicity on that day, understood why so many religions consider water and the bath, in other words, baptism, the indispensable, pre-supposed condition of initiation before a convert begins new life. The water's coolness penetrates to the marrow of the bones, to the very pith; it finds the soul, and thus, seeing the water, beats its wings happily like a young sea gull, washes itself, rejoices, and is refreshed. The simple everyday water is transubstantiated; it becomes the water of eternal life and renews the person. When the convert emerges from the water, the world seems changed. The world has not changed, it is always wonderful and horrible, iniquitous and filled with beauty. But now, after baptism, the eyes that see the world have changed. (quoted in *A Sourcebook About Liturgy.* Liturgy Training Publications, p. 3)

This is the first step and it will serve as the pattern for all life. Teilhard de Chardin picks up the image and extends it infinitely outward and inward when he writes, "Bathe yourself in the ocean of matter; plunge into where it is deepest and most violent; struggle in its currents and drink of its waters. For it cradled you long ago in your preconscious existence; and it is that ocean that will raise you up to God." Birth from the womb, birth from the waters, birth into the world and into the fullness of God: this is baptism, the sacrament of our initiation into the resurrection of Jesus and our first taste of the waters of the Spirit.

Each of us experiences this singularly, though we celebrate it communally, sharing it as our common source. Our entire person, our time, our bodies, our possibilities, relationships and being now belong utterly to God, and this source is as vast and deep as the oceans of the world. This awareness, this actuality is the living out of our lives from this moment forward. Karl Rahner wrote late in his life of what this means in his book *Encounters with Silence.*

> What else is there that I can tell You about Yourself, except that You are the One without whom I cannot exist, the Eternal God from whom alone, I, a creature of time, can draw the strength to live, the Infinity who gives meaning to finiteness? And when I tell You all this, then I have given myself my true name, the name I ever repeat when I pray in David's Psalter, "Tuus sum

ego" [I am yours]. I am the one who belongs not to himself, but to you. I know no more than this about myself, nor about You, O God of my life, Infinity of my finiteness.

This is the glory of our relationship with God, but it is "in Christ," and so we know a great deal of what it is to live in relation to the Holy One. This relationship, along with the gift of the presence of the Spirit seeded in our souls, is the first gift given to those who believe. We are given the same relationship with God the Father that Jesus knew and lived, and our initiation is an open door into that mysterious life, that intimacy and that communion, not only with God, but with all those who are one in Christ. Paul's letter to the Ephesians puts it succinctly.

> Blessed be the God and Father of our Lord Jesus Christ, who has blessed us in Christ with every spiritual blessing in the heavenly places, just as he chose us in Christ before the foundation of the world to be holy and blameless before him in love. He destined us for adoption as his children through Jesus Christ, according to the good pleasure of his will, to the praise of his glorious grace that he freely bestowed on us in the Beloved. In him we have redemption through his blood, the forgiveness of our trespasses, according to the riches of his grace that he lavished on us. With all wisdom and insight he has made known to us the mystery of his will, according to his good pleasure that he set forth in Christ, as a plan for the fullness of time, to gather up all things in him, things in heaven and on earth. In Christ we have also obtained an inheritance, having been destined according to the purpose of him who accomplishes all things according to his counsel and will, so that we, who were the first to set our hope on Christ, might live for the praise of his glory. In him you also, when you had heard the word of truth, the gospel of your salvation, and had believed in him, were marked with the seal of the promised Holy Spirit; this is the pledge of our inheritance toward redemption as God's own people, to the praise of his glory. (Eph. 1:3–14)

It is a long, long paragraph, part prayer, part summation of what we believe, part exhortation to live up to our being called in Christ, and part wonder that we live now in this grace, this forgiving love that God the Father has lavished on us in Jesus and shared with us in the Spirit. Three times we are reminded that this is all about the work of God and that we now live to worship and give glory and praise to God by our lives, our very being in Christ. We are to be "words of truth," to "set our hope on Christ," to "believe in him," to remember that we have been "marked with the seal of the promised Holy Spirit," and that we are now "to be holy and blameless before him in love, as his adopted children." All this is a freely given gift and all that we need, of wisdom and insight, every spiritual blessing will be afforded us. This is our meaning, our pur-

pose, our life now. This is why our first baptismal vow reads, "Do you promise to live forever in the freedom of the children of God?"

And Paul tells us again the specifics of this vocation, this mission and gift
to those baptized in Christ.

> But now in Christ Jesus you who once were far off have been brought near
> by the blood of Christ. For he is our peace; in his flesh he has made both
> groups into one and has broken down the dividing wall, that is, the hostil-
> ity between us. He has abolished the law with its commandments and or-
> dinances, that he might create in himself one new humanity in place of the
> two, thus making peace, and might reconcile both groups to God in one
> body through the cross, thus putting to death that hostility through it. So he
> came and proclaimed peace to you who were far off and peace to those who
> were near; for through him both of us have access in one Spirit to the Fa-
> ther. So then you are no longer strangers and aliens, but you are citizens
> with the saints and also members of the household of God, built upon the
> foundation of the apostles and prophets, with Christ Jesus himself as the
> cornerstone. In him the whole structure is joined together and grows into
> a holy temple in the Lord; in whom you also are built together spiritually
> into a dwelling place for God. (Eph. 2:13–22)

Paul is speaking here specifically of Jews and Gentiles, but Christ Jesus
who is peace has reconciled all peoples of the world to God and to one another. This is our life: to make peace, and to work with Jesus so that "he might
create in himself one new humanity," to "break down the dividing wall, the
hostility between us and proclaim peace." Now it does not matter where we
are born, what nation we live in, for we are sojourners on the earth. In reality
we are citizens of the Kingdom of God, members of the household of God,
and we ourselves are being made into a dwelling place for God in the world.
We, the baptized, the community of disciples of Christ, the church are to be
spaces of hospitality, havens and refuges of peace, actively and nonviolently, under the shadow of the cross that is traced on our bodies and marked indelibly
on our souls to break down the walls of hostility and to draw all people together, declaring peace as the way to be human and community in one family
as the children of God as the way to live now in the world. This is our belief
and our life's work as those who believe in the resurrection of Jesus that has
given us access in one Spirit to the Father of all. We stand before our baptisms
and ever after repeating our vow: we promise to live forever in the freedom of
the children of God.

Baptism is a threshold, a doorway that once we cross over, once we pass
through, once we turn into, we can in a sense never turn back, though we continue to walk in and out, back and forth across that threshold, that gate into
glory, that doorway to grace, again and again, ritually and daily in our lives. The

word "thresh," such as in the word "threshing," is the work of using one's feet (and sometimes a rake or instrument) to separate out seeds and grains from husks and stems, dried straw, and chaff. The origins of the word are identical to the words "turn," "contour," "return," and "thread." And Gary Thorp writes in "Crossing the Threshold" that "today, threshold not only refers to a doorway or gate, but also means both a new beginning and a limitation" [*Tricycle* (Winter 2002): 20–21].

This threshold or doorway into baptism, into the tomb of the Risen Lord, is the entranceway into another life, a life larger than ourselves, a life in community, inside the Kingdom of God, and we are commanded to turn from our old way of living and turn into our life in Christ, to live with one foot in the world and one foot firmly planted in the soil of the gospel and the sacraments, in the church. There is much to leave behind and much that is given as a gift to those newly drawn into the waters and those who serve as their teachers, their godparents, and their family, bound together in word, the wood of the cross, and the bread and wine of Jesus. What we are to shun, to avoid, to leave behind and resist is worded in our next vow.

Our second promise or vow is ritually phrased in a number of ways: "Do you reject Satan and all his works and all his empty promises?" or "Do you reject the glamour of evil and refuse to be mastered by sin?" Perhaps the most simple and the clearest question is one that I have heard any number of times in South America and Southeast Asia: "Do you promise to reject sin and refuse to be mastered by any evil?" It is blunt and covers it all. While it may seem overwhelming, we are reminded that it is the Spirit that does this work in us and that we are children now of the Spirit that breathes and moves in us as it did in the prophets and saints before us and in Jesus Christ. Paul, again in Ephesians, is praying for his readers specifically, but it is a prayer for all those who seek to live lives that make the gospel a reality daily.

> For this reason I bow my knees before the Father, from whom every family in heaven and on earth takes its name. I pray that, according to the riches of his glory, he may grant that you may be strengthened in your inner being with power through his Spirit, and that Christ may dwell in your hearts through faith, as you are being rooted and grounded in love. I pray that you may have the power to comprehend, with all the saints, what is the breadth and length and height and depth, and to know the love of Christ that surpasses knowledge, so that you may be filled with all the fullness of God.
>
> Now to him who by the power at work within us is able to accomplish abundantly far more than all we can ask or imagine, to him be glory in the church and in Christ Jesus to all generations, forever and ever. Amen. (Eph. 3:14–21)

We are wondrously to be like God, to be like Jesus. In one of the prefaces for Ordinary Time (Seventh Sunday), we hear the amazing words, "May you see and love in us what you saw and loved in Jesus, your beloved Son." Staggering! Such high expectations! Impossible! But this is what baptism, what resurrection, is all about—it is impossible, unbelievable, that we, the children of God, born in grace and freedom in the death and resurrection of Jesus should live in the Spirit of the Risen Lord, bearing witness, as Jesus bore his cross, speaking the truth and proclaiming with our lives, our moral choices, our ethical decisions, our presence, our solidarity with others, that we belong first and foremost to God and are children of the kingdom of peace and justice and citizens of the household of God! What does this mean: that we promise to resist evil and refuse to be mastered by any sin?

I have on a number of occasions heard the following extended second baptismal promise during the adult rite of baptism at the Easter vigil and am told that it appears in the sacramentaries in modified forms of other countries. It is specific, acting both as a call to discipleship, modeling life as a brother and sister to Jesus, and as an examination of conscience for those long baptized and struggling to live in that freedom of the beloved children of God. There are ten calls to resistance that translate Christian values and virtues into a call to live a radical life of belief in Jesus Christ, crucified and risen from the dead.

Do you promise to resist evil and refuse to be mastered by the sin of
1. Abortion, the death penalty, euthanasia, war, pre-emptive attacks
2. Violence in any form, physical, verbal, psychological, religious
3. Selfishness, greed, materialism, consumerism, capitalism
4. Lying, dishonesty, cheating, slander, calumny
5. Nationalism
6. Racism
7. Any domestic or international policy that gives unfair advantage to your own country and that does not honor the common good as first priority (the majority most in need)
8. Nuclear weapons (threatening to use them, using them, retaliating with them, or continuing to stockpile them or create new ones)
9. The destruction of creation and lack of respect for the Earth and provident use of resources, sharing them with all others
10. Any philosophy, any economic or political system, any "ism" that betrays the gospel or is in opposition to it

In parish missions, retreats, and workshops, I use these as a call to examine our consciences, to look again at our baptismal commitment to the Crucified and Risen Lord as individuals and as witnesses to the world as church, the sacrament of the Risen Lord. Reactions are swift, diverse, loud, mixed, stunned. Some are reduced to silence, reflection, and others reject many, if not all, of them out of hand. Yet, upon examination and reflection, these are all reducible to life-and-death issues, the fullness of life or a choice for sin, evil, injustice, and death. As with any promise or vow, this vow is a call to live into the future, to live into something alternative to the existing structures, beliefs, and practices. This is living into the "fullness of God" as revealed in Jesus and his Word of Scripture. It is the jumping off place, the diving into the ocean of God's grace and oftentimes learning to swim against the tide, against the prevailing forces in the world, as Jesus himself and his followers lived. These are what we turn from, what we leave behind, while the last promise can turn us toward what we are called to enter and practice ever more deeply.

The third promise of our baptism or vow, as it is written in the ritual now (#217), reads, "Do you reject Satan, father of sin and prince of darkness?" The commentary on the rite says that "besides these three formulas, the Episcopal conference may adapt them further." All the rites are base structures that are to be pastorally adapted to the needs and the lived experiences of the community and those coming to baptism. The third vow or promise that I pass on to others, after having heard it used powerfully and gracefully, is this one: "Do you promise to live under no sign of power but the sign of the cross—in the name of the Father, the Son and the Holy Spirit, our God the Trinity?" It is clear, and, again, it draws us forth into a future faith, seeking to transform us individually and as a community into the Body of Christ in the world, living and seeking to be a sign of hope and witness to others of our faith in the Crucified and Risen One. And again, this last promise is fleshed out in specifics, this time in positive practices of virtue. There are eight practices or disciplines that can be seen as marks or characteristics of the life of Christians.

> Do you promise to live under the sign of the Cross and practice
> 1. Forgiveness, reconciliation, and no retaliation
> 2. Mercy and the practice of nonviolence; resist evil without doing harm
> 3. Love one author as I have loved you, lay down your life for others
> 4. The bearing of one another's burden
> 5. The bearing of your share of the burden of the gospel
> 6. Atonement for evil: your own, your collusion with others, that of the groups you belong to, and others' evil
> 7. Restitution and repair the world (*tikkum olam*)
> 8. The offering of your sufferings for the healing of the nations, giving the sacrifice of your life for the worship of God, with Jesus's own prayer summarized in the great Amen of the Eucharistic prayer

Seeing these exhortations and disciplines all together can be overwhelming, yet they are no more than the basics for believers, foundation stones for lifelong response to the Word of God. It becomes immediately apparent that it is near to impossible to consider doing these alone. The support, the call to accountability, the prayer and presence of a community are as essential as breathing is to the body. And yet this struggle, this call to gloriously reveal the presence of the Crucified and Risen Lord to those around us, has been the core of being Christian since our beginnings. Paul writes to his church, to the saints, to the Colossians another version of what we have above, one that is even more detailed:

> As God's chosen ones, holy and beloved, clothe yourselves with compassion, kindness, humility, meekness, and patience. Bear with one another and, if anyone has a complaint against another, forgive each other; just as the Lord has forgiven you, so you also must forgive. Above all, clothe yourselves with love, which binds everything together in perfect harmony. And let the peace of Christ rule in your hearts, to which indeed you were called in the one body. And be thankful. Let the word of Christ dwell in you richly; teach and admonish one another in all wisdom; and with gratitude in your hearts sing psalms, hymns, and spiritual songs to God. And whatever you do, in word or deed, do everything in the name of the Lord Jesus, giving thanks to God the Father through him. (Col. 3:12–17)

The early church struggled from the beginning to put into practice the words and the grace that were given to it (and to us) in the death and resurrection of Jesus and the shared gift of the Holy Spirit. Clement of Rome, a martyr in the first century, prays:

> Almighty God, Father of our Lord Jesus Christ, grant, we pray, that we might be grounded and settled in your truth by the coming of your Holy Spirit into our hearts. What we do not know, reveal to us; what is lacking within us, make complete, that which we do know, confirm in us; and keep us blameless in your service, through Jesus Christ, our Lord. (*Prayers of the Martyrs,* p. 30)

At our baptisms, after the immersion or pouring of water in the name of the Trinity, we are anointed, as priests, prophets, and kings, with the oil of salvation, so that we will always live as members of the Body of Christ, sharing everlasting life (#224). We are confirmed in our belief, in our faith, and strengthened. The prayer and explanation put clearly what this grace of the Holy Spirit is for in our lives.

> The promised strength of the Holy Spirit, which you are to receive, will make you more like Christ, and help you to be witnesses to his suffering, death, and resurrection. It will strengthen you to be active members of the Church and to build up the Body of Christ in faith and love. (#229)

This gifting and anointing sets us aside and marks us out as witnesses, as presences of the Risen Lord in the world, as members of the Body of Christ, crucified and risen in the world. We are sealed, held in this Spirit by this chrism that alters us qualitatively. It is grace seeping through us and saturating our bodies and souls. The prayer is familiar and so are the gifts that are given to us in full measure for what the church needs to be and do in the world.

> All-powerful God, Father of our Lord Jesus Christ, by water and the Holy Spirit you freed your sons and daughters from sin and gave them new life. Send your Holy Spirit upon them to be their Helper and Guide. Give them the spirit of wisdom and understanding, the spirit of right judgment and courage, the spirit of knowledge and reverence. Fill them with the spirit of wonder and awe in your presence. We ask this through Christ our Lord. Amen. (#230)

This isn't all for just us, as individual believers, or even as church, but we are baptized, christened, christed, and made disciples for the world and especially for those most in need, most desperate, most often because of suffering, and those who live on the edges and fringes of death in our society. We are meant to be hope, to be lifelines, to be shining lights in the shadows of evil and despair, to be stars to steer home by, to be havens of help and communities that are publicly known for being truth tellers, and protectors of those society sees as expendable. We are to make sure that no one forgets that they are the beloved children of God, brothers and sisters of Jesus, our water and blood relatives in the Spirit. Again, Clement of Rome in the first century was praying for the larger family of God, not only asking God to do what he requests, but reminding himself and his people that the way that God does all these things that must be done is through us—or not much gets done at all.

> Lord, we beseech you to help and defend us. Deliver the oppressed, pity the poor, uplift those who have fallen, be the portion of those in need, return to your care those who have gone astray, feed the hungry, strengthen the weak, and break the chains of the prisoners. May all peoples come to know that you only are God, that Jesus Christ is your child, and that we are your people and the sheep of your pasture. (*Prayers of the Martyrs,* p. 14)

The earth is in desperate need of us, the Body of Christ, the sheep of his pasture, the family of the Father, the citizens of the kingdom of peace and justice. And we must look at all the peoples of the earth as God sees them, treat them as God has treated us, and bring everyone back home by our welcome, our witness, and our work in the world. No easy task, but it is what has been entrusted to us by the commission of the Risen Lord: "As the Father has sent me, now I send you!" (John 20). The world is not as it appears to be. No one is what is just there as face value. Because of the resurrection, we are all shining, spirit filled, and graced. There are many who have tried to describe what the earth's children look like through the washed out and cleansed eyes of baptism, but perhaps Thomas Merton's description is the most quoted in the last generation. It calls us up short and asks us how we see, if indeed the waters of our baptism have given us the sight of faith, the eyes of God.

> In Louisville, at the corner of Fourth and Walnut, in the center of the shopping district, I was suddenly overwhelmed with the realization that I loved all those people, that they were mine and I theirs, that we could not be alien to one another even though we were total strangers. It was like waking from a dream of separateness, of spurious self-isolation in a special world, the world of renunciation and supposed holiness. . . . This sense of liberation from an illusory difference was such a relief and such a joy to me that I almost laughed out loud. . . . I have the immense joy of being a member of a race in which God became incarnate. . . . There is no way of telling people that they are all walking around shining like the sun.

As baptized Christians, as those buried in Christ and rising in the Spirit, we view all of life through another lens, another angle—the angle of the cross, the eye of God our loving Father, with the vision of the Spirit transfiguring and transforming us into the Body of Christ. Once we see, really see, who we are and who others are in Christ, we can only treat them with respect, with tender regard and the ultimate love that we would reserve for the Body of Christ. Baptism situates us in the world in such a way that we are more intensely concerned with the world because of being rooted in the Kingdom of God as well. This is demanding, freeing, and absorbing and puts us in a strange position at times with others in the world. Listen to these words about baptism as a political act.

> When we wonder as adults whether we are loved, we know that we belong to God. But we also belong to the world. We are baptized into solidarity with the world in Christ at the level of deepest danger. In that sense, baptism is always a precarious political act. Because we have been baptized, we are linked to the sufferings of the world for which Christ died. Because we have been baptized, our hospitality always has room for the weak and the vulnerable. (Herbert Anderson and Edward Foley. *Mighty Stories, Dangerous Rituals: Weaving Together the Human and the Divine.* p. 73)

Other ways of speaking of this deep connection between those baptized and the rest of the world are found in many contemporary writings. The rule of Taize reads, "Love the dispossessed, all those who, living amid human injustice, thirst after justice. Jesus had special concern for them. Have no fear of being disturbed by them." And Frederick Buechner writes in *Wishful Thinking: A Theological ABC,* "The place where God calls you to is the place where your deep gladness and the world's deep hunger meet" (p. 95).

Baptism plunges us into the death and resurrection of Jesus as surely as it plunges us into the deepest needs of the world. We live by the sign and power of the cross at the crossroads where heaven and earth met, and God and human beings met and still meet. We are formed and made in the sign of the cross, designed to reach out to others as we stand firmly planted on the earth, yet standing in God's presence and in the kingdom of justice and peace that Jesus brought to earth in his person and presence. And in the end, that is all about music, about making music and being the song that is sung, the instrument, and the singers. Paul exhorted his community to sing hymns, psalms, songs, prayers. Baptism introduces us to the music of God, which is heard and known in silence, song, and prayer and known still deeper in the very rhythm of our hearts, our desires, and our hopes. Thich Nhat Hanh, a Buddhist monk, says, "The rhythm of my own heart is the birth and death of all that are alive." This is communion.

Strangely enough, if cells from a number of hearts are put together in a petri dish, it does not take long until all the cells are beating at the same pace and rhythm. We are created for harmony, for unity and communion. The rituals, the sacraments, the Scriptures, the community, the presence of God in all and in the Trinity seek only to draw us back together, to make us one, to make us a universe—one piece of poetry, of music, one expression of the glory of God. All our history, all the stories, all creation, all that God has done has sought this mysterious music. The mystic Mechtild of Magdeburg sang out, "Come, love! Sing on! Let me hear you sing this song. Sing for joy and laugh, for I, the Creator, am truly subject to all creatures." The incarnation, passion, death, and resurrection of Jesus are music beyond our fathoming that can only be learned by belief, by baptism, by passionate obedience, by listening with the heart and being immersed in this mystery, hidden with Christ in God as his beloved children. It is a way of life that is as intricate as a symphony, as simple as beginning with the basic chords and notes of any song, as singular as each voice and as harmonious as the music of the universe itself.

How to live out the sacrament of resurrection, to put flesh on the sacrament of baptism in our lives, from one extreme to the other of desire and joy to passion and death. Two stories can call us to make music that is unforgettable, unrepeatable, redemptive, and death defying. The first is taken from Elie Wiesel's *Night.* Wiesel has just arrived at a concentration camp, and he has lost everything, as has everyone else herded together, but he realizes that he knows someone among the new arrivals, his school friend Juliek. Juliek confesses to him that he has managed to bring his violin with him, and he is afraid that it will be confiscated. And he's afraid what will happen to him if he is caught, but he cannot live without it. Later that night, Elie wakes to hear the sound of a violin playing a fragment of a Beethoven concerto. Never had he heard a sound so pure. He wondered if the music was real? Could music such as this exist amidst such terror? Was he going mad for hearing it? Was the musician mad for playing it? No, it was Juliek, playing his very life, playing, as it turned out, as he never would again. In the morning Juliek was dead. The story haunts. The story destroys something in us, tearing down barriers and protections, making us want to cry out against such tragedy, such loss, such barbarity, and yet it stuns us into silence at such humanity, such beauty, such light in the midst of night. This is resurrection. This is baptism as a way of life, as a way of re-sisting evil and injustice, as a way of power that is nonviolent, freeing, forgiv-ing, and yet aware of horror and death.

The other story is from the tradition of the Ba'al Shem Tov, the Master of the Good Name, the founder of the Hasidim, Jews who believed that one of the ways to holiness, to intimacy with the Holy One, blessed be His name, was through singing, music and dancing, and telling stories. This route was as sure, and sometimes quicker, and of necessity the one to travel if you could not study the Torah for long periods because of work, responsibilities, or persecu-tion. This story is found in written form in Yitzhak Ber ben Z'vi Hirsh's *The New Community of Hasidism* (Lemberg, 1902; reprinted 1959–60, pp. 11–12). It is called "The Boy and the Flute." This is the way I tell it aloud.

It was the High Holy Days, the Days of Awe, and one of the poor villagers looked forward to these days. He would leave behind his sheep and his work and journey into the city to celebrate and to pray with the Baal Shem Tov, and this year he would bring his young son. His wife had died in childbirth and the two were inseparable, but they were inseparable also because the boy was slow, not very bright. The father never knew exactly what he understood or what he was thinking. He had tried and tried, but the boy hadn't learned his prayers, not even the letters of the alphabet, or the letters that were the name of God. He did not want to admit it, but he was ashamed of his only son. This year the boy turned twelve and it was time for his Bar Mitzvah. He had to take him to the House of Study to learn the law. He was afraid that the boy might do something against the law, even inadvertently. He had to ask the Baal Shem Tov what to do about him.

They arrived and went in almost immediately to the services. The young boy had brought his flute along with him. He couldn't be separated from it. It was his companion high in the mountain pastures where he tended the flocks. It was deep in the pocket of his coat, and he had not told his father that he had brought it with him. The service went on and on, the prayers rising and falling, but he did not understand a word; he could not pray them, with his father and the others. He remained silent for what seemed like hours, and then leaned into his father and told him quietly that he had brought his flute with him and that he had this strong, strong desire to play his flute now, here in the service. His father was taken aback, appalled, even frightened about what might happen if his son did play the flute. He gave him a hard look and told him that it was not the time or the place. Absolutely not!

The boy was quiet for the next set of prayers and then he pulled on his father's coat again and told him he had to play the flute. There was this need rising in him that he couldn't control. "Please," he asked, "may I play my flute?" His father grew angry and told him to be still and that it was against all the rules and that the only reason why he did not take the flute from him was that he could not touch a musical instrument on these holy days. Again the boy was quiet for a while. The boy pulled on his father's sleeve, his eyes filling up, pleading to play. He spoke in a whisper that could barely be heard, so that his father had to bend down close to his mouth. He said that his soul hurt and that playing the flute helped him when this happened in the fields. The father reacted by grabbing at his son's coat, feeling the flute inside the pocket and holding onto his coat so that the boy couldn't put his hand inside and get at the flute. They stood there together during the prayers, locked together until the service was almost over and the closing prayers were begun.

The father began to ease up on his hold and relax. The service was almost over, but the boy could not contain himself any longer. He had to play his flute. He yanked the coat out of his father's hand, reached inside, grabbed his flute and put it to his lips and blew with all his strength. A note came forth that was pure, strong, and shattering in its sound. There was absolute silence. The congregation turned and everyone stopped the prayers. His father was shocked. No one moved. The prayers had just stopped dead. But the Baal Shem Tov knew about the boy; he'd noticed him when he came in with his father and his heart had told him that the boy only knew how to pray with his flute.

The Baal Shem Tov picked up the prayer and raced through it to the end, much to everyone's surprise. Then he turned to them and spoke. "There is a young boy in our midst who has the voice of a flute. It is this child who has lifted up all our prayers to heaven and it is this boy who has lifted my own burden as your leader in prayer. This boy has been with us all day, silently standing with us, and as he sat and stood with us, a holy spark was ignited in his soul and the spark grew all during his silence, all day, burning into a raging consuming fire. Those of us who can pray use our prayer to channel this grace, this fire and holiness, but this boy did not know the prayers and he had no other place to put this holiness and fire of the Spirit. He had to play his flute before the Holy One. He had to play his flute to pray, to ease his soul and to release its goodness and praise. His father tried to keep him from playing and that made the desire just grow more bright.

He has torn himself free from earth. He has played his flute and he has lifted all our prayers to the Holy One. He has lifted all of us up to God, blessed be His name. His flute has been played and we are heard and now stand before God. Now we stand in awe and are saved."

The story is awesome, disturbing, freeing, and full of fire. We are baptized into Christ's prayer, Christ's obedience unto death, Christ's dying and resurrection. We are baptized into Christ's own Spirit, and we pray with him in that Spirit to the Father who hears us as one voice, one prayer, one beloved child, all gathered into one people, one heart, one mind, one soul, one strength. We stand before God unabashedly as Jesus stood before God to pray. And God stands behind us; stands with us, and stands for us. This is resurrection prayer that we are taught in our baptisms and learn and understand throughout our lives with one another. The music of our lives is revealed in worship, in prayer, in community witness, in the work for justice, in being peacemakers, in welcome and hospitality of those driven out and despairing and in our presence as the Risen Lord's power in the world, reminding earth and all her children that all belongs to God. It has all been given in the person of Jesus. We are reminded once again by Paul of the important things and how we are to live, knowing that we are always being watched by others who seek to know if we are the truth we proclaim, if we are good news for the poor and those who belong to God.

> [W]e proclaim Jesus Christ as lord and ourselves as your slaves for Jesus' sake. For it is the God who said, "Let light shine out of darkness," who has shone in our hearts to give the light of the knowledge of the glory of God in the face of Jesus Christ."
>
> But we have this treasure in clay jars, so that it may be made clear that this extraordinary power belongs to God and does not come from us. We are afflicted in every way, but not crushed; perplexed, but not driven to despair; persecuted, but not forsaken; struck down, but not destroyed; always carrying in the body the death of Jesus, so that the life of Jesus may also be made visible in our bodies. For while we live, we are always being given up to death for Jesus' sake, so that the life of Jesus may be made visible in our mortal flesh. So death is at work in us, but life in you.
>
> [B]ecause we know that the one who raised the Lord Jesus will raise us also with Jesus, and will bring us with you into his presence. Yes, everything is for your sake, so that grace, as it extends to more and more people, may increase thanksgiving, to the glory of God. (2 Cor. 4:5–12, 14–15)

The sacrament of resurrection is the blessing, the first blessing we know of new life, and from that moment on, our life is to be a blessing for others, a blessing that honors God in gratitude. We close with the ending of Paul's letter to the

Ephesians: "Peace be to the whole community, and love with faith, from God the Father and the Lord Jesus Christ. Grace be with all who have an undying love for our Lord Jesus Christ" (Eph. 6:23–24). Amen.

Or in the words of Evelyn Underhill: "The note we end on is and must be the note of inexhaustible possible and hope." Our lives, lived in the Body of Christ, sing hope, sing blessing to all the world. This is the music first sung in the tomb as the body of Jesus breathed and sighed once again in resurrection life, as he rose from the cold stone and stepped into the morning light. This is the music that was seeded in the earth itself and in each of our bodies and souls at baptism. We are such grace breathed upon the world.

10

Resurrection Now

Today is the day of the Resurrection: May all peoples rejoice and
  say:
"Friends and enemies alike—we forgive everything today!"
Christ is risen! He is truly risen!

—Orthodox liturgy

*W*e celebrate fifty days of resurrection joy and glory after the forty days of
Lent. The Byzantine liturgy reminds us bluntly of the transition between the
two and the bridge that connects them for all time. We hear in the canon sung
on Easter night: "Yesterday I suffered and was buried with you, O Christ, and
today I rise with you in your resurrection." Easter is the feast that encompasses
all other feasts, and in the eastern church, the week after Easter is called Bright
Week. It is meant to be an intense seven days, a preface to the seven weeks of
Easter time when we seek to absorb and integrate all the glory that has been
shared with us, and to imbibe the wisdom that has been given to us. We repeat, mantra-like, the great Alleluias, light the Paschal candle whenever we
gather, ring bells until the towers of the church rock, and bring flowers and
trees inside, making gardens once again of our earth and lives. We repeat the
refrain, drawn from Psalm 118:24, "This is the day the Lord has made, let us
rejoice and be glad in it." And this day is every day, but especially in this season of brightness, of hope and life ever more abundantly given to us. This is
our faith, and with every Alleluia and every song, every plant and tree, we proclaim life. We affirm life. We shout that God is alive, and that the tomb is
empty! We assert boldly that death is an empty threat and that life, because of
the Incarnation, the life of God dwelling with us, is indestructible, invincible,
impossible to destroy, everlasting, and that that life is ours now. And that there
are no limits to this life and its power to transform, transfigure, and redeem.

It seems in this season that every line from the psalms was prelude to the mystery of resurrection, that every story and promise makes sense and has come true in Jesus's being raised from the dead. We sing, "You give them drink from the river of your delights. For with you is the fountain of life; in your light we see light" (Ps. 36:8–9). The season begins in pitch darkness as we stand around the Easter fire and light the Paschal candle and then process solemnly into the opened gates and doors of our churches, singing the threefold blessing on this night: "Lumen Christi" and everyone sings back, growing stronger as the light grows surer, "Deo gratias." Thanks be to God. And we light each of our candles from the Easter Christ towering above us, risen from the grave. The Exsultet is chanted, a paean to the goodness of God and the Father's imagination, depth of love, and wondrous care for us since the beginning of time. All is redeemable. All are redeemed, kissed in the light of Easter dawn. Our God is light. And this light is loose in the world, and it is unquenchable. At vespers one night, we hear the words of Gregory of Narek (eastern church).

> Creator of Light and fashioner of the night, thou, life in death, and light in darkness, hope unto those who wait, and forbearance unto those that doubt; thou, who with skillful wisdom, turns the shadow of death into morning; thou unending dawn, thou sun without setting.

The church seeks words to describe this mystery, words that soar and almost disappear into reverence, into silence or song. How to sustain such joy, such wonder and delight in God, such praise for fifty days, let alone a lifetime! But that is resurrection life begun in baptism. It will be marked by rises and falls, times of doubt and confusion, flashes of insight and meaning, lonely times and times of comfort and companionship with other believers. There will be the pattern of the cross and death and resurrection, inseparable for all eternity now and being woven into the pattern of our lives, our bodies and our souls. It is the pattern, the weave, we seek to imprint on the very world, on history and all that transpires until the coming of the fullness of God in glory. Now we live suspended in hope between the violent reality of the cross and death and the ultimate last word of God: life, resurrection life.

Jurgen Moltmann, one of the great theologians of the last fifty years, originally began his studies in quantum physics, but was caught in the grip of world war, captured, and taken prisoner. His experiences in the tomb of that prison surprisingly led him in an altogether different direction for his life. While he was imprisoned, he learned what life was and how he wanted to live it out. Philip Yancey describes what happened to Moltmann after he was released.

> Upon release, Moltmann abandoned his plan to study quantum physics and returned instead to theology, founding a movement called "a theology of

hope." We on earth exist, he concluded, in a state of contradiction between the cross and the resurrection. Surrounded by decay, we nonetheless hope for perfection, for a restoration of the cosmos. We have no proof that it can ever be attained, only a sign in history, the "foreglow" of the raising of Christ from the dead. Yet if we can sustain faith in that glorious future, it can transform the present—just as Moltmann's one hope of eventual release from prison camp transformed his daily experience there. A future faith can alter the present, at the very least by allowing us to suspend judgment of God. A person without future faith logically assumes that the suffering and chaos on this planet reflect something of God; therefore, God is neither all-good nor all-powerful. Future faith allows me to believe that God is not satisfied with this world either and plans to restore the universe to its original design. Just as Moltmann came to believe in the possibility of life outside a prison camp someday, I can believe in a future time when God will reign with perfect justice. "Away distrust: My God hath promised, he is just," wrote George Herbert. I need that reminder daily. With future faith, I can trust in that as-yet-unverified justice despite all the apparent contradictions on this groaning planet. (Philip Yancey. "What Can We Expect to Find?" *Reaching for the Invisible God.* Grand Rapids, Mich.: Zondervan, 2000, p. 78, and Jurgen Moltmann. *Experiences of God.* Philadelphia: Fortress Press, 1980, pp. 7–8)

This belief is our root, our source and power base, and it is also the source of holiness that is this power expressed daily in our lives. Because of the Resurrection we live on impossible hope, with faith that is not rational in the face of the evil and injustice rampant in the world and yet superbly rational once the meaning of what the Resurrection might mean for the earth begins to reveal itself in history and the community of believers. Patrick Kavanaugh, the Irish poet, wrote "the resurrection—a laugh freed forever and ever." We live lives staked on this unbelievable reality, and it begins to form every response, every prayer, every decision, and even our own lives and the world we dwell in with such hope in resurrection's power. The theologian Karl Rahner wrote about what this might mean.

> God has entrusted this last, deepest, and most beautiful word to the world, in the Word made flesh. This Word says: "I love you, world, man and woman. I am there. I am with you. I am your life. I am your time. I weep your tears. I am your joy. DO not be afraid. When you do not know how to go any further, I am with you. I am in your anguish, because I suffered it Myself. I am in your need and your death, because today I began to live and die with you. I am your life. I promise you: For you, too, life is waiting. For you, too, the gates will open." (From a prayer card)

We are told by others, believers or not, what this means: "Once we bring life into the world, we must protect it. We must protect it by changing the world." (Elie Wiesel); and by Alfred North Whitehead, "Every act leaves the world with a deeper or fainter impress of God." This life impacts how we treat one another and every breath we take. One of the monks of old once said, "A brother once sorrowfully asked Sisoes the Great, 'Father, what can I do? I have fallen into sin.' The Staretz answered him, 'Rise again.' The brother said, 'I rose up and fell.' The Staretz answered, 'Rise again.' The brother answered, 'How often must I fall and rise up?' The Staretz said, 'Until your death'" (Ignatious Byranchaninov, from a calendar in a Rutherian Orthodox church).

Surprisingly, we live "trailing clouds of glory" and insistently are called to believe and to stake our lives on that belief. That call comes in whispers, in strangers, in the earth and its seasons, in good and evil, in all things saved in the blood of Christ's death and the wine we drink to proclaim his resurrection. The Muslim-Sufi poet Rumi writes intoxicating verse that echoes the joy and the extravagant life we are immersed in by our baptisms: resurrection life.

> How could the soul not take flight
> When from the glorious Presence
> A soft call flows sweet as honey,
> Comes right up to her
> And whispers, "Rise up now, come away."
> How could the fish not jump
> Immediately from dry land into water,
> When the sound of water from the ocean
> Of fresh waves springs to his ear?

These words, these pieces of poetry and prayer, sound too ecstatic, too lavish, too sublime to sustain, and yet we must know this, remember this glory and let it be seeded again and again in our very bones and hearts and minds through the Word, through the cycle of the Paschal mystery experienced and known intimately in our communities, if we are to sustain the practice of resurrection when the cross's shadow looms long, and the pain blurs out the vision, and the evil in the world is too close for comfort. It is only through faithful practice that the disciplines become the dance of resurrection, that the hard practices become the graceful, almost automatic responses to all that happens to us, and in the world we are sent to bring God's life in the Good News and in our presence as the living, viable, breathing, and sharing the life of God for others. And in this new millennium that began just three years ago with a vengeance, with hatred and killing that seem to spiral out of control and spread like a viral infection among all peoples regardless of religious belief, it is imperative to sustain the practice of resurrection: imperative for the very survival of hundreds of millions of people around the world, daily.

In her book *My Grandfather's Blessings,* Rachel Naomi Remen wrote of an astounding reality in a short piece called "Friction in the System." A number of media people were invited to fly the Concorde between the United States and Europe. They were given the royal treatment and invited up into the cockpit for a brief lecture on the plane's capabilities. The specifications were impressive: at a speed of Mach 2—1,350 mph—they could cross the Atlantic in less than four hours. She writes:

> One of these passengers was surprised to discover that no one actually kept the plane on course. Because of its phenomenal speed and the slowness of human reaction time, the course was actually maintained by two computers. The first computer took a course reading every few seconds, and if the plane was off course, instantaneously fed this information to the second, which would make the needed correction and confirm the new course.
>
> After a brief visit to the cockpit, [a VIP] returned to his seat aware that something had caught his attention but unsure of what it was. For the next hour or so, he puzzled over it without being able to identify it. Finally, he asked a member of the crew if he might see the cockpit once more.
>
> Once there, he realized almost immediately that it was not something that he had seen but something that he had heard. As the computers fed course readings and corrections back and forth between them, they made a certain sound. What he had noticed was that this sound was almost continuous. Turning to his tour guide, he remarked on this and asked what percentage of the time the plane was off course. The crew member smiled. "About ninety-nine percent of the time, sir," he replied.
>
> "And we will land in Paris at 9:03 P.M.?" said the VIP, marveling. "Yes, sir," the crewman replied. "Plus or minus sixty seconds or so." (pp. 365–367)

Amazing! To be off course 99 percent of the time! And yet, it makes perfect sense. The computers are in constant response once the course is set, and the entire process of navigation is to keep the destination in mind and stay the course. It sounds a bit like Paul assuring his people that he has stayed the course, he has run the race and looks to the glory of God to sustain him, no matter what he encounters and what is happening in the world that follows another course and often stands in opposition to the trajectory of the Good News to the poor, the Good News of resurrection life secured for all, let loose in the world to transform all things. And the early church soon realized that even after baptism, most of those who believed, who were followers of Jesus the Crucified and Risen Lord, were more often than not off course. They needed something to correct them, to steer them back into the way of the cross, the way of life, all the way to resurrection's fullness of glory. And the presence of the Spirit was given to the community, specifically in the wisdom and power of the Word of the Lord to keep the community on course, to abide with them, as Jesus had proclaimed: "And behold, I will be with you all days, even until the end of time" (last line of Matthew's

Gospel). The Resurrection is most clearly needed and most clearly revealed in those communities that are constantly seeking to correct and transform the world through the wisdom and the power of the Word of God made flesh in their lives and actions in history. The core of the message of resurrection can be found in simple, profound, and death-defying concepts. The first is found in this prayer from Byzantine Matins in the Easter season.

> Today is the day of Resurrection. Let us shine with the light of the feast. Let us embrace one another, brothers and sisters. Because of Christ's Resurrection, let us forgive all things to those who hate us. Then, with joy let us sing: Christ is risen from the dead. By death he conquered death!

It all comes down to this: we are forgiven. All is forgiven. All is given back as favor and grace. We must forgive because we know forgiveness. It is as constant as the breath that we draw into our lungs and expel once again, staying alive. This is the new truth that has entered our world and permeates all things. It undermines all sin, all evil and injustice. It is a way of life, a commitment to "living in the freedom of the children of God," the forgiven and forgiving children of God. This is the struggle along the way and the grace of every hour, the promise of every incident and experience. Forgiveness is the first radiant gift and grace of resurrection. This is the light of hope that has dawned on our world. Forgiveness shatters the darkness, subverts violence and hatred and opens a door in every place where sin has entered. The power to forgive and loose people from the hold of death and the power to bind—to hold evil bound, revealing its lie and resisting its destruction and stopping its death—this is the power of the Risen Spirit of our God breathed upon us, ordering us to go into the world and reorder it, reconstitute it with the balm of healing forgiveness (John 20).

In one of the most powerful and beautiful of the early Easter prayers, Jonn Chrysostom in his sermon sings of the power that is now our birthright and our legacy to share with the world. It is our source and what feeds our souls and gives our imaginations a way to save our world today. This is from a relatively new translation by Paul Roche that appeared in *America* (April 5, 1980):

> No one need mourn uncountable falls, be they over and over.
> For forgiveness itself has reared from the tomb,
> No one need fear death; for our Savior himself has died and set us free.
> He confronted death in his own person, and blasted it to nothing.
> He made it defunct by the very taste of his flesh.
> This is exactly what Isaiah foretold when he declared:
> "Hell is harrowed by encounter with him."

Of course, it is harrowed.
For now hell is a joke, finished, done with.
Harrowed because now taken prisoner.
It snatched at a body, and—incredible—lit upon God.
It gulped down the earth, and gagged on heaven.
It seized what it saw, and was crushed by what it failed to see.
Poor death, where is your sting?
Poor hell, where is your triumph?
Christ steps out of the tomb and you are reduced to nothing.
Christ rises and the angels are wild with delight.
Christ rises and life is set free.
Christ rises and the graves are emptied of dead.
Oh yes, for he broke from the tomb like a flower, a beautiful fruit:
the first fruit of those already gone.
All glory be his, all success and power . . . for ever and ever.

This power is ours! This freedom is ours! This life is ours! There is no power on earth—not death, injustice, sin, evil, hatred, violence, hunger, war, nationalism, greed, selfishness, and horror—that can stand against this Risen Lord. Forgiveness, its power, its presence, its reality as the person of Jesus in our midst, is now what we are to fall back upon, what we are to resort to in all situations and to turn to as a first response, and then again and again, staking our lives, and even our deaths if need be, on this gift of the Risen Lord. We are baptized into the waters of forgiveness, and it is the practice of forgiveness that renews our life, reseeds our souls when we have gone to seed, and allows us to mature in our adult lives as believers. Without this practice of forgiveness, individually in all our relationships and communally as witness and alternative to the ways of the world, we are dying, shriveled and lifeless as Christians.

Swanee Hunt, former United States ambassador to Austria, who now chairs the group Women Waging Peace, which is concerned with identifying the essential roles and contributions of women in preventing violent conflict, stopping war, and sustaining peace in fragile areas around the world, writes about our reactions to what happens in our world. She is the author of a forthcoming book, *This Was Not Our War*, the accounts of twenty-six women working in various ways to heal their countries. These comments appeared in an interview in *Hope* [33 (September/October 2002): 10–13, 47]:

A crisis like September 11 creates in many people the desire to go immediately to what is familiar and expressive. "We will fight fire with fire. We will get them back! What do we have at hand? Well, we have this arsenal." There are other people who, in a moment of crisis, say, "What we know how to do has certainly not worked up to this point. We need whole new paradigms." There is an opening up of ideas. Both happened within our society, and that's one of the reasons you get such anger from one side to the other—because both are natural reactions. (p. 12)

She states that "both are natural reactions"—perhaps, but because of baptism, because of the Resurrection, our natural reaction must be to get past our emotional reactions as quickly as possible and reflect on what has happened in light of the cross and resurrection and our own baptisms into that defining reality—to the life-giving and life-affirming waters of forgiveness and reconciliation. She continues later in the interview to say that she has a quote from Eleanor Roosevelt on her wall: "You must do the things you think you cannot do." And in response to the question, are there conflicts that feel unsolvable to you? she replies:

> I hear people say that about Africa or the Middle East. But I don't think that's an option. People used to say, "Why are you working on Bosnia? Those people have always been fighting." Someone said, "You are beating your head against the wall." In the back of my mind, I have this image that if you are there right by the big, big wall, and you can't get over and you can't get around and you can't get through it—stay there. Hit up against it over and over—and at some point something will happen. A crack will appear, and if you are there you will go through the crack. If you are not there, you don't even see it. Tough situations require us to be right there at the wall watching, experiencing, pushing, pulling. Eventually something happens. (p. 47)

This is practice. This is discipline. This is adherence to a way of life. This is faithfulness and endurance day in and day out, and it must be done in season and out so that when situations of horrific violence, of attacks and counterattacks, begin to swirl about, creating an ever-increasing spiral of violence, there will be communities of people committed to resistance, to forgiveness and reconciliation, to making cracks in the wall and seizing every advantage to redeem the situation, no matter how destructive it has been and how strong the hostility has become among those involved, and those on the periphery.

And it is not only those who would define themselves as believers who are asking these questions. In that same issue of *Hope* (September/October 2002), John Daniel writes in an essay, "The Roots of Renewal," about his own reflections and questions.

> On September 11, 2001 and during the weeks that followed, I turned where I usually turn for solace—to the natural world. . . . There is an ungraspable majesty in the movement of daylight into dusk and dusk into stars and moon. It is good to remember—at times it is saving to remember—that beneath and beyond and above our obsessive human busyness, our blaring

noise and lights, our wars and murders and torturings, there lives a universe of ongoing beauty that we can mar but never destroy.

. . .

Nature is as prone to violence as it is to peace. The redemption, the saving grace, is that every natural violence does good. A flood may kill many creatures, but it renews a river's fertility by flushing sediment onto the flood plain, creating new pools, and sweeping juvenile salmon out to sea in the spring. Fire, too, is a destroying creator. When allowed to burn periodically, it clears a forest of choking underbrush, maintains meadows and a spacious array of mature trees.

. . .

And so, when I look back now at last September, it's the possibility of redemption that interests me. It may seem an indulgence of one who suffered no personal loss in the attacks and lives a long way from Ground Zero, but I've been asking these questions: What good may come of that horrific violence? What thickets of blinding underbrush may have burned away, what possibilities may now have a chance to grow? In what forms might our renewal rise? (pp. 39–40)

And he continues later with suggestions on places to begin.

Courage can speak in many ways. It takes courage to say a kind word to someone we dislike or someone who dislikes us. It takes courage to examine ourselves for our biases and blindnesses and to listen carefully, respectfully, to those who see differently. It takes courage not to fear or shun strangers but to open ourselves to what we might learn from them—to what we might learn only from them. It takes courage to demand more of ourselves and our government than reactive anger and patriotic display, more than the hardening of defenses and the waging of war. It takes courage to inform ourselves about the diverse global community we Americans are a part of and to ask what we contribute to that community for good or for ill, and how we might give more of our best—more of the selfless bravery of the September 11 rescuers, more of the hard work and generosity we show time and again when our own citizens are in need. (p. 41)

It is amazing that remarkably good people are asking these questions and positing these alternatives of hope as human beings on this earth without even connecting to or asking what religion may have to say to this reality. Often as I travel and talk, I hear the refrain again and again: everything changed that day. And I find myself responding very quietly and surely, no. Nothing changed that day. The story and the long history of violence, of killing and retaliation with escalation is sadly the most rampant story of our sordid side as human beings. For believers there was a day, really three days, that did change everything for all peoples, for all times. Those days we call Good Friday, Holy Saturday, and

Easter Sunday, when the hateful story was stopped and the ending drastically altered and forgiveness in the person of God made flesh interrupted the telling and the killing and the seemingly inevitable reign of death and hatred of human beings for each other. Again, John Daniel writes of a more cyclic resurrection to describe why we should change and what the outcome might be as foretaste of, or even prelude to, the more radical and Spirit-filled graceful revolution of forgiveness and reconciliation.

> We say that everything is different because we sense that possibility has opened in some new way, and we are reaching, uncertainly, for what is to be. To find it will take many small acts of courage and community—acts of faith and hope, acts of boldness and acts of forbearance, acts we can't yet imagine, acts that may flower and bear fruit only after we are dead. Each alone may seem insignificant, overwhelmingly small, but so do the actions of raindrops and butterflies and the rootlets of trees. It is of such tiny movements, only of such tiny movements, that renewal is made. (p. 41)

This is the response of human beings intent on living with dignity, with integrity and goodness, aware of their place in the larger community of men and women. If this is the ground line then what is the ground line of our religion—our power base and intent as believers in the Crucified and Risen Lord? The Resurrection lived in community begins with the consistent practice, the daily devotion of forgiveness and the work of reconciliation as core to all our lives, all our vocations and relationships. And the second concept and power flows from forgiveness: it is the making of peace, the sharing of the peace of Christ. We are heralded as the children of God and blessed because we are God's peacemakers upon the earth, continuing the action and the presence of God among all peoples. This is where individual practice must essentially become communal practice and witness within and outside of the confines of church and community. The first words of the Risen Christ are not only greeting, but they are command, insistent imperative and blessing: peace be with you! There are many many groups and movements, but perhaps two might be singled out for mention.

One was birthed in the days of the Vatican Council (1962–1965), now forty years ago. It is the community of Sant'Egidio (St. Giles) conceived in Rome by a high school student, Andrea Riccardi, who is now a highly respected Italian church historian. Its name comes from the church where the group initially met to discuss what they were becoming, what they wanted to do and to worship together. It was an old Carmelite convent in the Trastevere district. They began, as the early church did, working and living among the poor who lived on the boundaries of the city and opening schools for the children in the neighborhoods. And in 1986 they were among the first to participate in the Assisi gatherings for world peace, seeking to unite members of all the earth's religions in prayer, and since then they have been integral to keeping this dream of praying together across religious lines as the source for peace in the world.

But their work has expanded to an international level, and they are found in the areas of the world that are most violent and where distrust, hatred, and long histories of conflict have separated groups blindly, where impasses are huge stumbling blocks to survival, and murder and destruction are the only realities some people can remember. They have been found working and struggling for peace in such far-ranging places as Mozambique, Guatemala, Yugoslavia, and Algeria. Their peace accord in Mozambique was not one of their first ends to armed conflict, but it is the one they are most proud of, describing it as "the first inter-governmental agreement ever negotiated by a non-governmental body." It was signed on October 4, 1992 (fittingly enough, on the feast of St. Francis of Assisi), ending a civil war that had left more than a million people dead.

Their work is both local within the city of Rome and in Italy, but that is often the base for their human rights work worldwide. In 2001 they began a campaign to abolish the death penalty, rallying all of western and eastern Europe together with over 2.7 million signatures that were presented to the United Nations. They have received a number of awards for their efforts at international peacemaking: the 1999 Felix Houphouet-Boigny Peace Prize (given by the United Nations); the 1999 Niwano Peace Prize in Tokyo representing the major world religions of Islam, Christianity, and Buddhism; and the 2001 University of Notre Dame International Service Honor. The group has also been nominated repeatedly for the Nobel Prize for Peace. They would rejoice in receiving that coveted prize because it would be public witness and recognition for the virtue and practice of peacemaking as central to the living out of the beliefs of Christianity and the passion of many in Catholicism to be that witness to the Resurrection and the peace of Christ in the world, not just on a theoretical level, but in the gritty hard work of peacemaking that is a never-ending process of belief, imagination, endurance, gracefulness, and passionate devotion. Their work on these national and international levels is sourced in the gospel, in community living and care for the poor that has led them invariably to the larger issues of injustice, despair, and massive economic inequities that are the roots of war and conflict.

We are elected, baptized to be peace, to bring peace to conflict and places of war, and to preach peace as the first word, the greeting and blessing of the gospel, the first words in the mouth of the Risen Lord: shalom! And the other group to be singled out is Pax Christi, the Peace of Christ, which is the international peacemaking and peace-keeping movement of the Catholic Church.

It was founded more than fifty years ago in a war-ravaged Europe by two men, French and German, who together vowed that something like world war must never happen again; that all avenues and options must be in position and used before war would be considered a response to conflict, aggression, and dis-agreement. It has chapters worldwide from the Philippines, to the United States, with its international headquarters in Brussels. It is not specifically a community, but a movement based on the principles of the gospel and nonvi-olence as a way of life and studied responses to evil and injustice. It confronts and seeks to relate local issues specific to each country, such as immigration, the death penalty, civil rights, racism, and poverty in the United States, to the overlapping issues of world hunger and poverty, war, nuclear treaties, land-mines, misuse of resources, addiction to oil and gas, child soldiers, torture and nationalism, and ethic cleansing around the world.

It seeks to educate people in the Catholic Church on both national and parish levels to the tradition of peacemaking and living resistance to injustice in communities that are steeped in the gospel, working together to be sources of hope and alternatives to dominant cultures that disregard human beings, tol-erating enormous levels of injustice, inequality, violence, and inhumanity as normative. The national offices in Erie, Pennsylvania, attempt to coordinate lo-cal chapters around the country and provide basic background information on peace and justice issues, the encyclicals and teachings of the church in these re-gards, while working as a nongovernmental organization affiliated with the United Nations to organize on international and national levels for issues that cry out for immediate response based on the Christian principles of love of neighbor, love of enemy, forgiveness, reconciliation, work for justice, peace-making, and the practice of nonviolent resistance communally to evil.

Its Web sites are www.PaxChristiUSA.org and www.PaxChristiInterna-tional.org, and they provide everything from information on the latest Vatican communiqués with the United Nations, to the U.S. Bishops statements, to vi-tal information on political, economic, and military issues that impact believ-ers and call for a response that reveals the values of the gospel and the church, often as alternatives to and contradictions of national policies. It is networking on a massive scale with other organizations and groups as well, as support for each local chapter and those seeking to gather new members. One of their goals is to have a community of Pax Christi active in every parish in the United States, acting as a viable body of peacemakers and justice seekers, wher-ever it is needed, encouraging others in the church to be more deeply com-mitted to being church, the sacrament of the Risen Lord in the midst of the world, especially the world at war, preparing for war and using war as the only response to world conflicts. They also provide educational and liturgical mate-rials for the seasons of the church year, for personal spirituality preparing people to take individual vows of nonviolence; resources for prayer services, vigils for peace and against acts of injustice, and preaching and teaching materials on issues as broad as the military draft (there are a growing number of groups on college campuses); civil rights, immigration and health-care issues, the use of natural resources, the death penalty, nuclear weapons treaties, the military budget and its effects on education, welfare, housing, medicines, poverty, racism, terrorism and Catholic responses to these issues in light of social teachings of the church and the Scriptures. It is at its root a movement, not an organization, and so a great deal of freedom is encouraged, urging each group to tackle injustice locally and practice nonviolence and peacemaking locally as integral to our Christian life and liturgy, as well as the need to come together nationally on crucial issues of war, preemptive strikes and violent aggression in any form.

These are the three concepts and practices core to resurrection belief and living: forgiveness, peace, and lastly the cross or nonviolent resistance to evil. Jesus in the upper room proclaims peace with his words and then shows his disciples his hands and his side: his wounds from the struggle to be forgiving and to be peace, resisting violence in his very person, his body, refusing to be violent and standing with loving resistance in the power of the Spirit, with his Father behind him, resisting even unto death. Again, this is not primarily practice as individual belief, but as community standing together at the altar of sacrifice and feast, and then standing together before injustice and in refusing to stand violently, they stand with the victims of injustice and violence or stand as peacemakers between those in conflict. At the Fellowship of Reconciliation (FOR) Conference in New York in June 2002, peacemakers around the world met and told stories of wounding and witness of word and bodies, although they did not exactly define them in that way.

One of the stories was told by Javier Sanchez, from the village of San Jose de Apartado in Colombia, which has declared itself a "Peace Community" for five years now. They find themselves caught in the deadly trap between the guerrillas and government-sponsored paramilitary troops, but they have vowed publicly and religiously to remain on their land and to carry no guns, not to take sides, and to practice nonviolent resistance. And they have remained steadfast despite the sufferings and hardships this has inflicted upon them, from almost daily raids and terrorizing and more than one hundred assassinations. FOR and other members of peace organizations responded to the peasants' request for aid by sending people to accompany them and help protect them. This support and solidarity, of literally massing bodies of strangers and friends together in places of conflict, is growing as a viable response to such armed conflicts with people caught in the middle who refuse to fight and to react with killing to situations, whether in regard to land issues, nationalism, tribalism, ethic disagreements, or longstanding hatreds fed by outsiders intent on their own interests.

There is a group called Peaceworkers, part of the Global Nonviolent Peaceforce, that seeks to intervene locally in situations that are explosive, violent, and capable of developing into conflicts that draw more and more communities into the violence. The executive director of the Peaceworkers was interviewed in *Turning Wheel: The Journal of Socially Engaged Buddhism* on who they are and how they operate.

> The Peaceforce is an outgrowth of Gandhi's call for a shantisena, or "nonviolent army," more than 70 years ago. We want to develop a trained international nonviolent group of civilian peacemakers who would be available, at the invitation of local peacemakers or human rights workers in areas of conflict, to go in as supporters of those local peacemakers.
>
> It's similar to the work that Peace Brigades International, Witness for Peace, and Christian Peacemaker Teams have been doing, and doing very well, but our project is on a larger scale. In Yugoslavia, in 1999, for example, NATO and our government leaders said the only alternatives were to do nothing or to bomb. But we know from our own firsthand experience in Peace Brigades that there is an alternative that most of the world doesn't know about yet.
>
> So, part of our motivation is to bring effective non-violent peacemaking to areas of conflict. But part of it is to get world attention, so that after a few years of some successes, the United Nations and regional organizational bodies will say, "That's a much more effective, and less expensive, way of dealing with conflict."

This group and others primarily work at humanitarian efforts across borders and with leaders of other religions to interrupt the process of conflict and its inevitable escalation, to literally put their bodies between those fighting. It is referred to as accompaniment. David Hartsough explains what this is:

> Accompaniment really means that local peace and justice workers are not alone. Death squads and paramilitaries don't like peace and justice workers. They rock the boat. So they kill them, disappear them, throw them in prison, thinking: Nobody will ever know. The idea of international accompaniment is to show those military leaders, those death squads, that the world is watching. These people are not alone, and the world cares. If they are harmed, there will be consequences. "A Global Nonviolent Peaceforce: Susan Moon talks with David Hartsough and Joanna Macy." (Fall 2002): p. 35.]

Groups such as these believe in risking their own lives to protect the lives of others in danger, to protect those seeking just to live in peace with justice.

They believe in what Brian Wilson said: "Our lives are not worth more, and their lives are not worth less." This movement is beginning to grow, and in the last twenty years, sizeable groups of religious people and people dedicated to nonviolence have been found in many places around the world. Hartsough continues by telling a story about the Island of Negros in the Philippines in 1988. It is an island about the size of Rhode Island, and it was torn by warring guerrilla factions and government forces, while being bombed by the U.S. military because of the suspected presence of "subversives." The population was fleeing in all directions, taking refuge in the churches and small chapels, carrying their children on their backs. Several delegates visited Bishop Antonio Fortich (whom the Quakers had nominated for the Nobel Peace Prize), and he was weeping:

> He was in tears, saying, "What can we do? These people have suffered so much." I told him of our experiences in Central America, with the Peace Brigades and Witness for Peace. His eyes lit up and he said, "That's what we can do! We can invite international religious people to come and be present with these refugees." So he dictated an invitation, and I went back to Manila and faxed it out. Within 30 hours we had about 25 international religious people there.
>
> We had a press conference in the church hall. We appealed to the death squads, saying, "These people are children of God. We appeal to you to treat them as brothers and sisters, and not to kill them. We want you to know that whatever you do to them you'll also have to do to us. And we're going to tell the rest of the world what happens to them."
>
> This statement was broadcast by local radio and television stations, and printed in the newspapers. The death squads didn't come back. It wasn't in their best interest to have the whole world know. (p. 36)

Information on groups like this can be found at www.nonviolentpeaceforce.org, and you can sign up for a newsletter and get on their mailing list at info@nonviolentpeaceforce.org as a fulltime peaceworker, reservist, or supporter. They plan on being in eleven different conflict places in 2003. Other materials are Yeshua Moser-Puangsuwan and Thomas Weber's *Nonviolent Intervention across Borders: A Recurrent Vision* (University of Hawaii Press, 2001), which gives examples of experiences of nonviolent intervention, or third-party nonviolent intervention, over the last fifty years. Another resource is Peter Ackerman and Jack Duvall's *A Force More Powerful: A Century of Nonviolent Conflict* (New York: St. Martin's Press, 2001). It is a book and video (available from Films for the Humanities and Sciences, 800/257–5126) about nonviolent movements of the twentieth century.

This is a growing international movement, but the history of even individual resistance to preparations for war is long and varied. Richard Deats, editor of the Fellowship of Reconcilation's *Fellowship Magazine*, once told a story illustrating the effectiveness of nonviolent direct action. In the 1950s the Eisenhower administration was considering a preemptive strike against China. FOR organized people to send notes to the White House along with small bags of rice, suggesting that rice might be more effective than bombs. More than forty thousand bags of rice arrived at the White House. Eisenhower's comment in response was, "If that many Americans want us to feed them instead of bomb them, we won't bomb." Perhaps it is time to start a new tradition of food packets to insist on no more bombing and as follow up in places like Afghanistan, Somalia, the Sudan, and the southern islands of the Philippines. Perhaps at least half of our military budget should be converted to food, clean water, and medicine, immediately as a shift in foreign policy. FOR is currently working with Pax Christi and the American Friends Service Committee on the Campaign of Conscience for the People of Iraq and a Nonviolence Training Program (845/358–4601); visit www.forusa.org. and www.afsc.org and www.endthewar.org. And in the Holy Land, Sami Awad of the Holy Land Trust in Palestine at www.holylandtrust.org is training young Palestinians nonviolent techniques, as a way to continue their resistance to the Israeli occupation of their land, realizing that suicide bombings do not help their cause.

As individual believers, as families and parishes, it must begin close to home and radiate out from the centers of our liturgies, prayer and relationships. We must practice devotedly the virtues of forgiveness and reconciliation, peacemaking and nonviolent resistance to evil and sin as expressions of our baptismal promises. It is essential if we are to live and practice resurrection life now, here, as a way of worship and belief. These are the ways we stand in solidarity and communion with, stand for and stand behind, what we believe, knowing that our God stands right with us against evil, sin, and injustice. This is what the power of the Spirit was given to us for and what it means to witness with our lives to the gospel of resurrection and good news to the poor. Here is a litany of things to do to practice and be reminded of who we are and what we are to do in the world. Some are very specific, some are rather vague, so that it is up to each person, family, and small Christian community and parish in the church to flesh out what it might mean for them and for others.

1. Wash the feet of those who may not walk tomorrow.
2. Stand with the victim, the outsider, the left out, those different.
3. Refuse any sort of violence and refuse to react violently.
4. Resist despair.
5. Scream silently in your prayer; remember the pain of others.
6. Bend the knees of your heart daily in conversion.
7. Learn to kneel and beg on behalf of others' lives and needs.

8. Bear the burden of the cross and seek to share the anguish and pain of others so that the pain stops here.

9. Let the Word of God in the Scripture come true in you daily, weekly, as you pray the readings of Sunday with a small community intent on change.

10. Speak the truth to power and learn to do it in such a way that they can hear.

11. Pray for your enemies and the enemies of your nation and ask forgiveness for them.

12. Absorb the international news and seek out alternative resources that give a more balanced and religious interpretation of events and why they happened.

13. Listen to the local weather reports and what is happening worldwide with the earth and its natural resources and wonder if our bodies and souls are also suffering from extremes of weather.

14. Do not deny reality. Face it down and accept what is wrong with you, the groups you identify with, your economic and racial group, your nation.

15. Support those who resist evil more than you do: prophets, conscientious objectors, peacemakers, and the like.

16. Think universally (the one, holy, catholic, universal church) and act locally and globally, join groups that seek to make peace.

17. Devise new and communal ways of being holy today in this world of violence.

18. Live simply, abhor greed, trust other people, and live a life worthy of mutual trust; share as much as you can, live with as little as you can, and be grateful.

19. End war and talk of war: on drugs, terrorism, refugees, aliens, ethnic groups, preemptive strikes, and so on.

20. Learn a language that is nonviolent. Drop words and concepts that are militaristic, belligerent, aggressive, and disrespectful. If need be, rewrite the media's reporting to reflect the fact that we are all human beings.

21. Treasure the Word of God, the Scriptures, and look to the Gospels for alternatives to what the world and nations say should be our response to any situation. Remember the ground line: we are here to call people forth from their tombs, back from death, and live death-defying lives

22. Resist sin with all your heart and soul and mind and strength (resources).

23. Act with others as much as you can.

24. Clutch and hold onto those near you; make families and relationships stronger than blood ties—ties that are based on water (baptism), bread and wine (the body and blood of Christ) and the cross, all those who suffer as Christ waiting to be taken down from the cross.

25. If you feel like you can't do anything, stand there, pray and resist with your soul force.

26. Live with invincible gentleness.

27. Forgive all, everyone, everything, and ask for it, bend and offer it graciously; learn the art.

28. Reconcile; walk with others as you follow the way of the cross to glory.

29. Remember to dance resurrection in the face of death.

30. Pray as though everything depended on God and work as though everything depended on you (it does) (the words of John of the Cross or Teresa of Avila; they were such good friends, even their words belonged to each other).

31. Learn the basics of another religion and practice some of its prayer and disciplines to better understand others, especially Islam and its mystical traditions.

32. Learn another language, if only a few words, such as "peace be with you," "hello," "thank you," "what is your name?" Learn especially languages of those labeled enemies: Iraq, Iran, the Palestinians, Afghans, Saudis, Egyptians.

33. Tell stories of hope, of resurrection and new life, of justice and peace, and refuse to be caught in the trap of name calling or demeaning others.

34. Think in terms of us and we, and drop the ideas and phrases that prolong the dichotomy of us and them.

35. Practice kissing fists, opening hands, and bowing to all others profoundly.

These are baby steps in learning to walk the way. It is a way of life for the rest of your life, life after baptism, life lived in the community of the Risen Lord, life renewed in the baptismal promises and the bringing of new Christians into the waters of joy and freedom and lived and deepened whenever life is revealed as stronger than death. We Christians need to do some hopping, skipping, and jumping to catch up on this walk, this dance of resurrection. There are others from other religions who speak sometimes more clearly than we do as Christians.

Someone once asked the Dalai Lama after a talk, "Why didn't you fight back against the Chinese?" The Dalai Lama looked down, swung his feet just a bit, then looked back up at us and said with a gentle smile, "Well, war is obsolete, you know." Then, after a few moments, his face grave, he said, "Of course the mind can rationalize fighting back . . . but the heart, the heart would never understand. Then you would be divided in yourself, the heart and the mind, and the war would be inside you" (compliments of my friend Anthony Cowan, who was in the audience).

Thich Nhat Hanh gave a talk at Riverside Church in New York City, September 25, 2001, with the monks and nuns of Plum Village and musician Paul Winter. He began with a poem that has become very famous.

> For Warmth
> I hold my face in my two hands.
> No, I am not crying.
> I hold my face in my two hands,
> To keep my loneliness warm
> Two hands protecting,
> Two hands nourishing,
> Two hands preventing
> My soul from leaving me in anger.

I wrote this poem during the Vietnam War after I heard about the bombing of Ben Tre City. The city of 300,000 was destroyed because seven guerrillas shot several rounds of unsuccessful anti-aircraft gunfire and then left. My pain was profound.

All violence is injustice. Responding to violence with violence is injustice, not only to the other person but also to oneself. Responding to violence with violence resolves nothing; it only escalates violence, anger and hatred. It is only with compassion that we can embrace and disintegrate violence. This is true in relationships between individuals as well as in relationships between nations.

What needs to be done right now is to recognize the suffering, to embrace it and understand it. . . . The violence and hatred we presently face has been created by misunderstanding, injustice, discrimination and despair. We are all co-responsible for the making of violence and despair in the world by our way of living, of consuming and of handling the problems of the world.

And he ends with a call to do something unbelievable, radical and freeing.

If we look and listen deeply we can see that when we pray for the victims, we must also pray for the attackers. They are also victims of confusion and violence. If as a nation, America wants to be safe and secure, it has to help other nations, other peoples, feel safe and secure.

I have the conviction that America possesses enough wisdom and courage to perform an act of forgiveness and compassion, and I know that such an act can bring great relief to America and the world right away. Such

an act would be a statement of the willingness to embrace all suffering inside and outside the nation, to look deeply in order to understand better the
cause of the suffering and to act according to that insight. The act could be
a project to bring relief to those who actually suffer within and outside the
country.

This call is not a single cry, but it has been echoed again and again by
leaders of the religions, including John Paul II, soon after September 11, 2001,
and ever since. On the first anniversary the pope was reported speaking to a
general audience, saying "it was necessary and urgent" to address the global injustices that created the conditions for terrorism. At the same time, he said that
while no situation of injustice could ever justify terrorism, which "is and always will be a manifestation of inhuman ferociousness," he also prayed at the
end of the audience an Arabic-language petition asking God to help believers
of all religions to reject every form of violence and make a commitment to di-
alogue to resolve conflicts. And he asked for prayers for the terrorists, saying in
Polish, "May God show mercy and forgiveness for the authors of this horrible
terror attack."

He reiterated that "armed violence and war are decisions that only sow
and generate hatred and death. . . . Reason and love are the only valid means
to overcome and resolve strife between persons and peoples."

> The pontiff called international terrorism a "true crime against humanity"
> that "represents a formidable and immediate threat to world peace." He said
> an "essential part" of fighting terrorism must be political, diplomatic and
> economic initiatives aimed at relieving "the scandalous situations of gross
> injustice, oppression and marginalization which continue to oppress count-
> less numbers of the human family."
>
> The building of such a global culture of solidarity is perhaps the greatest
> moral task confronting humanity today. For developed Western countries,
> this task will prove particularly challenging because a spreading "exagger-
> ated individualism" there had called into question its long-held Christian
> principles and values. This has led too often to "indifferentism, hedonism,
> consumerism, and a practical materialism that can erode and even subvert
> the foundations of social life." [*America Magazine* (September 23, 2002); and
> *Zenit*, the online Vatican newsletter.]

Addressing these underlying causes for terrorism and for all wars is the
practice of compassionate justice, of resisting violence by providing alternatives
that nourish life, the family, values of forgiveness, reconciliation, and peace. Perhaps the positive statement that equals nonviolent resistance is to cultivate and
practice compassion. Often when I teach and preach on resurrection and use
the story of Jesus in the upper room, seeking to dispel the fears of his disciples

and greet them with shalom, I call the talk "In Their Justice Is Our Peace" and focus on the wounds of Christ that empower his words of peace. It is in the actual corporal works of mercy, taking care of the bodily needs of the poor (now reckoned at more than 85 percent of the world's population, slowly starving to death, let alone those caught in the vise of war and bombing, sanctions and strikes) that peace is experienced and made a reality. The practice of compassion, passionate devotion to easing the pain and suffering of others caused by injustice and violence, is the practice of nonviolent resistance to evil, sin, and death. And alongside the practices of the corporal bodily works of mercy must stand the principle of mercy, which underlines why there is such need for massive compassion. It is the power of mercy to confront and stand against injustice as faithfully as one bends before those who need to wash their feet and feed their bodies with food and their souls with hope for a future without violence and lack.

This is part of humanity's heritage, and Christianity's, as well as that of many of the other world religions. What follows are quotes taken from the National Historical Site dedicated to Martin Luther King Jr. [wherever it reads "men" perhaps the word "people" could be used, but they are carved in stone and it was the way they were originally spoken]:

> When evil men plot, good men must plan.
> When evil men burn and bomb, good men must build and bind.
> When evil men shout ugly words of hatred, good men must commit themselves to the glories of love.
> Where evil men would seek to perpetuate an unjust status quo, good men must seek to bring into being a real order of justice.
> A religion true to its nature must also be concerned about man's social conditions. . . . Any religion that professes to be concerned with the souls of men and is not concerned with the slums that damn them, the economic conditions that strangle them and the social conditions that cripple them is a dry-as-dust religion.

The principle of mercy, the practice of compassion, is to do everything in one's power, alone and with others, to stop death, to ease pain, to act as a healing balm, to bind up wounds, to redress grievances, to provide refuge and sanctuary for those running for safety, to provide a haven of security for all peoples, to stand silent witness with those who die violently and to cry out against anything that destroys human lives. We are to be known by our baptisms as those who are faithful to life and compassionate to all, especially to our enemies, to those we fear and to those we feel have done us harm or intend us evil. This is what makes us the beloved forgiving children of God, brothers and sisters with Jesus, peacemakers, with our hearts ever wider to embrace those who suffer and to offer consolation to more and more who seek solace and the word of life that is shalom and resurrection.

Because of resurrection everything bears within it the possibility of redemption, of grace and life. It can be as simple as the example I found in a Japanese magazine. There was a picture of a butterfly on one of its pages. It was a dull and lackluster ashen gray until I discovered by accident, rubbing my finger across it, that it began to turn before my eyes. It was a unique printing process that with the warmth of the human hand caused the inks to react and the butterfly was transformed into a flashing shimmering rainbow of color, as though it was flying off the page. This is the principle of mercy, the power of the Resurrection, seeded in us at our baptisms waiting for our hands, our touch, and our bodies, our presence in the world to release the light and life buried in everything.

And this principle is pragmatic, practical, and absolutely necessary to be translated into politics, ecology, economics, laws, corporations, international bodies, and all local and national issues. Ben Cohen, who was one of the original founders of Ben and Jerry's Ice Cream, now works with business corporations and groups interested in alternatives to existing practices nationwide. He calls his new brainchild TrueMajority, and he works with over five hundred CEOs and corporate presidents in Business Leaders for Sensible Priorities (BLSP) and Religious Leaders for Sensible Priorities, representing forty denominations believing that business must be transformed to reflect values that practice social responsibility, acting as a positive force for change in society. They believe, along with many others, that there is no reason that twenty-four thousand people a day should die of starvation and that poverty can be eradicated for a fraction of the military's existing budgets. He has used everything from Oreo cookies to pigs to demonstrate the huge gaps between the military budget and the portions allocated to education and health-care initiatives. Last Independence Day, three pigs roamed the streets of Boston to put in perspective what is happening in our country. The biggest, most massive pig was the one for $396 billion proposed for the military in fiscal 2003, more than $1 billion a day. Then next size pig was much smaller, designated for the $33 billion for federal K–12 education, and the tiniest pig was $10 billion, for all humanitarian foreign aid. The overall health of society must be a major priority for all businesses, as well as churches and nonprofit organizations. This is about the soul of the American people, he proclaims.

He has, along with the members of TrueMajority, come up with ten principles for sustaining a kinder world that is its philosophy (and a free congressional monitoring service), and all of these ten principles could be funded completely through "reductions in unnecessary Cold War–era weapons that no longer contribute to our national security." These principles are worth noting.

1. Attack poverty and world hunger as if our lives depend on it. They do.
2. Champion the rights of every child, woman, and man.
3. End our obstructionism to the world's treaties (at the moment, the ABM, child soldiers, landmine, Kyoto agreement, world court).
4. Reduce our dependence on oil, and lead the world to an age of renewable energy.
5. Close the book on the Cold War and end the nuclear nightmare forever.
6. Renounce Star Wars and the militarization of space.
7. Make globalization work for, not against, working people.
8. Ensure equal treatment under the law for all.
9. Get money out of politics.
10. Close the gap between rich and poor kids at home.

Good places to start. All of these are Christian values spelled out in very pragmatic terms. You can find more information about TrueMajority at www.truemajority.com. As Ben Cohen says, "These are things that are based on the traditional American values of compassion, equality, and social justice."

Along with the pragmatics and the practice, there must be stories. There must be attitudes, and there must be those who stand together living belief in Jesus, the Crucified and Risen Lord, remembering, reminding, speaking out again and again, collecting the bits and pieces that make resurrection take on life and flesh, and laughter, joy, and concrete vision. They can be short pithy insights or stories passed from mouth to mouth (always better than the ones you pick up electronically online) or old prayers growing into new ones that tear at our hard hearts, seeking to bring us back to life again. A friend of mine, Eva Silva, once wrote this short piece in the Dominican newsletter *Touching In*.

> Somewhere, sometime, someone pointed out to me that in every opera, climax comes when the hero or heroine meets a tragic death. In *Romeo and Juliet*, Juliet takes her life. In *Carmen*, she is stabbed. In the opera *Tosca*, the heroine jumps from Castel San Angelo into the Tiber River to her death. In one particular production, the woman playing the lead role was athletic enough to jump off the stage, so as to give the impression that she was jumping to her death. Below was a mattress for her to land on but it was a hard jump. She talked to the crew and they in turn added another mattress, but it didn't make much difference. In the final production of the opera, without telling her, the crew switched the mattresses for a trampoline. In the final scene of the final production, she sings her solo, jumps and to her astonishment and the audience's, she bounces back up!

It is a grand piece, evoking laughter, but underneath the laughter is the undying belief in "coming back," in "bouncing back," in redemption. And there must be people who do this for others, a vocation, a lifestyle that is consciously intent on bringing people back to life and instilling heart, courage, and hope, again and again, in situations lacking grace. Storytellers, musicians, dancers, dreamers, weavers, potters, all those who make things out of other things, imitating the Creator-Keeper God, must be honored members of every parish, community, neighborhood, and nation. They overlap into preachers, prophets, and teachers, those who pass on the tradition's stories, especially those found in the Scriptures and lives of those who have gone before us. We must remember and take heart from them, lean on them and pray that they will continue to be present to us in the power of the Resurrection. There is an old anonymous prayer I found once on a card in my Nana's dresser that says it well.

> We thank you, O God, for all the saints of the ages;
> For those who in times of darkness kept the lamp of freedom and faith burning;
> For the great souls who saw visions of larger truth and dared to declare it;
> For the multitude of quiet and gracious souls whose presence has purified and sanctified the world;
> And for those known and loved by us, who have passed from this life into the fuller light of life with you. Amen.

I love its simplicity and its vagueness—I can add in those contemporary to my life who sustain me, scattered around the world and close to home—and I love it because it was my Nana's, a piece of what she prayed and held onto for a dearer life in hard times. Here there is solidarity and communion that defies death and reconnects us to those who have gone before us in faith, known and unknown, yet part of the Body of the Crucified and Risen Christ.

And this last story was told to me by a friend in New York, and I save it for the last, because it's not just the best, but it catches you off guard, spins you around, and throws the world into right relationship again, and you laugh and you sing while it happens. My friend had the good fortune to actually be there, and the written version falls a bit flat. As you read it, when you get to the part you can sing, sing it out loud—it helps immensely.

> Once upon a time a young mother wanted to encourage her children to love music, and so, since she had loved playing the piano growing up, she insisted on providing piano lessons for all her children, who happened to be four boys. It was the last one, the youngest, who really seemed to get into the music and soon progressed beyond banging the keys and grousing about practice. His mother thought to encourage him even more, and when she saw an ad in the *New York Times* for a Paderewski concert at Carnegie Hall,

she decided to buy tickets for the youngest and herself for the only matinee. The tickets were outrageously expensive, but it would be worth it. She got front row seats so that he could see just a few feet away the master pianist's fingers as they raced across the keyboard, making marvelous music. Surely he'd enjoy it and want to make music like that himself someday.

The day arrived, and he was as excited as she was at going to the concert. They settled into their front row seats, and she noticed a friend a few rows back. She told him she was going over to say hello and to stay put in his seat because the show would begin soon. The lights would flash off and on, and then the theatre would be dimmed and the curtain open for the concert to begin. And off she went to chat with her friend. And after a few minutes of fidgeting in his seat (they're made of wooden slats and he was only six), he slid off his seat and promptly disappeared behind a curtain off to the side of the stage, with a sign over it saying, "No Admittance."

The lights blinked, and she hurried back to her seat and realized instantaneously that he was gone! At that moment, the stage lights came on, and the curtain opened to a grand piano alone on the stage, and her young son sitting on the bench playing the piano with glee and concentration. She gasped along with the entire audience. But Paderewski was striding onto the stage. All watched fascinated as he bent over the child and began playing along with him. He slid onto the bench beside the child and began with one arm on either side of him. The song he was delightfully picking out so carefully on the piano was "Twinkle, twinkle little star, how I wonder what you are. Up above the sky so high, like a diamond in the sky . . . twinkle, twinkle little star." He whispered to the child, "Don't stop, keep playing!"

And the little boy did. And so did Paderewski. He filled in a bass part with his left hand and then around the child he added a running obbligato. And they played on, the old master and the young boy, faster and faster, slower and slower. He would whisper every once in awhile, "Don't stop, keep playing." And the experience that could have been frightening for the child, embarrassing for the mother, disastrous all around became a creative, mesmerizing experience for the audience. They played on and on and on with Paderewski inventing and ad libbing, as the child played louder, skipped notes, and began to improvise himself. They played for almost twelve minutes! And when they were finished, they both slid off the bench and stood together, bowing as one. The audience went crazy, laughing, crying, stomping their feet and clapping.

My friend was way up in the cheap seats in the second balcony and watched. When he saw the maestro bend so tenderly over the child and whisper something in his ear, and how the child responded, he said that all he could see, through his tears, from that moment on was God the Father bending over Jesus, bending over all of us, whispering words of love, of encouragement, of life into our ears. When he heard backstage later that the words were "Don't stop. Keep playing," he cried again. God is always saying that to us, whispering and shouting. Ever since God bent over the torn, destroyed, and dead body of his beloved child and drew him back into life, raising him from the dead, our God is with us, bending over us, sliding next to us in all the situations of our life, standing with us and making music out of all we do.

We may only be playing and singing "Twinkle twinkle little star, how I wonder what you are—up above the sky so high, like a diamond in the sky," but even out of such simplistic and childish renditions our God can make incredible music, a masterpiece performance of our lives. Our God, our Father, has stood with us, stood behind and stood up for us always, and most powerfully in the raising of Jesus, his firstborn beloved child, from the dead, and in the power of the Spirit given to us in baptism, our God Father stands with us forever, making music, unbelievable music, and redeeming us, all of us, everywhere. We, like our God, with Jesus, in the Spirit that sings in our breath and blood, are baptized and commanded to make music and make the world a place where all the children of God can live in freedom and dance together in the joy and gladness of life, resurrection life, to which there is no limit—here on earth in the church and the kingdom of peace with justice and in the age to come when all the earth and its children will know the coming of the Lord of Easter glory in fullness upon the earth. This is what we stake our lives upon and how our God plays us in the world. This is Jesus's prayer, drawing us all into the Oneness of the Trinity, the dance of the Father, the Son, the Spirit, and all that they have made and loved, lived, and died for and with, and seek to raise again to life unbelievably holy even now. Every day is the day that the Lord has made and we are to rejoice in it for Christ is risen! He is alive! Death is swallowed up in the warm whispering breath of Life that is our God kissing us and drawing us all to live as one in His embrace. Practice resurrection! It is how we live until we die. It is life everlasting even now.

Closing Prayer

EASTER PRAYER OF THE EASTERN CHURCH

Simon, the New Theologian (949–1022)
Today we awaken in Christ's body as Christ awakens our bodies.
And my poor hand is Christ. He enters my foot and is infinitely me.
I move my hand and wonderfully my hand becomes Christ, because all of
   Him, God, is indivisibly whole and seamless in His Trinity.
I move my foot and at once He appears like a flash of lightning.
Do my words seem blasphemous to you?
Then open your heart to Him and let you, yourself, receive the One who
   is opening to you so deeply.
For if we genuinely love Him, we wake up inside Christ's body.
We are all our body, all over, even the most hidden part of it, is realized in
   joy as Him.
And he makes us utterly real in everything that was hurt and seemed to us
   dark, harsh, shameful, maimed,
ugly, irreparably damaged is in Him transformed and recognized in the
   whole world as whole, as lovely, as
radiant in His light.

Bibliography

Arnold, Duane W. H., comp. and trans. *Prayers of the Martyrs*. Grand Rapids, Mich.: Zondervan Publishing House, 1991.

Boismard, Marie-Emile. *Our Victory over Death: Resurrection*. Collegeville, Minn.: Liturgical Press, 1993.

Bonhoeffer, Dietrich. *The Mystery of Easter*. New York: Crossroads Publishing Company, 1997.

Boulding, Maria, SPCK. *Marked for Life: Prayer in the Easter Christ*. London: 1979.

Brouwer, Arie. *Overcoming the Threat of Death*. Grand Rapids, Mich.: W. B. Eerdmans Publishing Company, 1994.

Brown, Raymond E., SS. *A Risen Christ in Eastertime*. Collegeville, Minn.: Liturgical Press, 1991.

Bruteau, Beatrice. *The Easter Mysteries*. New York: Crossroads Publishing, 1995.

Catchpole, David. *Resurrection People: Studies in the Resurrection Narratives of the Gospels*. London: Darton, Longman and Todd, 2000.

Davis, Stephen T., SPCK. *Risen Indeed: Making Sense of the Resurrection*. Grand Rapids, Mich.: London and Wm. Eerdmans, 1993.

Davis, Stephen; Daniel Kendall, SJ; and Gerald O'Collins, SJ; eds. *The Resurrection, An Interdisciplinary Symposium on the Resurrection of* Jesus. Oxford, U.K.: Oxford University Press, 1997.

Esquivel, Julia. "They Have Threatened Us with Resurrection," in *Threatened with Resurrection/Amenazado de Resurreccion: Prayers and Poems from an Exiled Guatemalan*. Elgin, Ill.: Brethren Press, 1982

Fuller, Reginald H. *The Formation of the Resurrection Narratives*. New York: Macmillan Company, 1971.

Gibbins, Ronald C. *The Stations of the Resurrection*. Collegeville, Minn.: Liturgical Press, 1989.

Goizueta, Roberto. *Caminemos con Jesus: Toward a Hispanic/Latino Theology of Accompaniment*. Maryknoll, N.Y.: Orbis Books, 1995.

Hendrickx, Herman, CICM. *Resurrection Narratives of the Synoptic Gospels*. Manila: East Asian Pastoral Institute, 1978.

Hillesum, Etty. *An Interrupted Life: The Diaries 1941–43*. New York: Pantheon, 1983.

Lapide, Pinchas. *The Resurrection of Jesus: A Jewish Perspective*. Minneapolis, Minn.: Augsburg Publishing House, 1983.

Lorenzen, Thorwald. *Resurrection and Discipleship: Interpretive Models, Biblical Reflections and Theological Consequences*. Maryknoll, N.Y.: Orbis Books, 1995.

Malin, David. *The Invisible Universe*. New York: Little, Brown and Company, 1999.

McAlister, Elizabeth. "Resurrection Ironies," in *The Other Side*.

Meynell, Alice. "Easter Night," in *The Poet's Christ: An Anthology of Poetry about Jesus*, compiled by David Winter. London: Lion Publishing, 1998.

Moore, Sebastian. *God Is a New Language*. Westminster, Md.: Newman Press, 1967.

———. *The Crucified Is No Stranger*. New York: Seabury Press, 1981.

Perkins, Pheme. *Resurrection: New Testament Witness and Contemporary Reflection*. Garden City, N.Y.: Doubleday & Co., 1984.

Perry, John Michael. *Exploring the Resurrection of Jesus*. Kansas City, Mo.: Sheed and Ward, 1993.

Quenot, Michel. *The Resurrection and the Icon*. Crestwood, N.Y.: St. Vladimir's Seminary Press, 1997.

Remen, Rachel Naomi. *My Grandfather's Blessings*. New York: Riverhead Books, 2000.

Rutledge, Fleming. *The Undoing of Death*. Grand Rapids, Mich.: Wm. Eerdmans Publishing, 2002.

Index